LEGACY FROM THE STARS

By

DOLORES CANNON

OZARK MOUNTAIN PUBLISHERS
P.O. Box 754
Huntsville, AR 72740

First Printing-1996; 2nd-2010; 3rd-2011; 4th-2013; 5th-2015; 6th-2018; 7th, 8th & 9th-2019; 10th-2020; 11th-2021

Library of Congress Cataloging-in-Publication Data

Cannon, Dolores, 1931-2014

Legacy from the Stars by Dolores Cannon

Information obtained through regressive hypnosis about several cases where the subjects relived other lifetimes as inhabitants on other planets in strange environments.

1. Hypnosis 2. Reincarnation 3. Extraterrestrials

I. Cannon, Dolores,1931- 2014 II. Reincarnation III. Title Library of Congress Catalog Card Number: 96-067899 ISBN:0-9632776-9-3

Book Design: Tom Cannon
Cover Design: Jenelle Johannes
Book set in: Times New Roman, Marigold
Arrus blk BT,Ribbon 131 Bd BT

Published by:

OZARK MOUNTAIN PUBLISHING

P.O. Box 754
Huntsville, AR 72740

Printed in the United States of America

Whoever undertakes to set
himself up as a judge in the
field of Truth and Knowledge
is shipwrecked by the
laughter of the Gods

Albert Einstein
1879-1955

Books by ***Dolores Cannon***

Conversations with Nostradamus, Volume I
Conversations with Nostradamus, Volume II
Conversations with Nostradamus, Volume III
Jesus and the Essenes
They Walked with Jesus
Between Death and Life
(Formerly:*Conversations with a Spirit*)
A Soul Remembers Hiroshima
Keepers of the Garden
The Legend of Starcrash
Legacy from the Stars

Conversations with Nostradamus is available in abridged form on audio tape cassette.

For more information about any of the above titles, or other titles in our catalog, write to:

OZARK
MOUNTAIN
PUBLISHERS

P.O. Box 754
Huntsville, AR 72740

Wholesale Inquiries Welcome

TABLE OF CONTENTS

CHAPTER ONE

THE ALIEN MEMORIES SURFACE

The majority of human beings on Earth today tend to think that aliens and extraterrestrials are to be feared. They look different, act differently, show emotion in different ways (or the lack of emotion). Since they seem to be different they cannot possibly understand humans. Therefore they must be evil and coming to Earth to harm us in some way. This is normal human logic. We always fear what we don't understand. But this book will expose how this concept is basically false. We have been conditioned to think this way through science fiction movies and literature that we have been exposed to all our life. Even UFO investigators have focused on presumed negative qualities of the cases. In the last several decades TV shows and movies like "Star Trek," "E.T. the Extraterrestrial," "Close Encounters," are trying to present a more positive picture.

In my work I have discovered they are more *like* us than different from us. This is because we have *all* been aliens in other lifetimes. We are *all* extraterrestrial, because none of us originated on the planet Earth. This is merely a temporary stopover. Compared to the enormous age of the universe in which we live, the Earth is a relatively young planet. Thousands of other worlds throughout the galaxy have been peopled, and were evolving for millions of years before our planet reached the stage when it cooled down enough to support life. The advancement of other civilizations and cultures in the far reaches of our universe is so incredible that it cannot be imagined by our mortal minds. Thousands of worlds have been born and have died before ours was even conceived. Our eternal soul is immortal, it has been around forever and it will continue to be around forever, even after the demise of this small planet. Thus it is logical to say this has not been our only home. Through the process of reincarnation we have all lived on other planets and in other dimensions, and we will continue to do so after our lessons on Earth have been completed. Earth is merely a school, one of many in our long education. When we leave here we hopefully graduate to another grade, otherwise we have to come back and repeat lives (or classes) until we have learned the lessons. The terms "old soul" and "young soul" are often used in connection with spirits incarnating on Earth. An "old soul" is considered to be one that has had many Earth lives. A "young soul" is one that has recently decided to come to Earth. They may have lived many other lives on other worlds, and just recently decided to accept the unique challenges and limitations of our world. Our wonderful planet Earth is unique because it has been granted free will. It also is one of the few left in our galaxy that still experiences violence and war. A soul coming here has to be prepared to learn harsh lessons of how to cope with others of a violent nature, and of how to experience emotions. The emotions on Earth are much stronger than on other worlds. There is pain and suffering here that would never occur in other realities. On some worlds emotion is not known or understood. This explains the curiosity of some alien species who are observing our culture. It is difficult for them to understand how human beings can harm each other so callously. By incarnating on this world we have agreed to accept the limitations, the challenges, to experience emotions, and to learn lessons. It is not easy, because the lessons are often tremendously harsh, but the rewards to the soul's growth are tremendous.

Once the soul comes to Earth it is caught up into karma. Then the soul must continue to come back until all of the incurring debt has been paid. Even alien spirits, or as I prefer to call them, the "Star-children," know the risk they are taking by incarnating here. They cannot escape being caught up into karma, because they are interacting with human beings. They know the risk before coming into the human body, but many of them have agreed to accept the challenge because they know that Earth needs help. This help will most likely come from these gentle souls that have never experienced hate and violence. They are the infusion of new blood, that hopefully will turn our world away from violence, and lift it into the new vibration, the new world that is to come. I believe these beautiful creatures have difficulty existing in our chaotic world, because they can be overwhelmed by the emotions and conditions here. They have had no experience to prepare them for what they will find. The subject of these aliens' souls incarnating in human bodies is explored in depth in my book, *Keepers of the Garden.*

Another definition of a "young soul" is one that is having its first experience *ever* in a physical body. There are a countless number of spirits that have never left the side of God since the creation of the universe. These are the ones who have been "minding the store," so to speak. There are innumerable jobs for them to do in the spirit realm. Many of these have had no desire to incarnate, but prefer the quieter life on the other side. These are beings referred to as angels, guardians, guides or master teachers. They have important roles to play, and when we are between lives, in the so-called "dead" state, we are very much aware of these beings, and we have much communication with them. This subject is explored more fully in my book *Between Death and Life.* If these entities were to decide to come to Earth, it would be for a specific purpose. They would be noticeable because their purity and lack of prejudice would cause them to stand out. I have often thought that individuals such as Jesus and Buddha were divine masters, who had no remaining karma to repay on Earth, but merely came to try and teach the human race how to live in peace and harmony. We all know what happens to brave souls such as these whose message is misunderstood.

I was unaware of all of this when I began my work in regressive hypnosis in 1979. I have been greatly educated by the subjects I have worked with. The information I have gained is enormous and has resulted in the writing of ten books to date, and it seems as though I will continue to gain knowledge and to write about it the rest of my life. My work has been in the field of past-life therapy. This field of therapy has grown tremendously since I first began to practice it. In those early days it was considered to be "off-beat" or "off-the-wall," something only practiced by New Age "kooks" It is now being considered a valuable tool, and many professionals are desiring to learn it and add it to their repertoire. It has passed the test of time, and been proven to be very helpful in the treatment of difficult cases. Past-life therapy is a form of hypnosis where the answers to problems in this lifetime are often found in other lifetimes. Often answers can be found by regressing the subject into the forgotten early years of *this* lifetime. But there are many other cases that defy explanation by any events occurring in the present lifetime. In these cases the solutions can often relate to events that occurred hundreds of years ago. Many times it is related to trauma, especially the manner of death in the former life, and sometimes a repetitive pattern has been set up through a series of lives. In these cases the soul pattern is caught in a rut, so to say, and they don't understand how they can get out. The answers can often be found by examining the lives and the pattern. The subconscious is the record keeper of all the events that have ever occurred in our present life, and also all the events from our other countless lives.

People often ask me, "Why can't I consciously remember these past lives?" It is easy to see why it is best that these be repressed. It would be overwhelming to our conscious mind if we were walking around with the memories of other lives and other injustices constantly bombarding us in our waking state. The subconscious has wisely chosen to suppress these so we can concentrate on the job we have to do in this life. They are there in the memory banks and they can be accessed if needed. But for a healthy, normal life it is better if they stay repressed.

One of the problems that can arise is that the subconscious has no sense of time. It does not realize that it is now inhabiting a different body, where certain physical problems no longer exist, and do not apply. In its role as protector and guardian of the body, it can often innocently create problems where none should exist. An example is a case I worked on where a woman greatly desired to have a child, yet all her pregnancies were resulting in miscarriages. The doctors told her there were no physical reasons for this to keep occurring. In past-life therapy it was discovered that she had died in childbirth in her last lifetime. So through the logic of the subconscious mind, it chose to protect her in the only way it knew. It decided to keep her from becoming pregnant so she would not die again. My hypnotic therapy was designed to convince the subconscious that the soul was now in a different body that was healthy, and pregnancy would not cause the same problems. Once the subconscious agreed to cooperate the woman had a normal pregnancy within the year. Amazing results can often happen in only one session if the cause can be tracked to other lives or a pattern of lives. Still, it is not a magic formula, or a magic button one can push and have instant results. As in any therapy, you must have the cooperation of the subject. Past-life therapy has given them the answer, but it is then up to them to apply it to their life. No one can do it for them.

I work mainly with the somnambulist state of trance. My technique quickly puts the subject into this deep level. I have been doing this type of past-life therapy since 1979, but now my work in hypnosis has mostly become associated with history. This is because in the course of my work I have found many fascinating cases where the subjects relived lives in important times in history, or when they were associated with important people. When the subject is in the somnambulistic level of trance, it is similar to going through a time tunnel. Their present lifetime fades away, and they are totally immersed in the other lifetime. They are literally *there* in every respect, and thus can provide enormous amounts of information, that cannot be uncovered by conventional methods. I really believe history should be studied in this way, because the information is so accurate. I have done extensive research in these lives, and have recovered missing parts of historical data. I consider myself the reporter, the researcher, the accumulator of "lost knowledge." This soon became obvious when I saw that my books were following a pattern. They were recapturing historical knowledge that has been lost, distorted or incorrectly recorded. It seemed to be my job to get this important knowledge back and present it again to mankind. The hidden, the unknown, greatly fascinates me and I seem to be drawn to anything I do not understand. Thus I have been led down many strange pathways in this pursuit, and my patience in research has been rewarded. But I often feel as though I am only scratching the surface, and that there is much more for me to explore. To this end I have dedicated my life.

In 1987 my work was extended and took yet another strange twist. I began investigating UFO cases, and I was called in to conduct hypnosis in suspected abduction cases. These resulted in two books about my findings: *Keepers of the Garden*, and *The Legend of Starcrash.* I have so much information now about this fascinating topic that I have had to categorize it into several books. A future book will contain specific cases and my theories about them.

This present book, *Legacy From the Stars*, will follow a different direction. These were cases where no alien involvement was suspected. In supposed abduction cases the subject had conscious memories of strange events, or strange dreams. In my early days as an investigator I thought the person had to have a conscious recollection of a sighting or an encounter. Then I discovered this was not always the case. Many times in my work I found the stories of alien involvement coming forth through what I thought would be a normal pastlife regression. This was totally unexpected and often fervently denied afterwards. Neither I nor my subject knew it would come out. But once the door had been opened, I always felt obligated to explore it. I had to know why the story had chosen that time to come forth. The results have often been startling. So this book contains the cases of people who were aliens in other lifetimes, or had encounters that they tucked away in their subconscious and never remembered again.

Since my book *Keepers of the Garden* came out I have received many letters from people who feel so alienated and out-of-place here, that they are sure they must also be Star-Children. Mostly out of curiosity they desire to explore this possibility through regressive hypnosis. In my work I have found it is better to seek understanding of the life you are living now, then you can have better understanding of what you were in past lives. There are many people who have difficulty accepting the idea that they have lived more than once. They would have an even greater difficulty accepting the thought of living elsewhere in the universe and being something which they would term utterly alien. In these cases it would do them more harm than good to seek this knowledge. The present lifetime is the most important lifetime of all, and is the one that should be focused upon. Any other information gained from past lives should be treated as a curiosity and applied to the understanding of this life.

In this type of work it is important to have an open mind. Once you say, "But that cannot be. It does not fit the pattern of what I believe exists," then you close the door on wonderful possibilities. When an incredible case presents itself I can think of a million questions to ask. I feel I must try to understand the ununderstandable. In this way my mind has been expanded by many new ideas and theories that I would never have considered if I had continued in what I knew or believed to be true. My mind would never have been opened to these new possibilities if I had contended that they did not fit the accepted pattern, or that because they sounded crazy they could not be true. Truth is relevant. My truth may not be the same as someone else's truth, but that does not make either truth invalid. It just means that it has to be looked at from a different viewpoint; perhaps a viewpoint that has never been considered before. And thus my world and viewpoint continues to expand. I hope my books will provide the same avenue to other adventurous souls who want to know what lies beyond the accepted norm. So read this with an open mind, with all preconceived notions pushed to the side. Suspend belief and see where it leads.

I have promised to protect the identity of my subjects, because in some areas of our country past-lives, reincarnation, plus extraterrestrials adds up to ridicule. So in the cases that follow "the names have been changed to protect the innocent," as the saying goes.

CHAPTER TWO

ALIENS AS ANGELS OF OLD

Terry was a young man in his thirties, whose occupation involved electronics. He traveled and repaired equipment in various factories in our area. He had been raised as a strict Roman Catholic, but did not consider himself especially religious. When a regression of this type occurs, the first thing I am asked about is the subject's religious beliefs, as though that may influence the material in some way. I have found that it does not matter whether the person is religious or not. It makes no difference what faith they belong to, or even if they have no religious beliefs at all. When they are in deep trance all such dogma is bypassed. You are dealing with the subconscious and its memories of all of this life, as well as all of the former lives. The information and the answers always follow a pattern, and are untarnished by any religious training or lack thereof. This is one of the unusual phenomenon involved in my work.

I had been working with Terry for a few weeks. The past lives that had been coming forth were mundane, yet they seemed to have importance to him. This is often the case. I may see nothing relevant in the past life, yet it may contain one small piece of information that holds the key and only makes sense to the subject. This is the reason I tape record all my sessions, and I always give the subject the tape to take home with them. It is important for them to hear their own voice relating the story.

Often the answer may lie in a certain phrase or the voice inflection while describing a scene. There are many details that could escape notice by the therapist, but could hold a world of importance to the subject. After all, the session is very personal to them, and often they are the only one who knows what they are really looking for.

At this session in 1984 I was expecting more of the same simple lives to come forth, but the results were totally unexpected. At the time I was working on the first drafts of my book *Jesus and the Essenes.* I do not know if that influenced my mindset, but I had enough material to work with on that book. I wasn't looking for any more along that line, especially dealing with alien involvement.

In that book there was an indication that the Star of Bethlehem may have been something other than a natural phenomenon. The description definitely sounded more like a spacecraft (or several appearing together). It was also indicated that UFOs had appeared on a regular basis at Qumran, the home of the Essenes in Israel, where Jesus was taught in his early years. The Essenes said that the Watchers were pleased with their preservation of the ancient knowledge that had been handed down to them from their forefathers in Atlantis. These indications were startling enough, and I was not expecting to find any more information dealing with the story of Jesus. I apologize if this story disturbs anyone's religious beliefs. I respect beliefs, and I try to never go against anyone's theological education. I am only the reporter telling what I uncovered.

In 1984 I had not yet begun to work on UFO cases, so I was surprised at the alien overtones of this session. The tape has been filed away waiting its inclusion in one of my books. I believe it belongs in this one, despite the religious connotations.

Terry was in a deep trance and moved into a past life. We had been working in the time period of the 1800s, so I was surprised when he saw himself in desert surroundings. I presumed his subconscious had brought up this past life for a purpose, so I listened as he described the scene he found himself in. He saw himself standing on white sand with a mountain in the background. He also saw tents with striped canopies that he said belonged to a traveling caravan.

When he looked at himself, he saw that he was a dark-skinned old man dressed in a one-piece tunic and wearing leather strapped sandals. I asked what he was doing out there in the desert.

T: We're getting water and supplies for the women and children who are at the camp which is in the hills. We had come down from the hills to this caravan of merchants to buy supplies for those who are in the hills.

D: *Have the people in the hills run out of supplies?*

T: They have not depleted their supplies, but have used them to a point where it is necessary to replenish them. This is a traveling caravan of merchants who travel the deserts and wilderness to supply the groups of people who live in these remote areas. There is a trade which flourishes by supplying those who live in the desert and wilderness.

D: *I see. What is your name?*

T: Hassan. (Phonetic)

D: *(I repeated it.) I have difficulty with these names sometimes. Do you know the name of this country? Does the country have a name?*

T: It would be in what is now Israel. It was called something at that time, only not in those words. There was a translation.

D: *You said you are an old man?*

T: Yes, (uncertain) ... sixty-eight ... years ... old.

D: *Did you come a long way from the hills?*

T: Several miles, approximately three ... three and a half miles.

D: *I think that's very good if you can walk that far at your age.*

T: The health is good for there has always been work to do, and work is healthy. So I have been blessed with this healthy body. The journey was not rugged, it was merely long. For the hills were not steep but were sloping, and so it was as walking down a sloping path.

D: *Were there many of you that came for the supplies?*
T: They numbered around fifteen.
D: *How are you going to get the supplies back to the people?*
T: There are mules, which are pack mules. The supplies are packed and carted on the mules.
D: *Where you live in the hills, is that a town or a city or something?*
T: It is merely a loose band of people who have decided to live in the wilderness, in order to observe God's laws and to purify themselves and to learn. For there is much to learn, without the distractions of the cities.
D: *You said to learn God's laws. What God do you worship?*
T: Yahweh (Ya-way) is his name.
D: *And you thought you must isolate yourself to worship him?*
T: To learn of him, for those in the cities do not learn of him. They do not wish to learn of him. It is necessary to remove oneself from the noise and the bustle of the cities and to listen to the quiet. To the voices which speak. And in this way one can learn and can hear Yahweh speak to him.
D: *That makes sense. Does your religion have a name?*
T: We call ourselves the "Group of the Whispering Sands," for we believe we hear Yahweh speak in the whispering of the sands. In the wind which blows through the desert.
D: *Wasn't it dangerous to locate yourself where there would be a lack of supplies?*
T: There is no danger from the animals. We are not afraid. And it is merely a matter of contacting one of these traveling caravans and explaining where the group is. The caravan will then see to it that a route is established.
D: *What do you buy the goods with?*
T: There is bartering which is done.
D: *What do you use for your medium of exchange to barter with?*
T: We use money. Shekels is one term which is used.
D: *Is that a coin or what?*
T: Yes, it is a coin, a Roman coin.

D: *I was wondering how you would get money out there in the middle of nowhere.*

T: There are those who are of wealth who have money. There are also sales of lambs and sheep, for we raise sheep.

D: *Is there any other form of money? Other names for money?*

T: We wish not to speak of money, for those who speak of money are not interested in anything *but* money. So we please ask not to speak so much of money.

D: *That's all right. I was just trying to get some facts. I'm not interested in money myself, so I can understand what you mean. What is your occupation with this group? What is your work?*

T: Goat-herder. Raise goats and kill goats, for we use much from the goats. Their milk and their hides and their meat, and so I raise goats.

D: *Do you know what year this is? Does the year have a number?*

T: There is no record in our group of the time, for we are not interested in marking time.

D: *You don't keep track of the seasons or the years in any way then.*

T: We note the seasons of course, for the seasons change. We find no need to mark the time however. (His voice sounded old.)

D: *Is your religion similar to the Jewish religion? Do you know that name?*

T: We feel we have no religion other than a belief in "He-Who-Is-and-Protects." This is not a religion, this is a belief. There is not an organized religion here. It is merely a group of people who share a common belief and wish to live in these beliefs.

D: *Can you tell me a little about the beliefs of the group?*

T: We believe Yahweh is the creator of the heavens and the Earth. Who is the ultimate, supreme being. This is given to us by those who are of the fair skin, and who travel in the skies at night. This is ... not to be spoken outside this camp.

That statement sparked my curiosity and let me know this would not be a normal regression. What type of beings was he speaking of? In a situation where secrecy is involved, the hypnotist must gain the confidence of the other entity or the information will not be shared.

D: *You can trust me because I am also searching. I wish you no harm at all. I'm interested in the fair-skinned ones that come from the sky. Can you tell me more about them?*

T: These are our friends who visit us frequently and bring us tidings of much to-do on this planet. For they have educated us to the fact of there being life on other planets. This is knowledge which would cause us to be stoned, were we to speak of it.

D: *Yes. There are many people who don't understand these things. I can see why this would be one reason you felt you must isolate yourself.*

T: The friends would not come to us were we not isolated.

D: *Would it be dangerous for them?*

T: They would not come. They would not put themselves in danger.

D: *I'm very interested in them. I would like to count to three and move to a time while you are living in your community when one of these ships come from the sky. I would like you to describe it for me. I will count to three and we will be at one of these times, when they make a visit to your area. 1, 2, 3, we are at one of those times. Tell me what is happening.*

T: There is a fire built which is customary to bring them forth. Part of our ceremony, of sorts. There is a fire built and the group is standing around this fire. We chant and sing and hold hands and praise the God of Heaven. Suddenly we see a light below in the valley, for we are on the crest of this mountain. And we can see this light skimming across the desert below.

D: *This is at night?*

T: Yes. It is night for all others in the area would be asleep at this time. The light comes up the path on the side of the mountain and stops several hundred yards from the circle. There is a door which opens from below, for this is somewhat circular in shape. And ... three friends come from the light.

D: *How do they come from the bottom? Are there stairs or anything?*

T: They hover or float, there is no contact with the earth. They are white or give off white light in appearance. And speak to us with their minds for they do not speak by tongue. We hear them in our minds.

D: *Can you see their features or is the light too bright?*

T: They have but a small mouth which never moves, and very large round eyes with ... no eyebrows. They are very tall in stature.

D: *Taller that your people?*

T: Yes. Six ... between six and seven feet tall.

D: *Do they have any hair?*

T: No, they are bald.

D: *What kind of clothes are they wearing?*

T: They have what appears to be a robe with long sleeves, which comes down and covers their feet. Their feet are not visible. They stand on disks or plates and it is on these plates that they move.

D: *Oh, I see. This is how they are able to hover.*

T: Yes. These are very beloved friends who come to us and give us words of great hope and encouragement of the Messiah which is to be born on this planet. For these are precursors of the coming of the Messiah, and we cry when we hear these words. For many have waited entire lifetimes and not seen the coming. And here we are being told He will come in our lifetime. There is much love from these creatures. And we believe them and trust them and listen to them. For they are obviously of angelic proportion.

D: *How do they know these things?*

T: They are of the spirit world and have knowledge from that which is from the spirit world.

D: *Why are they telling you these things?*

T: They know that we are studying in the light. We wish to learn. They understand our purpose for being in the wilderness and so they bring this news to share and to enlighten. The first time they came we were terrified. We thought we were going mad, for it happened then just as it did and does every time. The light skims across the desert from the river, the river Jordan. All who know about the Messiah would understand what these people speak to us about. Yet only those who are of high mind would be allowed to receive these visitors from Heaven.

D: *Do you have anything in your own teachings, beliefs, about the Messiah?*

T: He will be of fair skin, we are told, and his face will shine like the sun. He will be of the heritage of these light beings yet He will be man. He is the Son of God, they say, and is to teach our world that which is God's love on Earth.

D: *Do they say where he will be born?*

T: In Bethlehem. He will be born of parents who are meager in resources. He will lead a very normal life as a child and will then begin his mission as a young man. This is all we can say for there is none other given to us at this time.

D: *Where is Bethlehem in relation to where you are?*

T: It's north from where we are now.

D: *Very far?*

T: Fifty miles ... approximately.

D: *You said that He will come to teach God's law. Can you tell me what God's law is, as you have been taught?*

T: The law spoken is merely an interpretation of how one feels toward his fellowman. For the words all fall short of the practice. The intent of the law is to foster good will and love and understanding and patience and virtue and chastity.

D: *Are there many people in your group?*

T: There are twenty-five to thirty, approximately thirty.

D: *Are there women and children also?*

T: There are no young children, merely brothers and sisters of those who are in the group. No infants, for this life would be extremely hard for an infant to tolerate. (His voice at times sounded very gruff.)

D: *But there are a few families?*

T: Yes. We consider ourselves one family.

D: *I see. Do you live in houses or what type of dwelling do you have?*

T: There is a cave on the top of the mountain which is suitable for housing. There are bees around the entrance to the cave, which present a problem at times. However, they have soon grown accustomed to our wandering around the mouth of the cave. They are no longer a problem. The cave is dark and dry.

D: *Does everyone live in the cave together?*

T: There are those who stay outside and guard the cave at night. In order to watch for wild beasts or to be alert for someone who might stumble upon our camp.

D: *I see. You are mostly in that one cave then. It must be a large cave.*

T: For the most part, all sleep somewhat around in and out of the cave. Somewhat half in and half out of the cave. And there are tents around the mouth of the cave as well, to accommodate those who live in tents.

D: *Are there any other groups of people living near you?*

T: There is another group to the south and to the east, who live on a mountain similar to ours. We know of these people through the caravans. We have not met them however.

D: *How are you able to get your water way out there?*

T: This is brought with the caravan.

D: *It takes a lot of perseverance to want to live so isolated. Can you tell me how long your group has been together? I mean, has it been several years or was it gathered before you were born?*

T: This group has seen many come and go. It, however, has been a group of varying members for fifteen years in different areas. For the group has not always lived in the same place, but have moved throughout the wilderness for these fifteen years.

D: *Then it does move around. It doesn't stay in the same place.*

T: There would be the move when situations arose which made it necessary. However, there was no moving done simply to find another place. If another group happened to set claim to land and built a house which was too close to this group, then we would move to find another place, which was more isolated.

D: *But could your friends in the ships still find you?*

T: Yes.

D: *I imagine they wouldn't let anything happen to you.*

T: They have nothing to fear from us nor do we from them. They are quite capable of protecting themselves.

D: *I meant they would probably take care of you if you did have need.*

T: We are not under their charge, nor they under ours. We have our own lives to live. They simply would not intervene in case of tribal warfare or the like. And we would not expect them to.

D: *Have you ever heard of the word Essene? Is that familiar to you?*

T: This is a group who is similar to ours in that they are studying the laws. This does not apply to our group however, for our group is loosely banded and is under no jurisdiction or mandate or charter. But is simply a group organized to learn and to love.

D: *Then you have heard of them. Have you ever seen where they live?*

T: It is said that they are from Qumran. (Pronounced: Kum-a-ran.)

D: *Is that near where you are?*

T: No, it is to the west and south, so it is said.

D: *Do you know if these friends of yours from the sky have any contact with these people?*

T: They visit the other group, yes. For they have told us this. And there are others. There are four groups in this wilderness which they said they have visited. For this is something which is somewhat popular at this time. They have spoken of these groups in the wilderness.

D: *Did your friends say how long it would be before the Messiah would come to Bethlehem?*

T: Soon they said, for the preparations have been made. All is in ready. The parents have been selected, and all is now in the Father's hands. For there was much preparation to do, on Earth as well as in heaven. For there is always much work to do.

D: *Can you tell me some of the preparations? You said that the parents were chosen? Did they have a part in that?*

T: We do not know this, for this is simply something we have been told. The parents have been chosen, the preparations have been made. Those who are to participate have been told and have agreed, and all is in order at this time. There is simply now the final word from of the Father.

D: *They are just informing everyone of the event to come then.*

T: That is correct. For we are merely observers and are not taking an active part. We send much love and hope for this effort. For this has been waited for and looked for, for generations.

D: *Will any of your group go to where this is to happen?*

T: We know not at this time who will travel, or if there will be any travel. We have not made any plans to do anything different than what we have been doing for the past fifteen years, for this suits our purpose well. If we are asked we will go. The friends know where we are if they need our assistance and they will ask us.

D: *They are taking care of everything.*

T: They are assisting as all those who are in the flesh.

D: *Are the friends flesh like you are?*

T: They are from another world and are assisting at this birth, this birth of mankind.

D: *Will the friends let you know of any future events that happen with the Messiah?*

T: We have no idea for they tell us only what they wish. We gladly accept what they give us and ask for no more.

D: *Do they have any set times that they come to visit you?*

T: We know when it is time, for we feel it. And so they come.

D: *Did they say, is there any way you will know when the time comes for the birth of the Messiah?*

T: They said only that the time was near. That it was at hand. That we would know when it was. They did not say *how*, they said merely, we would know. We do not question them, for it would be unthinkable for a man to question an angel.

D: *I see. They didn't tell you to watch for anything.*

I was thinking of the Star of Bethlehem.

T: They said we would know, that is all.

D: *Apparently it is important for your group to stay isolated from the cities. And this is important in the communication with these friends. Wouldn't they appear to others that live in closer groups?*

T: There are several reasons why it is important to isolate. For in the cities there is much activity, mental activity as well as physical. And it is recognized that thoughts are perceived by those around us, and we from those around us. And so to close one's thoughts one must put himself in a clean environment. So the wilderness affords this quietness for the thoughts without interruption from the neighbors and those who also dwell in the cities. There is also the act of aggression, which is in the cities, which would be carried to the visitors were they to simply walk into the cities. They would be stoned.

D: *Why? Wouldn't the people understand?*

T: They would be terrified. They would not understand. They would not be receptive to this experience and so they would react in a typically human fashion.

D: *Well, you said you were terrified the first time you saw them too. So that would be a normal reaction, wouldn't it?*

T: It is a normal reaction. We, however, were not of violent natures and so we did not react violently.

D: *Are there any large cities near where you live?*

T: Only wilderness and the river.

D: *Did you come from a larger city to begin with?*

T: I, please, wish to ask not to answer this question, for I speak not of my past. I speak only of the present and the future. For that which is done is done and is as dust on the ground. And is not to be kicked about and made hard to breathe in. That which has been done is done and is not to be repeated, nor is it to be spoken of. The past is done, let it lie as it would, dust on the ground. This is one of our beliefs and we practice this belief. Looking only to the future and practicing God's law in the present.

D: *I had no way of knowing that, so I didn't mean to offend you.*

T: We understand. We wish to explain however.

D: *I was just asking questions.*

T: That is understandable, for our beliefs are considered eccentric to those around us who would not understand us.

D: *I respect beliefs. I believe anyone should believe the way they want, that's why you have nothing to fear from me.*

T: That is all right, for we accept you as a friend and we wish you to know our beliefs, for we have no intentions of forcing them on you. You do not have to accept them. We wish merely for you to understand them.

D: *That's what I'm trying to do. I'm very interested in things like this. Have you ever heard the term "Watchers"? Does this have any meaning to you?*

T: That is them. They are the Watchers, for they watch in the evening when the sun is down and the stars are above. They are always watching and waiting. And when they move, they move with light. They hover and glide and never touch ground, for the ground would harm them were they to touch it. It would *ground* them. These are the Watchers, that is correct.

D: *This is why they glide on the plates then, they never touch the ground.*

T: They are not to touch the earth, for there would be a reaction which we do not understand, but we acknowledge that this is so. We never attempt to touch them for we are of the ground as well. We are of the earth and they are not, and so it is that they must not touch the earth. Who is to say why? Who is to question? This is what has been told and so we must accept this. For we have no knowledge of their reasons, other than what they tell us and we accept that. For they are good, they are holy. They are of the light.

D: *But they never come in the daytime, only at night?*

T: They never come in the daytime, they come only at night, *only* at night.

D: *Is there any special reason for this that you know of? For instance, does the light that shines on the earth in the daytime have any ....*

T: (Interrupted) It is too strong for their bodies, for they are not equipped to deal with the sunlight as we are. They are not of this universe, for they come from another universe which has a sun which is totally different from that which this one is. And so the light from this sun would have a damaging and lethal effect on them were they to receive it in full strength.

D: *Maybe that is one of the reasons they have this glowing appearance.*

T: The glowing is not from their sun, it is from their energy which they are exuding. This is a natural phenomenon which occurs because of the energies which they are channeling through.

D: *I see. I have heard of the Watchers in my travels and I wondered if these were the same people.*

T: These are the same, for they come from the same planet. They may be called many names in other places, but they are the same.

D: *I would like to count to three and let's go ahead to the next time that the friends return to your group and they give you more information of what has happened. 1, 2, 3, we have moved ahead to the next time they come to your little community. Can you tell me what is happening?*

T: (Long pause) There is much sorrow in the camp for the old man has slipped and hit his head on the rocks and they are mourning him. And the friends come and tell them the old man is "in the light" and not to cry for him, for he is in a much better world than those who mourn him. And they understand.

D: *Did they tell the group anything else about the Messiah?*

T: No, for they came to console the group, for the old man was their leader, their guide. And now there is much confusion as to what the group will do after his death and departure. And so this meeting was to bring reassurance and love and understanding.

D: *Was the old man Hassan?*

T: Yes.

D: *Then you are watching this. What do they decide to do?*

T: There is a younger man who is deciding, contemplating whether he is capable of accepting the role of leader.

D: *Is the group still the same, or has it grown or diminished in any way?*

T: Two have left to live as married couple in the city, for they have decided it is time for them to live as man and wife and so have left. The rest are, at this point, all deciding whether to stay or go.

D: *How did the friends, the Watchers, know the old man had died?*

T: The energies, the thought energies were there, for they monitored and watched and were in touch on the thought level. They could tell.

D: *Did you ever hear any more news about the Messiah?*

T: He had been born, was sent. He had been born in Bethlehem, and so there was great rejoicing. There was not the consideration to go to Bethlehem, for it was feared it might lead those to Him who wished to do Him harm.

D: *I see. That was the last news you heard?*

T: He has been born and that is all.

D: *About the old man, if you had been able to observe his transition, where is he now? Or where is his spirit?*

T: He's looking down on the group from above them and to their side, and glad to be out. For the body was getting hard to move around. Hard to move those bones, for they were beginning to feel like dust, which they would soon become. They yearned to go back to the dust ... and so they did.

D: *Can you see what happened to the body?*

T: It lies now on a bier with the arms crossed.

D: *As you're watching this, what association do you have with this old man?*

T: We are the same.

D: *Okay, I thank you very much for talking to me.*

T: It was time for the story to be told. Now is the time, for the centuries have waited for this time. There is much work to do between the two, the storyteller and the listener. For the listener then becomes the storyteller and on and on and on and on. And so the word spreads, for this is the law, the plan, the preparations. And He will come again just as surely as the sun will rise and set.

D: *Are the Watchers planning any part of the preparations* now *as they did then?*

T: Yes, they are the same. And they are still coming to those who are isolated. There are those groups who still find the need to isolate themselves and to learn and to open their inner selves. And so there are those who still see and talk with and meet the Watchers, the Friends. You have been selected to be given this information, for you are one who is to make the best use of it. They will make use of whomever is, by opportunity, the most suited. And you are at this point, one of those who is being given this information. For it is time to tell. There is the story to be told from both perspectives. From the side of the light and from the side of the Earth. For these are cousins, brothers, the light and the Earth are brothers and this is not understood at this time. And so it must be made known that the brothers in light wish their brothers on the Earth to see them as such and to not fear them. For they wish only to help and to assist.

D: *Is this message going out in other parts of our planet?*

T: The ego would like to believe that this is particular to this area, but the Earth as a whole is receiving this same message. For it would take centuries were it to evolve from one point only. The message that they are our friends is being spread throughout the world, not just this point.

When Terry awakened we discussed this strange session. He could not imagine where it came from, because it surely did not conform with his religious upbringing (or with anyone else's, for that matter). I could understand it better than he could because of the work on the Jesus material that is contained in my books. My mind had been broadened during that work, and had been opened to many possibilities that do not exist in our normal frame of reference. Thus I did not reject this information, but filed it away for future use. Since this session in 1984 the pattern has become increasingly apparent to me, and now many sessions have been interlaced as similar information came from several subjects. Compiling the information in this book was like putting a puzzle together, and I watched as the pieces found their own little niche. There was continuity and confirmation rather than contradiction. This case opened the suggestion that perhaps many of the angelic visitors mentioned in the Bible were actually extraterrestrials. One of the definitions for angel is "messenger". The people who lived in Biblical areas could have been using the only words they knew to describe highly unusual visitations. These encounters were so extraordinary that they left an indelible impression on their minds, and were carried down to us through verbal and written accounts. Similar cases have been recorded in the form of legend and folklore throughout the world.

CHAPTER THREE

THE NATIVE AND THE UFO

Penny was an attractive young woman in her twenties living by herself in Fayetteville, Arkansas, the nearest large city to me. She had gone to New York to try her luck as an actress. After a few years she decided the glamour world was not really as glamorous as people think it is. She returned to Fayetteville where her parents lived, and was taking classes in business college. When I met her in 1987 she wanted to try past-life regression out of curiosity. She had problems with various allergies and was on medication, but she was not really looking for the cause. At the time of this session UFOs were the furthest thing from my mind. I had only been working on a few cases with Leu Farish by this time, and did not have much experience with it yet.

I used my normal cloud method to induce the deep trance. Her voice was so soft it was difficult to hear, and later caused problems when I transcribed the tape. When she descended to the ground from the cloud she found herself standing in front of a primitive wood hut with a round shape and a pointed roof. The surroundings were desert-like and desolate.

When she examined her body she was amused to find she was a man. She was a young African native wearing hardly any clothes, but adorned with gold bands on his wrists, and earrings.

As she saw herself standing holding a spear she was surprised to find that her head was shaven.

D: *I wonder why it is shaved.*

My question caused her to enter into the scene, and she began to report it from the first person viewpoint. She immediately became this other individual.

P: Because I'm in this country now.
D: *What do you mean?*
P: It's like a different place.
D: *Do all the people in the tribe have their heads shaved?*
P: Yes. It is the custom. It is to show honor. Your head ... it means ... it has always been that way. My people are strong.

She became aware that fellow tribesmen were near. They were singing and dancing and generally making noise.

P: They have bands around their neck, jewelry. Kind of a goldish color. Maybe brass or something. I'm not sure what it is really.
D: *Do you feel good about these people?*
P: I'm not sure. I stand alone.

This was the first indication that all was not well between him and his tribe.

D: *I want you to go to where you live, and you can see what kind of place it is.*
P: It is the hut that I'm standing in front of.
D: *Do you want to go inside, and see what it looks like?*
P: I know what it looks like. I could go inside. I see pots with things in them. Colorful pots. Food in it, and dyes.
D: *Dyes. Is there any furniture?*
P: No. There are blankets to sit on.

D: *Where would you eat?*
P: There's a ceremony when I would eat outside with a group of people. But I can eat inside if I want to.
D: *All right. See yourself eating. I was wondering who else would be with you.*
P: (Pause) A woman there. She has a shaved head too, and a wrap around outfit. She is my wife.
D: *Is there anyone else in your family?*
P: (Proudly) A baby boy. I love him.
D: *Is that your only child?*
P: Oh, there's a new little baby. A newborn. It's a girl.
D: *Then you have two children?*
P: Yes, but I am proud of my boy. He will follow me. He is very young. He is ... (unsure) four? Three?
D: *I want you to see yourself doing whatever it is that you do with your time. Your occupation. What is it that you do?*
P: I hunt with my spear.
D: *Are you good at it?*
P: Yes, I think so.
D: *Some people are not very good hunters. They can't hit what they aim at.*
P: I'm good. When I throw it, I usually hit it. (Pause) I have my family. They love me. But I'm different from the others. (Sadly) I feel alone.
D: *Do you know why that is?*
P: (Sadly) They alienate me. I want to change things. And they don't like that.
D: *What things do you want to change?*
P: Ideas about things.
D: *What kind of ideas? I'm interested, and I won't judge you.*
P: (Seriously and quietly) The sun ... and why it is there. What it means. What it means.
D: *You mean you think differently than the rest of the people.*
P: (Almost distressed) Yes, I do.
D: *What ideas do they have about the sun?*

P: They say it's only for the crops. But I know it means something more. It *does* mean more. I *know* it. (A whisper) It means so much more. It talks to me.

D: *Do you try to explain this to the others?*

P: Yes. They don't want to hear it. I am alone. No one stands with me. It frightens me. My family loves me, but they don't believe me either. They are afraid too, because they are related. They fear for themselves.

D: *Is that the main reason? Your ideas about the sun, or do you have other ideas they don't understand?*

P: (Confused) Something ... something talks to me. And I don't know what it means. I don't understand it.

D: *I think they should be more understanding of you. Does your village have a leader or a chief of some kind?*

P: Yes. He wears a big headdress. He is strong, forceful. He wants everyone to follow *him*.

D: *How does he feel towards you?*

P: He doesn't like me now. He disagrees with me.

D: *Are your ideas different than his?*

P: Yes. And that's why ....

D: *But I understand, and if there's anything you want to tell me, I will listen.*

P: (Barely audible) I want to know about the sun. I want to know what it means. Why it talks to me. I want to understand more. (Pathetic) I know there's more.

D: *But these are mysteries people have always wondered about. And I don't think anyone really knows all of the answers.* (I tried to gain his confidence.) *They shouldn't criticize you. I think you're a good person.*

P: (Almost in tears) But they humiliated me.

D: *I don't think it's wrong to ask questions, and want to know more.*

I did not yet realize the importance of what he was trying to tell me. I asked him to move ahead to an important day in his life. It was a celebration. His son had reached the age of thirteen and had become a man.

P: There is dancing. And they're singing. He's happy. I'm happy. Mother is there. She is pleased. And now everyone's happy again. I'm proud of him. When the initiation parts are done, he is initiated to the tribe.
D: *What do they do when they initiate him?*
P: There are feathers that they wear. Put on feathers and paint. He must pass a test. He must be strong and not be fearful. To prove his manhood.
D: *Is this a test that all of you must pass?*
P: Yes. All the men. He must spear an animal. He must ... do something else. I can see it now. He must drink something. He must battle someone, and be successful.
D: *Do you think he can pass these tests?*
P: Yes. I have worked on training him well.
D: *All right. Let's move ahead a little, and see if your son passes the tests that he has to take. Has he taken the tests?*
P: Yes. He succeeded. But he hurt his foot in it. He cut it. And it hurts him sometimes. It was during the battle. It is better, but it's sore. He complains of it.
D: *But he was able to pass the test into manhood.*
P: Yes. He is brave.

I then moved him ahead to another important day in his life. This time it was the wedding of his daughter.

D: *Does she have to dress a certain way?*
P: Yes. Flowers adorning her. She has special jewelry that her mother gave her to wear. She is very beautiful.
D: *Is she marrying someone that you know?*
P: Yes. He is all right. I'm happy for *her*. They will have children. They will be together.
D: *But this is a natural thing.*
P: Yes. (She showed signs of distress.)

D: *What's the matter?*
P: I'm concerned for *her*. I do not trust him.
D: *Why? Do you feel something about him?*
P: Yes. But I cannot change her mind about the marriage. I don't want her to marry him. I feel he will not be good enough to her. He has lied before. And I found out about it. He does not know I know. I don't know if it will work, but I hope that it will.
D: *Yes, that's all you can do is hope that everything will work out all right. Do they have any kind of ceremony they must go through?*
P: The priest of the tribe, he marries them. Words are spoken. And then they are together. And there is a great celebration. And they dance. And they are happy.
D: *How does your wife feel about the marriage?*
P: She's happy for them too. But she's sad to lose the children. She misses them.
D: *But this is natural. Is your boy gone too? (Deep Sigh) What is it?*
P: Can't find him. He is alone. They alienated him too. Because of me.
D: *Why? Does he think like you do?*
P: Yes, I taught him to. I wanted him to see what I saw in the sky. (Barely audible) I saw something.
D: *Can you tell me what it was? I will understand.*
P: *No one* understands. No one believes me.
D: *I believe you. You can always tell me anything.*
P: It was flying ... it was silver ... through the sky. It talked to me. Talked to *me*.

Her voice was so soft I was having great difficulty hearing her. Even on the tape it is barely audible.

D: *Was it the sun?*
P: No, but it flew toward the sun. I thought it was *from* the sun.

D: *How large was it?*
P: I could not tell. It was high up. But it talked to me.
D: *With words?*
P: It's hard to explain. It was so real. It was saying to me ... it was saying to me ... and I understood something I cannot explain. It is difficult. No one believes me. It was a message to *me*, to speak to the others about the sun and light. There is more. I know it. (In awe) I saw it.
D: *Do you mean it was like words inside your head?*
P: Yes, the message was like that. I have never seen *anything* like it before.
D: *Was it only one time?*
P: Yes. I wanted it to come back. I did everything so it would return. But it didn't. That made me sad.
D: *That was what the people didn't believe.*
P: My son believed me. (Almost crying) Now they don't believe *him*. And he is alone.
D: *If you only saw it one time it must have been really important to have left such an impact on you.*

This whole part was barely audible. Some words were almost a whisper and hard to transcribe. As though he was talking to himself.

P: It changed me. It changed me. I'm all changed. I must change ... this way ... I want to. If I do this now to plant ideas that are so ... so new. Ideas. (Big sigh)
D: *Is that what you mean, the ideas were like inside your head?*
P: Yes. It is like it ... yes. That's why they don't understand, because they don't know how such a thing can be.
D: *Did you see it for a long time in the sky?*
P: It was light out. I was taking a walk. It was through the forest. The trees ... I walked. Alone, I was alone. I had to think things over. I went to the top of a hill, and there it was. I thought it was *God.* It was in the sky. It hovered, kind of. These words (English) are foreign to me now. I

use other words. I don't understand why they sound this way.

D: *That's all right. Did the shape of the ... thing remind you of anything that you have seen in your life?*

P: No, I never saw anything like this. The sun shone on it and it shined. Like the sun it sparkled. I thought it was God talking to *me*. It was round. A disk, silver, round. Round like the sun.

D: *But a different color.*

P: Yes. It moved very fast. It went west toward the sun.

D: *Did you see it go past the sun?*

P: No, it disappeared.

D: *When did the words come? When you first saw it or what?*

P: Messages. Messages. I did not understand them. They were just there. And I had ideas, new ideas I never fathomed before. And it changed me.

D: *What were the ideas about?*

P: About *me*. That all things will change. How they could be different. How we could raise crops different. This is all so new. I was afraid to tell them. I was so afraid they would kill me. I tried not to ... I wanted to tell them because it was *God* who spoke to me. I knew I had to tell them, or he would be angry with me.

This whole part sounded as though it was coming from a person with a childish (or primitive) level of understanding. He was explaining things in the simplest way, because apparently that was the only way he could understand it.

D: *But these are good things that would have helped your people.*

P: They thought I was crazy. They said I made it up. They did not want to change. They isolated me, and my family. Only my son did they accept, because they had hoped he would not believe me. But he *did*. Then they eventually treated him the same as me.

D: *Maybe in time he will be able to make them understand.*

P: I hope he will. I prayed to God. I asked him to reappear for *him.* To show *him* what he had shown me. I cried. I cried. Oh, I did not want him to see me cry.

D: *Do you think your son will also be allowed to see it?*

P: (Sobbing) I hope so. I want him to. And I went back and I waited on the hill. (Sobbing) I waited there.

D: *The same place?*

P: Yes, I went back again and again. And I asked it to come back. (Crying) And it didn't.

D: *Maybe this was one of those things that only happen once in a lifetime.*

P: I prayed to it. (Softly) I prayed to it.

D: *The people apparently were just not ready to see there are better ways of doing things. Well, at least your son believes you. That is very important.*

P: I love him so much.

I had a feeling there would be nothing gained by pursuing these scenes any further. So I took him forward to the last day of his life in that lifetime. Often things can be clarified when viewed from the spirit side after death.

D: *Let's move ahead to the last day of your life, and tell me what is happening. What are you seeing?*

P: My wife is here. She helps me. I'm sick. I'm older. I have a blanket over me. My son ... he visited me. He is sad because I am not well. He came, and he put his head on my body, and cried. It made me sad, but I know he will be all right.

D: *Did your son ever marry?*

P: He is not married yet. The women of the tribe are afraid of him because the tribe has still not accepted him. And it would hurt them ... they would be alienated if they married him.

D: *I see. What about your daughter? She was married.*

P: It is different for the man than for the woman. She has a child. She cries sometimes. She is sad now because I am not well. But she is still married to him. I feel better about him now. He has been a good father. He has loved her. He helps her. But I am bitter. Because no one still believes my story. And I know it means something.

D: *But it is important that you believed it all this time.*

P: My son is the only one. My wife loves me anyway, but does not completely believe it. She does not understand it. My son leaves, he is a man now, like I was. And I did not want it that way.

During this death portion Penny's speech was chipped and sounded rough, not like her normal voice. Of course, the major portion of this session was so soft as to be almost inaudible, so the voice may have been that way throughout and I might not have caught it.

D: *But the experience must have been very powerful. That's why you believed it all ....*

P: (Interrupted) It changed me ... inside.

D: *That's very good. I'm going to ask you to drift away from that scene. It's over now, and you can look back on that life. Tell me, what do you think was learned from that? What do you think the lesson of that life was?*

P: Lesson? *Many* lessons. I learned many. Change must come. A change *will* come. (Her voice was finally louder.) It is inevitable. You must believe what is unbelievable. You *must* believe it anyway. Believe in your*self*. You must believe in yourself, and never doubt. You must hold that precious truth in your heart, to your death. You must not worry about what others say. That 'tis all that matters.

D: *Those are important lessons. I think that's very wonderful that you learned it all. All right, I want you to leave that scene and drift away from it.*

I conditioned her with a keyword to make it easier to conduct future sessions, and then I brought her forward.

When Penny was awake we talked about the session. She did not remember what it was about, verifying that she was a somnambulist (a subject that can go into the deepest possible level of trance). I explained to her the rather strange past-life of a native seeing a UFO, and how it affected his entire life thereafter. She said she had no real interest in UFOs, but always had a secret desire to see one just out of curiosity. She said the closest experience she could associate with one, was once as a child when she saw a strange light in the woods next to her home. I did not take this very seriously as a suggestion of an encounter, because this was in the early days of my work on UFOs. So I dismissed it. I still had a lot to learn about the way these incidents are manipulated, controlled and covered over. I was yet to learn the remarkable and inconceivable part the aliens and the human's own subconscious mind had to play in the scenario. At this early time in my investigations I thought the subject had to have a conscious memory of a visual sighting or an encounter in order for it to be valid. I did not know the memory could be very skillfully suppressed. Thus I brushed Penny's remark off, until I later talked to Lou Farish on the phone. He is the publisher of UFO Newsclipping Service, and the man that I work most closely with on my investigations. He suggested there might have been more to the incident. I did not think so, because all she remembered was a strange light. Nothing else had happened. But Lou thought I should pursue it and ask her more about it under hypnosis. I didn't think anything would come of it, but I agreed to try it. This led to several sessions as we explored the childhood event and found it to be a valid encounter that had been wiped from any conscious memory. It did not have any negative affect on her, so it had not come forward in dreams or in any other manner. This was my first experience in discovering that everything is not always as it seems. That memories, no matter how vague, could lead to something much more profound. This opened up an entirely new way of looking at UFO and alien investigations, and was to lead me into many strange cases that were to test my entire perception of reality.

I do not know the purpose for Penny's subconscious bringing the native life forward, unless it was to revive interest in the area of the strange and paranormal. This had been an incident that had changed her life as the native, and had cost her much, in the respect of her peers, when she stood up for what she believed in and would not renege.

CHAPTER FOUR.

A CHILDHOOD MEMORY REVISITED

A few weeks later I again went to Penny's apartment for another session. We discussed what she remembered consciously of the childhood event we were going to explore. Penny didn't remember how old she was, but she was in school so she couldn't have been too young. She was living in Kansas and she liked to play by herself in the field and woods near her home. All she remembered was seeing some strange lights in the woods. She didn't recall anything else about the incident, but she always wondered what the lights were. She thought sometimes it could have been her imagination or a dream, but she thought it must mean something if she had never forgotten it, but had wondered about it all these years. Since Lou had suggested there might be more to the incident I thought I would pursue it and see if I could find anything out. Penny agreed, even though she could remember nothing but the lights. I used her keyword, and it immediately put her into a deep level of trance. I then counted her back to when she was living near Olathe, Kansas.

D: *You were a child and you liked to play by yourself. And on this occasion, you were near the woods, and you saw some lights. I'm going to count to three and we'll go back to that time, and relive it and find out what happened on that day. I will count to three and we will be there. 1, 2, 3, we've gone back to that day. What are you doing? What do you see?* (She took a big breath, and she seemed confused.) *What is it?* (I could tell something was bothering her.) *You can talk to me. You can always talk to me.*

P: I have pigtails. Braided pigtails.

D: *I bet you're a pretty little girl.* (Her eye movements indicated that something was going on.) *Are you playing outside?*

P: I'm standing still. Looking. (Pause) I'm having a hard time seeing much. I see trees now. And there's some kind of orange light out there. Right behind the tree.

D: *What made you notice it?*

P: It's different. (Long pause) I sense something ... metallic looking. (Soft, hard to hear.) Like a round ... dome. I don't see lights now. Oh, yes! All around the edge of it, there's some kind of reddish light. It's like a pie-shaped ... something. And it's real low on the ground. And I don't know what's in it. It's kind of like an octogram. The sides are kind of squared off like a octagon.

She had difficulty with the description. She used hand motions, but they only added to the confusion and her frustration of not being able to amply describe it.

P: It's kind of like a three-dimensional piepan. Lights in the center, and around the edge where the two piepans meet, like one was a regular ... (had difficulty) in a position where you could put a pie in it. One that way, and then there is one going the opposite way right on top of it. And you put them together. But the edges are kind of octagon-like. And then right where they would meet, right there is a band of a red kind of light.

D: *Like two piepans put together. But kind of odd shaped. Is that right?*

She again had difficulty with the description, but she seemed to be determined to get it correct, and tried to supply as much detail as possible.

P: Yeah. ... Metallic. ... But the edges. It's important. The edges are ... they have that sharp change like an octagon. And it's kind of flat on top. And there's a red rim with light, all around the edge in the center.

D: *Are the red lights on now?*

P: Yeah. That red-looking thing is all around the whole edge of it. That red *rim*, like a tube of the lights. Actually a tube .... And it doesn't want to harm me. Orange lights probe me ... probers ... checking out. That's what I saw earlier, but it was higher. They were like a robot prober. The orange lights were kind of checking out the area. To protect them.

D: *What do you mean, like a robot?*

P: A probe. It was a type of probe to just check out things. The beings didn't want to come out themselves, until this prober went out first. It was an orangish light that was projected from the craft. To search around, to let them know what species were out there. And not expecting to run across *me*.

D: *They didn't know you were there?*

P: They found out. (Childish laugh) When I saw the lights I went over to investigate. And the lights are all I remember, up until *this* time. Now I can see the craft more clearly. But they were like balls of orange light, kind of dancing around. You know, like ... a dance. Kind of popping around.

D: *Outside the craft?*

P: Outside. To analyze organisms, and any species that were present. And they told me this. They conveyed this to me in a certain state of consciousness so I would not be fearful. And I tranced-out at that time. I was tranced-out to protect my consciousness.

She was still having difficulties relating this. Hesitating and moaning.

D: *What happened?*

P: (She sounded woozy and dizzy.) Oh, I just feel ... being there ... I kind of saw them for a minute.

D: *What do you mean, you saw them?*

P: Inside a ship. And there's a kind of reddish light inside. The beings are very short ... and a round head. ... And thin arms. And some fingers, but not many of them, on each hand. Long, they're long. ... And they almost seem bent over or something. I don't know what they're doing, but I saw that red light in there. And their heads are big. And dark eyes. And short, they're short.

D: *Are they wearing anything?*

P: (Pause) Clothing hard to ... I more sense the jewelry. A jewelry-type object around the neck.

D: *Can you make out what it looks like?*

P: (Pause) Some kind of crystallized stone ... a kind of a crystal-type looking stone attached to a band around the neck. And a really weird feeling from them like nothing I ever experienced before.

D: *What kind of a feeling?*

P: (Difficulty) Zombie. I felt kind of zombieish, tranced-out a little. I wanted to talk and I couldn't talk really. They were in control ... of me. And they wanted to look at me. And I was small enough that I was able to be inside the craft somehow. ... I feel like a light shown on me.

D: *A light?*

P: I was not able to get out of it. It must have been after the orange light, probers, that this light shown on me. I tranced out at that time. And then I was taken on board. And I was put back in a similar fashion.

D: *About how old are you? You said you were small.*

P: Oh, I'm eight.

D: *Are you about as big as these beings that you see?*

P: I'm a little bigger than they are. And they felt my ... (Childish giggle) they were kind of intrigued with my pigtails, my braided pigtails. (Laugh) With the hair, because they had no hair. And I remember them pulling my braids up, and looking at it. Like they thought it was strange.

D: *Were there many of these?*

P: I only feel a sense of two of them. This craft is a pretty small craft, and very low off the ground. But the top part of the craft slanted up a little, with edges on it, like octagon-type edges. They communicated some things to me. They said ... for later use. I was too young to utilize it at that time, they felt.

D: *Utilize what?*

P: Information from them. Different messages in my head. (Big sigh) A blueprint of their solar system ... where they come from. They thought it would be safe in my subconscious, stored there.

D: *Can you see it?*

P: I see a map, like a map-type thing, but it's really a ... (had difficulty) it looks kind of like a map. But it's like a galaxy map. (Giggle)

D: *Is it on paper or what?*

P: Well. (Pause as she studied something.) It kind of looks like it is on a paper-type substance, something. There are folds in it. Something they were able to fold, and to open up. I don't know ... probably it's not real paper. (Giggle) Maybe it's out of something else. But it is of a lightweight substance, and I see folds in that paper somehow, or whatever the substance is. And I see stars kind of like a ... um, astrological star system. It would be similar to that. And there's a very bright ... it looks like a very bright star. That's where they come from. But you have to travel through ... it's past some other stars and planets to get there.

D: *Do you think you might be able to draw what you see, or is it complicated?*

P: Well, I just see mostly the major part, the big stars. (Pause) If I saw a bigger map of the galaxy, I might be able to recognize it. In a star constellation. Putting it together, it kind of looks triangular, but ... this top star. It's almost like tracing the dot to dot. (Laugh) Which I've been very good at that. It's one of my favorite things to do.

D: *Well, I'm going to give you a suggestion that you'll remember the pattern that they showed you.*

P: I've got to take a closer look again, because it was real fast when they showed me this.

D: *Can you get a closer look at it?*

P: I see them holding it up now. And pointing. Their long fingers pointing where they're from. They don't really show me exactly how to get there. I can just see ... I think they pointed out planet Earth *from* there, so I could have a better idea.

D: *Yes, some point of reference.*

P: But there are so many stars out there. Yeah, I'll do the best I can to draw it.

D: *I'll give you a suggestion that you remember the pattern so you'll be able to draw it for me later. That you can fix the picture of the* main *pattern anyway, the main ones that stand out, and the one they are from, so that later you'll be able to draw it for me. All right. You said you are inside the craft when they are showing you this. What does it look like?*

P: It's one room. It has reddish lights inside. They have a little more orange cast, but mostly red. And I do see ... they have control boards that they use to aviate the craft. And there are some blue and white lights as well as ... it's another universe. (Laugh) But it's right on their control board.

D: *The same picture?*

P: Well, similar. But this is a much brighter scale. And they tune in and tune out. (Laugh) I think they tune in to a certain frequency and vibration of where they want to pop up. And they scan it first to make sure there won't be an obstacle in their way when they appear there. That's why these craft disappear out of the blue, because they just pop in and pop out.

D: *They don't actually travel through the air?*

P: Well, they can do that. They can hover. And they can ... (Positive) they can travel through the air, yes! But sometimes to actually get to the place where they zoom in, they just kind of pop up there. They are tuned in to that vibrational frequency and they set their controls at that same frequency of where they want to go. And they just pop in that vicinity, in a certain range of that vibration. And then they can go down. They can make a landing if they wish, or they can go anywhere they choose to.

D: *It sounds like it's not a foolproof method, because they didn't know you were there.*

P: Well, yes, they pick up the general area. But at least they didn't *land* on me. They probe the area so they won't land on something, you see. I've never heard of any of those type of craft landing on anybody.

D: *I don't think I have either. -- Why did they pick that particular area? What are they planning on doing there?*

P: Taking samples.

D: *What kind?*

P: Of everything there. Plant life. Animal life. And I was more of an animal life form to them. I'm the most advanced of the animal life that *they* saw. Maybe that's why they were very intrigued with me. And with my consciousness, they weren't sure how I would react. This was their first encounter with a human.

D: *Oh, you mean they don't normally deal with humans?*

P: These two had not traveled to the planet before, and they wanted to pick a state that was more desolate for this purpose. But they didn't know exactly what to expect. They knew there was a lot of activity going on, and there were beings moving about. They could see this, and they knew this ahead of time about this planet. But they had never actually gotten close enough to really take a good look at the beings. They weren't totally sure how the other beings were going to react to them. And that's why they put the beam out, because they did not want to have their ship attacked by any being. And that protects them from that.

D: *You said they are short, and have large heads or bald heads?*

P: Large, but wide at the sides on their heads. They have almost *baby* type bodies, but their backs seem kind of hunched. Their arms are awfully long, longer than their legs.

D: *Their arms are hanging over?*

P: Yes, the fingers and the hands hang down because their arms are so long. It is the weight of the hands and fingers, but they can move them very easily.

D: *Did you say they don't have as many fingers?*

P: No. (Pause as she studied them.) Three, and the fourth thing is really a ... where you would think a thumb would be, it has more of a suctiony-type thing on the end of it. The fingers ...three, they're long type fingers. But this other thing enables them to grip things. The thumb-type finger is shorter, and has a suction-type thing on the end of it. Their feet remind me of a mitten.

D: *What color is their skin?*

P: A whitish color. Yellowish-white, actually.

D: *Do they have any clothes on, or are they just naked? You said they had the jewelry.*

P: No clothing. One had a crystal "neckatar" on. The other one seemed to have a band around the neck, but I think the one that had the big stone is more of the commander of this craft, and more the one in charge than the other one. But they both are together.

D: *Can you see their features?*

P: Dark eyes. I don't sense any eyelids really. They probably have them. I just see their eyes open. And hardly any nose. A little bump kind of, where a nose would be. I don't remember any nostrils, so to speak, but a kind of a bump there. It could be a nose, where a nose would probably be placed. I can't remember a mouth at all.

D: *Nothing there at all?*

P: I definitely don't see a mouth opening at all.

D: *Then how are they communicating with you?*

P: Mentally, mostly.

D: *What about ears? Can you see anything on the side of their head?*

P: Now I am getting it. Yes, there is the top of an ear. Like an outline of an ear, of an opening. But it's not a full earlobe, it's not even defined, but there's like a rim, kind of a skin.

D: *Not like ours.*

P: No. The upper rim part of the earlobe is kind of large. -- And they tested me to find out how intelligent of a species I was.

D: *How did they do that?*

P: They asked questions. (Giggle)

D: *What kind of questions? I'm curious.*

P: About space travel. Had I seen beings like them before? Does my kind have craft like they do? What type of aircraft is used on this planet? What type of vehicles are used? (Laugh) That seemed to give them a lot of information, immediately, about the level of intelligence on this planet, because of their travel systems. Immediately they seemed to shake their heads, as if to know what type of being they're dealing with here. And that's why I was placed in the animal category. (Laugh) I mean, the most advanced of the animals, of course, but they were much more advanced.

D: *Of course, they don't know that you are a child, and you wouldn't know as much as an adult, do they?*

P: No. But they were able to read my mind. And they could see pictures in my mind of other things going on with me. And they were able to see other people in my life that were in my mind. And by reading my picture thoughts they were able to see many things. And see that there were larger beings. And some animals. They were intrigued with the animal life. In my mind picture they could see a dog. And they really were curious about it. They wanted to get a sample. They wanted to examine other animals. They mostly had to take samples of the plants of where they were, and the type of smaller species, because there were no other bigger animals around.

D: *What type of smaller species?*

P: Oh, worms and insect life. And soil also. They showed me samples. And oh! ... a bird. (Laugh) They beamed a bird and took it onboard. But I think the bird didn't handle the beam very well. It asphyxiated it or something. It just didn't stay alive. It was too much of a shock to its system. So it was in there and they were examining it as another species of this planet. They, I think, were going to dissect it since it was already expired.

D: *Can you see where they are putting these samples?*

P: Yes. It looks like plexiglass containers. Kind of round on the bottom with just a flat top on it. Some sort of clear translucent jar-type thing, but it is a peculiar shape. And the lid doesn't look like a regular lid. It is like a flat square on the top. It is kind of different. They would put their samples in these jars.

D: *Are the jars very large?*

P: No. They have a special cabinet kind of thing. And they put them down inside of it, and closed it to protect it. So that during all their movement they would not be unsettled too much.

D: *I'm thinking of plant life, did they keep it in the dirt so it would still be alive, or how did they do that?*

P: They just put it in a jar.

D: *Can you ask them why they're taking samples?*

P: I'll try.

D: *They're asking you questions, you can ask them some.* (Laugh)

P: Well, you see, before it was difficult for me to say anything, because of the state of consciousness I was in when I first was beamed aboard. But I can try to mentally communicate.

D: *Let's see if it works. It's fun to try anyway.*

I was unprepared for the physical reaction that simple question would have on Penny's body. It was proof to me that she was reliving an experience in the presence of physical beings, who could produce a definite physical reaction in her. Because it was an unpleasant reaction, I do not believe it was fantasized. There was a long pause as she tried to mentally communicate. Then her body jerked with a sudden jolt, and she took a sharp intake of breath. It almost gave the impression that she had been struck by something. "Ooooo!" she moaned. Penny was breathing heavily and showing signs of physical discomfort.

D: *What's the matter?*

P: Well, I tried to tune in, and I immediately felt something like a miniature lightning bolt coming forth, statics of electrical stuff shooting out from their head. This is why they can communicate mentally so powerfully. They have a protection system inside their head so others cannot enter in without their permission. It kind of shocked me. I was trying to read their mind. Let me try another approach.

D: *I don't want you to feel uncomfortable.*

P: It just surprised me.

D: *Just mentally ask them questions and see if they can answer you. That way you won't have that same feeling.*

P: Yeah, I was trying to almost probe, and they didn't like that.

D: *Okay. Just mentally form the question of why they're doing this sampling.* (Long pause)

P: That time it worked. This is the message I received, "We are trying to find a new planet to inhabit. For our planet is being destroyed by the elements right now. And we're trying to find a new place to continue. We are checking out other planets, too. It's too early to interfere on the species here. We must take samples to see if they would be compatible to our bodies. If we could exist in this type of environment without receiving bacteria that could be harmful to our existence. This is why we prefer to take samples. And are in a protected area, so they are handled in such a manner that we are not contaminated by the substance." And *I* ... ummm, that is the message I am getting now. I sense now that even I myself am in a plastic cylinder that is surrounding me, so as not to contaminate the beings. I think I was beamed with the light right into this. The craft opened and I was beamed into this cylinder. Clear like plexiglass, but it's not. It's a substance, and it is surrounding me. And they are able to penetrate mentally through anything, just about.

D: *This was for their protection. Then when they showed you things, you were looking through the glass?*

P: Well, I must have been. It is clear, so I can see through it. And that's why the samples are also put in cylinder-like bottles. Because they do not actually touch the substances with their hands. They cannot risk that. I don't know exactly ... I'm trying to think how they did pick them up. They just beamed me up. I don't know if they beamed substances right to the big cylinder first and then transferred them. I can't see ....

D: *Well, it makes sense that they wouldn't want to be contaminated. I can understand that.*

P: I feel like one of them did get out of the craft to look around a little. But he put on a special suit. It was silverish looking. Zipped up the front or something, some opening in the front, to protect their bodies. Even while they were out there they could not let anything touch their skin, as you would call it. What was peculiar, they talked in a language I am not familiar with.

D: *Talked to each other?*

P: They mentally talked to each other a lot, but there is a voice-like transmission coming forth from one to the other, back and forth, a conversation.

D: *You said they didn't have any mouths?*

P: I just don't remember seeing a mouth.

D: *Do you mean there were particular sounds they were making?*

P: A language, a type of language.

Penny had difficulty describing what it sounded like. A few weeks after this session she found something similar to it on a record of space-type music. She said it was not exact but sounded very much like it. When I listened to it I found she was correct, it was difficult to describe. It sounded somewhat like a babbling, scraping series of sounds. Not mechanical or computer oriented, but similar to sounds that could be made by humans if need be, although it was not in words like our languages on Earth.

D: *Can you ask them, is this small craft the main ship, the only ship?*

P: No.

D: *Because I thought it was awfully small. Where do they take these samples?*

P: I'm trying to get it. (Pause) I think if I was there, I could just find this place. If I was in Olathe, I think I would just be drawn to that area. There were trees there, but there was a bit of a clearing for them to land. It's in and about Olathe, and my grandma lives pretty close. I don't get a very ... it's off a street and near Stephenson ... farther out. And that's the closest street, because it's not a residential area. It's just a wooded area.

D: (I tried to get her back to the question.) *I was wondering, where do they take these samples in these plexiglass bottles or containers?*

P: To a mother craft.

D: *Can they give you a mental picture of what that looks like?*

P: Larger in size.

D: *Does it have a certain shape?*

P: Similar shape, but much larger. Like this is a baby ship, and that's kind of like mommy. (Laugh) Instead of just a red rim around it, there are some dark things supporting it. I mean, in the midst there's a darker color, like a very dark blue, or maybe black or something in a darker shade. Like an interspace between the red and the light going around it. Maybe windows perhaps. And, oh, it would be much more noticeable if it landed. It would probably frighten a human being. It would be too large to not be noticed easily. This smaller craft is used for landing, because it is less noticeable.

D: *Is this the first time that this mother craft has journeyed to Earth? You said it was these beings' first time.*

P: Well, this is the first time these beings had left the mother craft and actually landed right on the planet with the opportunity to get out of the ship if they wanted to. Actually it was these two beings' first time leaving their planet. And they decided to go with the mother ship to come here. The mother ship has a camouflage system.

Clouds. It can hide behind clouds very easily. And that is why they cannot be seen. The smaller ships come out of it. There is a compartment on the side of it, like a metal wall that slides up, and small craft can come right out and go wherever they want. The large craft will be in the general vicinity of where the small craft are. They will stay over the same continent, for instance, because they must keep an eye on their craft, and their beings. It's a form of protection for them. And they have to be careful not to disrupt the harmony in the universe. There are certain reasons they have been informed of, prior to visitation of the Earth. Of universal law. So they know the rules.

D: *Then this is not the first time the mother ship has come?*

P: Let's see. It's been here before. Other areas. Peru mostly. At an earlier time in the history of man.

D: *Well, how do they go back and forth to the planet they are from? Or do they go back and forth?*

P: Yes, they must go back. They cannot stay very long. They go back and forth. They're here for a mission, and when the mission is completed, then they return. It's been a while since they came back this time, but it was necessary. You see, there was an atomic bomb and this alarmed them. They had to get certain data of the effect on this planet, for their research. And the effects that it was having on nature in different parts of the planet. It was a disruption in the universe. It was felt throughout the universe. And an abomination to their type of thinking. They're trying to understand *why* this came about, and what could be done to help it in any way. But they were concerned for our planet. It had actually helped in some ways. Unknown to many, after this took place they, and other space beings, too -- a conglomerate of systems working together -- banded together to prevent any more of this type of activity. That is why you haven't seen another atomic bomb since then. They have had a very strong influence. That is another reason why there are space beings around now. To prevent another disruption in the universe. It won't be allowed. And mentally people are being set in their mind to avoid a great nuclear disaster. And you will see the influence in your governments.

D: *If they don't come very often, does it take them a long time to get back to their home planet?*

P: Well, there is not time as you know it.

D: *They don't consider time like we do?*

P: No. And ... (had difficulty) the speed of light is easy for them to go past, beyond it. Actually, first they come in close to the vicinity of the planet. They are still in outer space. They don't project right on to the planet. But there's like an orb around the planet. They are still pretty much in the far outer space. And then they travel, and keep projecting closer and closer and closer, till they can land on the planet. It's like little jumps. There's a major jump past the speed of light. And then it's a series of smaller jumps once they're in closer range to the planet, that they have tuned their vibrational equipment to be near. And that is why they will be in that vicinity. And they want to make sure there is not an obstacle there, too, when they take that super jump. (Laugh)

D: *Then when they go back, it's the same kind of a procedure?*

P: To planet Earth?

D: *Or when they go back to their home planet?*

P: That's what I was describing.

D: *It's the same procedure then. It's difficult for us to understand without thinking of time and how long it takes.*

P: Well, that is the thing. Time, well, let me see. I'm speaking through my voice, yet I'm getting a lot of visualizations and mental messages now. They're willing to communicate with me if I don't try to force my mind on theirs.

D: *I know they probably don't even understand our concept of time at all.*

P: They aren't concerned with it. Except when there's a disruption in the universe, and that will call their attention. That was a *moment* in time. Big events happening on the Earth. A shift in the Earth's axis, for instance. Major things. Tidal waves. Big things affecting the whole planet will attract their attention. But it's just a *moment* in time. They're more concerned with how it's going to affect over a long period of time. It just depends on exactly what kind of occurrence is happening. There are no days to *them*. But light years have some measuring, and light years mean something. They measure time in light years in a way. That's the best I can tell you.

D: *Well, you said this type of beings, or this type of mother ship, are doing sampling of the Earth, and animal life. Do they ever do any samplings dealing with humans?*

P: Well, they did take a sample of my hair. And they wanted a sample of my skin. And I didn't even notice it. It was such a small piece. I didn't feel any pain when this was occurring. But from one cell they can discover a lot about the makeup of a human body. And they wanted a dog like they saw in my mind pictures, to test, to compare. There wasn't one in that area, and they were kind of disappointed, I think. (Laugh)

D: *How were they able to take the samples if you were inside that glass?*

P: Well, that is a good question. (Laugh) Because I do remember them touching my hair.

D: *You said they were fascinated by your braids.*

P: Yes. Actually, this glass thing, now that I'm getting a better sense of it, is more like a clear force field. But so strong, it's like you would think plexiglass or glass would be. The force field was clear. It had a form and dimension to it, when projected. So there are ways that they could, with gloves on, put an arm through and pull something out. And they put my consciousness in a trance state, because they didn't want to frighten me. They knew that I was frightened. And even there I guess I was showing signs of this shock almost. And so they particularly did not want to induce more of that feeling.

D: *Well, that was understanding of them, anyway.*

A similar situation occurred in my book *Keepers of the Garden*. When Phil was taken onboard the spacecraft he had the impression that he was placed in a jar, or rather that his *personality* was in a jar while they worked on his body. In this way he would have no physical sensations. He then discovered that the "jar" was indeed an energy force field that he was encased in. So the experience can actually give the impression of being inside a solid container.

P: Even though I was in a trance, they could still sense a shock-type state. I mean, a sense of fear coming from me.
D: *So they took samples of your hair and a sample of your skin. How did they do the sampling of the skin?*
P: Well, right now I'm getting a feeling from my arm that there's a metallic type of instrument used for this. And after this was over I couldn't remember, and I just thought that I'd run into a tree or something.
D: *It was like a scrape?*
P: Yes, so I really didn't think that much of it. But I can see now that it's red and kind of bloody there, but I thought it was more of a scrape.
D: *Did they do any other sampling on you?*
P: Well, they had a machine that they ran up and down my body. And with this machine they were able to see the inside of my body. Plus their own sensory equipment was pretty amazing, with what they could tell automatically. They were able to find out a lot just from probing my mind. And everything is there, all the information they could want to know about me.
D: *Did they make any remarks about the body, whenever they were looking inside it?*
P: I think they pointed at my reproductive organs. (Embarrassed laugh.) They did point at that. And I think they were just acknowledging that that's an area for ... that's how humans multiply. (Laugh) It's kind of weird now to think of it. But they needed to know about that. I feel like I'm naked now. At first I felt like I had clothing, now I feel

I'm naked in this thing. That's when they're pointing at that part of my pubic area. But I'm still behind this field, because they can't physically touch me, or they would be contaminated.

D: *Is that the only thing they thought was unusual?*

P: Well, they just wanted to understand how that worked. I couldn't really show them. (Embarrassed laugh)

D: *Because you are a child.*

P: I needed another human being to show them, right. I had never had sex. They saw a book in my head, one my parents showed me, a" facts-of-life"- type book. It had pictures of how the baby comes out of the mother and everything. And they searched me for that. And that's how they were able to find out about the male and female body, because they got it from my mind pictures.

D: *Can you mentally ask them how they reproduce and multiply?*

P: I'll try. (Long pause) Let's see, I'm getting some kind of confusing pictures. Let me try to clear it up without my own consciousness interfering. I'm going to have to ask again so I make sure I get it right. (Pause) (Big breath) Oh, ho, ho, wow!

D: *What?*

P: Well, I wasn't kidding when I said their minds are pretty spectacular. You see, when they want to do that sort of thing, two beings get closer together, just standing apart from each other though. Physical contact isn't necessary. But the head of one being projects energy, it looks like, into a womb area, the lower area of the other being. And I saw something kind of swelling up in that area, like there is a ... oh, well, oh! Now I am getting the message that both beings are capable of this. One can take the turn or the other.

D: *Neither is one sex then?*

P: No. Androgynous type. But they can be either. Both of them can reproduce. I saw that one will emit out of their head something like a little miniature light. An electric show like you'd see in the sky, lightning. Something to that effect, pretty powerful, is projected, with a visualization in mind of what is to be produced there. The two beings are connected at that time. And something will start to grow inside one of the beings. But that being that the new being grows in also can turn around and use their mind and shoot out that electric surge into the other being. It doesn't matter. They're all one. And it just is a matter of choice which one wants to produce it. The ... babies, as you might call them, are produced at a very rapid rate. In fact, immediately after that mental transference takes place, an electrical charge actually touches the abdominal area of the other being. You can see it shooting forth and actually touching and actually going into that area. Immediately after that happens, a swelling starts. And those kind of beings are produced at a much more rapid rate than our kind of beings are.

D: *How do they come out of the body then? Can you see that?*

P: Let me see. Well, I'm getting a feeling of ... through the stomach. Not out through the legs. But they can open up their bodies in the stomach area, and it just kind of comes out there.

D: *Is there an opening there?*

P: Well, you see, there is a glowing light about their body, so you can't really see. I get the feeling that openings can open and close, and you would never see the openings. I mean, it's automatically sealed up. That glowing light makes it more difficult to see, but I did get a visualization of it coming out, just like a caesarean would be. And sealing back up immediately. And it's tinier. It starts off smaller, and grows to full size in a very rapid rate. And the children are very advanced very young. They are taught, and immediately put into a type of training, as soon as they are able to walk around. At that time they are already shown pictures of the universe. They are already being trained to be familiarized with galaxies in the universe. Even at that age, they can comprehend what is shown to them, as far as the universe and the galaxy. As soon as they are just barely able to walk, their comprehension is amazing.

D: *That's very good and I thank you. Can you see any kind of symbols or insignias or any kind of designs if you can look around that room?*

P: (Sigh) I'm trying to look. Let's see. First my attention is drawn to a crystal in the upper portion of the ship. But this is like a cut crystal, red in color. It's set in a round circle with a golden rim around it. Actually this could be where the red light comes from. I see that. At first I thought it was a symbol because it was placed inside a circle-type thing. But let me see what else I might ... I'll try to look around. (Pause) Ummm, well ... I don't know what that means.

D: *What?*

P: Zigzags. I see ... on the side of the ship, upper area again. I guess it could be an emblem, but it's a zigzagging type of design in a goldish kind of tubular rimming. Perhaps it comes from the way the ships fly, they kind of zigzag in the sky. And it represents something. It also represents a type of a space council. It's an emblem, something to do with that, too.

D: *Do you think you could reproduce that for me afterwards?*

P: I could try. It's not real clear. I mean, I can just get part of it, because there are a lot of lines to it. It's more than just one line. It's three or something.

D: *Well, try to fix it in your mind the best way you can.*

P: Okay. Let me look at it again, and try to get it imprinted better.

D: *Okay. Well, then did they return you to the outside?*

P: Yes. It was like nothing had happened. My eyes were closed, and I opened them up. And to me it was as if I just blinked. (Laugh) It all happened so quickly. All I remember is seeing those orange lights moving around. I did not see the craft at that time. It was behind the lights. They were in front of it. But they were aware of me.

D: *You said it was just like blinking your eyes?*

P: Yeah. Apparently when it was aware that I noticed it, then a beam was shot out almost automatically, because it didn't want me to see the craft, and it had to protect their identities.

D: *Is the craft gone now?*

P: I don't see anything there now. Oh! I think it kind of dematerialized. I had a visualization about it. It just kind of vanished. And for a moment I thought I saw something. After I opened my eyes, I actually thought ... it was like there was a flash of light that went by. And I looked again, because I thought I saw something. I think it was that craft, it could vanish that quickly. And to me it appeared as a flash of light. It could have still been more of a beam light emitance. I don't know. Oh! I can see it dematerialize now. Oooo, this is quite unusual. I think that's what it did. It didn't really take off this time. I can see it just fading into nothing. Kind of blotting out till finally there's nothing there.

D: *But anyway, you didn't remember anything about this afterwards?*

P: Well, like I said, I saw what I thought was a flash of light. And I just remembered something orange. I felt rather fatigued after the experience. I just wanted to go home and go to sleep. And then I forgot about everything.

D: *All right then. I want to thank you for what you've been telling me, and I appreciate it very much. And I would like to come again and ask you questions like this at another time, if it's all right.*

When Penny returned to full consciousness we discussed the session, and I reactivated the suggestions that she would remember some of the details well enough to draw them.

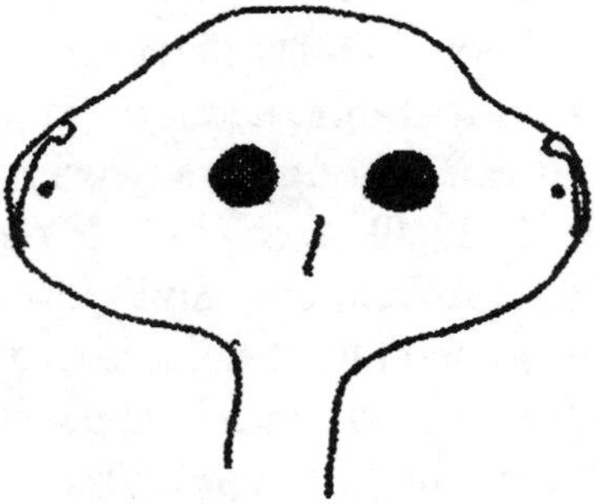

Oct. 27, 1987 creature

Foot

Description of creatures:

Head (sideways) oblong shape. Eyes very round and solid black. Nose a mere bump, no nostrils visible. Ears had a rim and top tips, but close to head. A hole where sound would enter. Mouth not visible. Later she thought the mouth was visible one time but then it seemed to disappear again. At that time it was more of an uneven jagged type of opening. She said, "Does this make sense? That it could appear and disappear?" She seemed to relate it to the way the creatures had their offspring. The abdomen area seemed to open and close over again. They seemed to be enveloped in a type of glow which made some details difficult to see.

Hands: three fingers and a suction cup-type device on the thumb. Creatures' arms were longer than their legs. Their posture and stance monkey-like, stooped over with dangling arms hanging down. When at rest the hands were bent at the wrists and almost touched the floor. The feet were enclosed in a mitten-type of skin covering, and a longer thumb-like appendage. She compared the feet to duck's webbed feet, because she could tell there were long bones inside the skin covering. She thought the foot was capable of gripping.

She had the feeling that her conscious mind was not registering the answers given on the tape. It seemed to be "tranced-out," but her subconscious was reporting what it was seeing. She remembered feeling a sense of cringing when she first saw the creatures, because they were not pleasant to look at. She thought there was probably more done to her than she reported. She thought her young eight-year-old mind shut out a lot of it.

Upon awakening, the area just above the inside elbow joint of her left arm was hurting. She thought this was where they scraped the skin off. This was a case where the body was also remembering an experience, as well as the mind. Care must be taken by the hypnotist to prevent any physical symptoms from carrying forth into the waking conscious state, so I removed any feeling of discomfort.

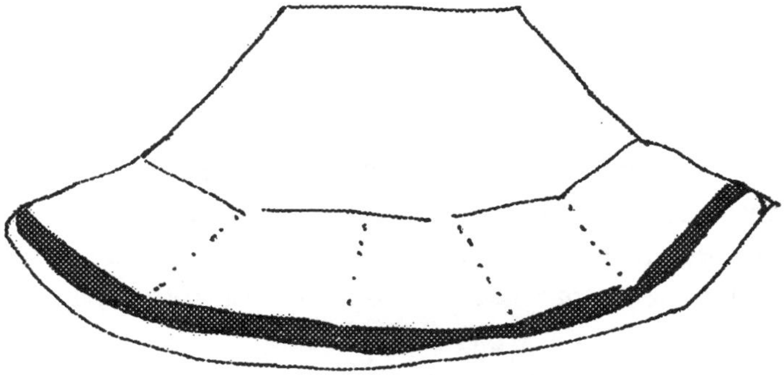

After much trial and error this was the best we could come up with on the shape of the spaceship. She had a compulsion to correctly portray the shape, yet she felt it was still not accurate. She said the flange was more bent than seamed, as though there were structural supports underneath. A red light ran all the way around the edge of the flange. It had a small interior, only one room, yet it was large enough to stand inside. It held only two small beings.

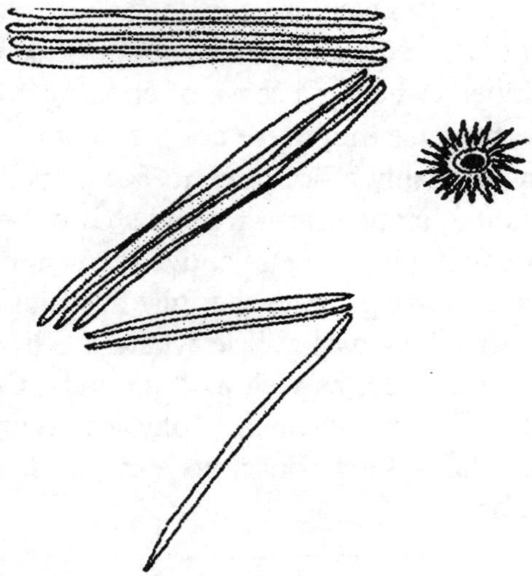

Emblem on wall of spaceship. Note: Four bars on top, then three bars, two bars and finally one bar coming down. She was most emphatic about this arrangement. The star-like emblem on the right meant that the ship was a member of the space council.

Enlargement of emblem to the right of the larger one composed of bars. It showed a silhouette of jagged mountains, definitely some kind of rock formation, against a red sky. She had the impression from the emblem that the sky was red on their planet. This was why the lighting on the ship was red. It was the light spectrum they were used to.

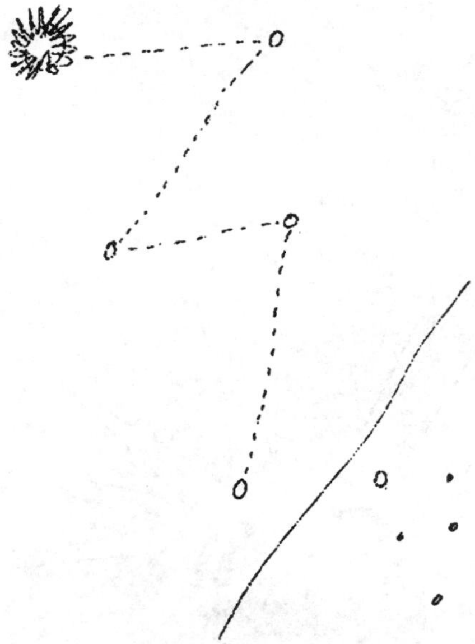

In the lower right corner is the arrangement of the stars on the Star Map. There was a large one on the upper left, which seemed to be their home planet. Then the smaller ones, with the bottom one furthest away. They apparently then traced the zigzag pattern for her, which her eight-year-old mind associated with dot-to-dot drawings.

They tried to communicate to her that there were small jumps from dot to dot, then a larger jump to the last one (Earth?). This last one required more energy or more effort or whatever to make the jump. It was easier to go to the first dots, but harder to the last one. Almost as though they had to shift to a different type of speed or process or something. (Maybe going through a dimension?)

When she awakened and was drawing this, only then did we notice the similarity between the star map and the emblem on the wall. The same zigzag design.

In answer to the skeptics that might think this session was the result of the subject relating a fantasy to please the hypnotist, I do not think that is the case. Penny had no conscious memory of an experience, and thus had no motivation for inventing a story. I have had cases in my UFO abduction research where the subject was convinced they had experienced a real encounter, yet under hypnosis the truth came out. In many cases there was no UFO or alien experience, but something ordinary and perfectly normal. The subconscious has many reasons for hiding an experience, the least of which is alien involvement. It is always wise in therapy to accept the simple explanation before the more complex one. But I have found that if the subject is in a deep enough trance, the conscious mind can be pushed to the side and the subconscious will supply the correct information if the right questions are asked.

In my opinion this was not a fantasy invented to please me. And the next session a few weeks later further convinced me of the validity of the memory as the subconscious supplied more information.

At the next session I wanted to ask a few more questions about the aliens that Penny saw when she was eight years old. I used her keyword and took her back again to that time.

D: *Let's go back to the time when you were around eight years old, and you had the unusual experience with strange-looking little beings. And you were in that room inside the enclosure-type thing. You were asking them questions and seeing all the different things that were there. I will count to three and we will be there. 1, 2, 3, you've gone back to that time when you were eight years old, and having that experience. What are you doing? What do you see?*

P: (Big breaths, then slowly) I'm standing up. My arms are out to my sides. Oh? What do I see? (Pause) (Childish) Them beings, they're still pointing at me. Pointing at me, and I can't respond verbally. Restraining me. They don't want to harm me, but they are curious about me. What else do you want to know?

D: *Why are they pointing at you?*

P: Different parts of my body. To find out how I reproduce, and studying the organ structure. They have a lot of it already figured out with the experiments. And they wanted to take samples. My body is kind of resisting it. I just can't believe it. That I'm really here, because I've never had an experience like this. And it kind of scares me. And these beings kind of frighten me. They try to communicate with me, but I just don't know what they're going to do next. Because I don't know *them* at all. It just happened so quickly, and I am in a slight state of shock about it all. I feel kind of afraid, and I don't know what they're going to do next. And I don't like that feeling.

D: *Didn't you say they had some kind of machine that could look at the different things inside your body?*

P: Yeah, it looks like what you might call a flashlight (unsure of word)-type thing. The light comes on, but it's shaped flatter. You know, like a flat, flat, flat flashlight. But there's a beam of light that comes forth from that. And they move it up and down my body, kind of like a scanner. It scans me. And with that it makes pictures come up on a screen. And they can see what's inside my body with that particular instrument. It's black on the outside of it, a black tool. And it has a beaming light that comes forth from it, it shines on my body. And they went up and down and around. Mostly up and down with it.

D: *Is it like an x-ray?*

P: Yes, but they hold it in their hand, and the pictures come up on a screen. It's similar to a computer type screen. Like the front of a word processor, but without the rest of it, just the screen part. There are no keys like a typewriter. There's something like a computer thing that they have with it, so they can punch in data, and analyze the specimens with this device. They can break down, analyze the cell structure and the chemical structure. And they compare it to their structures, and see the differences and the similarities with this computer-type screen. But it's like nothing I've ever seen before. There are colors on this screen, that are also significant. The body organs and things, the colors mean different things.

In the beginning Penny was reporting this episode through the eyes and vocabulary of a child. As she progressed it was obvious her subconscious mind was drawing upon concepts in Penny's adult mind to give the descriptions that a child would obviously not understand. This was apparent because there would not have been computers when Penny had the experience at the age of eight. She was using the modern concept of computers and word processors to help in the identification. Yet the idea of colors on the screen was surprising to her and to me, because in 1987 color computers were still a futuristic concept.

D: *Oh. That really does sound different. Earlier we were mentally asking them questions, and they were giving you answers. They said they didn't mind doing that, did they?*

P: Only with their permission. I can't just tune in without them being very aware of it.

D: *They said they didn't like that.*

P: As long as *they* don't feel violated, then they will permit a mental exchange of communication.

D: *Because I had a few more questions I wanted to ask them. I want to find out more about* their *physical structures. Can you ask them if they eat or drink?*

P: I'll try. (Long pause) Hmmm, hmmm. I'm getting mental pictures. Fluid has to be absorbed into their system. Their skin ... this surrounding material around the body can absorb things. And there are substances, even in the air, that they can absorb if they choose to. There are fluids that can be done this way. They don't have to use a straw to be filled with the fluid they need to exist. They don't need water as we do. They use something similar to a water substance, but it's translucent looking. And on their planet there are areas that are similar to a pond with water on the Earth. Or a lake or ocean. There are places on their planet where there are fluid substances, but they're of a different texture and cell structure than water. They don't have to drink it, but just be next to it and absorb it. With their system, they get a feel of whatever they need. Mentally they can transfer these substances. And the outer layer of their body is made such that it easily can absorb things into it, without it being seen ... very much. It's sort of a *mist* type of experience that happens. A steam or mist that is absorbed into the steamy ethereal part of their body. And as far as food goes, there is a plant type substance that they do eat. A darker, leafy, green type of plants, that they partake of with much enjoyment. Let's see ... they do have a mouth that can be used sometimes to eat this leafy green stuff. I don't know what that's called. But they can absorb things to get the nutrients they need. They're very interested in our plant life here, and in comparing it to the plant life on their planet.

D: *Earlier you weren't sure if they had a mouth or not.*

P: Let me take another look at them. It's just barely ... they can almost cover it up. There's an etheric part of the body, you see. It's so bright that it kind of covers it. There is an opening under where their nose is, but it's just a *real small* opening. It's not very big ... circular ... in structure. It's just a slip in the skin, almost, that opens up. They can seal it up so you don't even see it most of the time. I thought it was very peculiar seeing beings with no mouths. But then when I heard them talking without lips, I knew they had some kind of mouth.

D: *They were making some kind of sounds.*

P: Yes, and that's how they were able to do that. I don't know if they have teeth, because they eat plant stuff. I don't think they eat any meat-type substances. There are things that are on their planet that they can turn into food. But their bodies don't really need a lot of bulk. Actually it makes it easier for them to transport and to do some of the wonderful things they are capable of doing, with less bulk in their system. Food is actually a secondary thing to these beings.

D: *We are always comparing to what we know of our own bodies. And I was curious about how they are different. You said there are wonderful things they can do? Could you elaborate on that? Do you mean this going between planets?*

P: They can dematerialize. That's pretty major to us, but it's pretty second-hand to them. To them, their bodies are of that type of structure. They are capable of doing this because they're more advanced. And they can travel places more easily than other beings of alien type nature, because being able to dematerialize gives them more mobility. They're able to pass through major obstacles in the universe, in the solar system, with *ease*, because of their mental advancement. And they are in complete control of their system. Their bodies are a tool for them. They are observers in a sense, too, observers of the universe. And very knowledgeable. They have taken records from *many* civilizations. And they will compile it into their ... like a big book that they have on their planet. They try to learn as much as they can about every type of species available. In fact, they specialize in collecting things for their planets. There are other alien civilizations. Some of them would look up to these beings, because they're pretty high up there. Even as far as ones that can travel in these alien ships. There's even different degrees of knowledge. Some are more advanced than others. And these are one of the more advanced groups. They have like a center of information for the universe. They welcome any other alien civilizations. They have their own protective systems, so that no undesirables will be able to penetrate their force field.

D: *You said there was a larger ship up in the clouds that they came from. Can you ask them, are all the beings on that larger ship the same type of beings as they are?*

P: Well, I got a message that there are some androids there. Androids like robot beings. They perform certain duties that these beings would rather not waste their time doing. They program the android and it will just do tasks. In fact, they are considering making a human-liker android, because they think the human species is an attractive looking species. They're considering that at this time, but they need more data first. (Pause) The androids that I see there are more of a triangular shaped box kind of thing. Moving around the aisles, really more metallic looking with lights on them. And they can do many things. They really don't like using too many of those. They rely on their own skills which they think are superior to the android.

D: *I was thinking of an android as being at least part machine. Would that be accurate, or are they made differently?*

P: I don't know how they make them. It's a robot type machine.

D: *It doesn't have a face or features or anything?*

P: Well, the ones they have just move around the floor. They do have probers, but that's a different function. Actually, a beam of light is projected forth from the ship. And it's a scanner, it's almost like eyes from inside the ship. They can see through it, and they make it move wherever they want to look. But there is a density to that light that makes it able to pick up textures or things they wouldn't get with just the vision of it. Does that make sense?

D: *I think so. That would be what you saw in the beginning, that was scanning out the area. But on the larger ship the intelligent beings all resemble these ones you have contact with?*

P: Most of them. Well, the robot-type things are different. But those aren't really beings, they're more mechanical. Let's see ....(Pause) My consciousness is mixing up pictures here. (Mumbling) I must get the accurate ones. (Pause) They are all pretty similar, but there is a main one in control. He wears a robe with a high collar and a big jewel around his neck. And he sometimes projects himself to the area near the pyramids in Egypt.

D: *Does this being look physically like these others?*

P: Yes. And he can dematerialize and materialize and never be seen. I saw a mental picture of him, and I sensed him being *in* a pyramid, actually, in Egypt, because that energy is very conducive to their bodies. The pyramids are like a signaling station for extraterrestrials. Messages can be sent from these to higher places.

D: *I have wondered what the pyramids were for.*

P: They have been used for many different things. But the energy there is such that it's conducive to transmitting energy as well as being very receptive for it. It can energize anything within it. It stabilizes things. Messages can be sent toward the craft, because if you are inside a pyramid, your telepathic abilities are naturally increased. So if you have a very intelligent alien being in a pyramid, it is logical that they could transmit a higher frequency to reach any aircraft that would be in the area, if they wanted to. Different frequencies affect different crafts. It's like a signal. Like the air force might send a signal and only their craft would recognize it. And they would give the right message out. Plus they have other instruments that can send a frequency of a *sound* that is so high that our regular physical type hearing wouldn't hear it. It is a similar phenomena to the way a dog can be affected by sounds so high than humans can't hear them. They have a little tuning instrument that they can adjust, and project a certain frequency. Now if it is done in a pyramid, it is exaggerated. Plus it's a safe place for them to be without being seen and upsetting people by their form. That's another reason why they were in some of the more secluded areas. They can tell whether there are any people around before they manifest. Some people that are attracting that type of experience are ready to see them manifest. But they can tune a certain frequency, and it can be projected out. And then the craft of that frequency range will be attracted to it, and might send a message back.

D: *Did they find out by accident that the pyramids would do this?*

P: For somebody visiting from above, when they look down,

the pyramids are something an aviator would notice. They stand out. And someone in the sky, in the heavens, would notice it moreso than another type structure. Plus pyramids, even in the far stretches of the universe, have a great symbolic meaning.

D: *Then they knew it would do this.*

P: They were curious at first. They wanted to go inside one. And once they were there they tried it and it worked. The dimensions were created perfectly in the pyramids. The conditions were accurate to create the pyramid energy. So they probably knew it would work ahead of time.

D: *Now let's leave that scene. And drift away from that scene when you were eight years old, and you were having that strange experience. And it won't bother you to remember that at all. We'll drift away from that experience and move forward in time. I want to ask your subconscious if Penny ever had any other experiences like that, while living in this life? Is that the only time she experienced anything like that?*

P: (Pause) No. There have been other times. These same beings tried to contact me again. When they try to monitor me.

D: *How can they monitor you?*

P: Something was placed in me.

D: *When was it placed in you?*

P: The time the information was placed in my head. That's part of it. This is to create a certain frequency in my system, and this frequency attracts them. It's almost like a radio antenna.

D: *Do you mean when you were eight?*

P: Yes. Alien beings are attracted to this similar frequency, and they want to use me to observe things going on on this planet and to provide information for them.

D: *Was it some kind of device?*

P: They didn't want me to know for a while. I didn't understand it when I was younger. Now it's starting to be more revealed to me. Let's see, it's something planted in my head. (Pause) And it was almost mentally projected there, but there is a form to it. It's mentally projected but it has a texture to it. They can manifest things with their mind. But it's almost triangular in shape, a piece of metal. But to them it's like an antenna.

D: *Do you know where they placed this?*

P: (Pause) The top part of my head. I sometimes feel the affects of it. About once a year I get a weird feeling in my head. It's like a throbbing. It's helped me with some things, you know. It really doesn't interfere with my normal biological functioning. It's more like they can tune in to me very easily, and I can send them mind mental messages. When they want to tap in there they can.

D: *Do you think an x-ray would reveal anything like that?*

P: Maybe it could. I don't know. It's not a regular type metal. So could you check something that's not a type of metal as we know it? It looks metallic in nature, but it's just for data. It hasn't really affected me. I'm not a robot for them. I just keep up with things going on in the world. They want to know what we're doing down here so they can help us more easily. What they put there is not obstructive to my growth in any way. If anything, it's an asset. Because they're very advanced, they know what they're doing.

D: *About how big is this?*

P: I think it's ... I'm getting different pictures now. First I see a tube in my head and then a ... maybe a tube was put there to place it. I don't know. It's weird. And then I see a triangle, very small, very small indeed, microscopic almost. I want to say microscopic. But I'd have to put it next to something to really know how big it is. And my skin layer is kind of woven around it.

D: *Do you think there might be more than the one on the top of your head?*

P: No. I only feel there was one placed, because that's the age I was at. If I was more completely grown .... See, they knew that my skull was going to grow in size. And they didn't want to put anything too large there, so it could grow without having any obstructions.

D: *That's why they put it on the top of your head?*

P: Yes, it's a signal. But it can only be activated by certain frequencies. They will try to communicate with me sometimes in my dream states. But they don't really try to interfere with my everyday progression. It's like I'm an observer for this particular species. They study us. There are quite a few people on this planet who are utilized in this way. To someone else it might seem rather violating, but it really has not caused me any problem. If anything, it has enhanced mental abilities for me.

D: *Do you have any way of knowing when they are having contact with you?*

P: I'm starting to become more aware of that frequency. When my vibration is raised to a higher level, I'm more sensitive and aware of them tuning in to me. I feel like my heart's speeding up or something. I feel like a rush of vibrating energy descending on me. Higher beings are vibrating at faster levels. It's intense, but it's a comforting good feeling, too. It just automatically happens. It's not anything that distresses me. I'm getting more sensitive to it as I naturally progress, especially more now in this time of life than ever.

D: *Do you ever hear any sounds or anything?*

P: I've sometimes heard a humming noise. But I don't know if that's what it's from.

D: *Does it come from any certain part of your head?*

P: I don't know. It's just a vibration noise. (She made a low pitched sustained hum.) That kind of a noise.

One of the reasons I wanted more specific information about the tone was that I have encountered similar reports in my work with UFO abduction cases. Some subjects have reported hearing a tone or hum just before an experience occurs. Often it was reported as high-pitched, similar to the sound of a Skil-Saw. In Penny's case she said it was low-pitched. It could be that a variety of tones are use.

P: But that doesn't always happen simultaneously. I can sense when there's a high energy being around. I can feel its vibration, because it interacts with mine. It almost makes me feel a little shaky, because I'm adjusting to the higher vibrations. But it doesn't make me upset or anything. I am kind of programmed, you know.

D: *What do you mean, you're programmed?*

P: To be an observer for them. But they had an agreement with my will before this took place.

D: *What do you mean?*

P: Well, I guess I was attracting that kind of experience. And before I took embodiment I chose to have some of these type of experiences. I wanted to reach out to help others. I subconsciously wanted to be a mediator between lower man's nature and higher man's nature. Or between the lower beings and the higher beings, a mediator. So in this way I am like a bridge, while being in this body. And helping to bring forth ideas of great creativeness and great intelligence to help advance man in many ways.

D: *I can understand that. Some people can't, but I can understand that way of thinking and looking at it. But it won't bother you to know these things about yourself. They haven't bothered you all this time, have they?*

P: No. There was one time when I could tell someone was making some adjustments in my head. I definitely was feeling like a robot, but I knew I wasn't. But I had something altered, and I don't know exactly what. Maybe an adjustment to that thing or something. I couldn't see things, but I could *feel* it. Physically, consciously feel changes going on in my head, like things being adjusted or something.

D: *When did that happen?*

P: It was about ... eight years ago. Eight or seven. I was going through a crisis at that time, and I asked for assistance, for help, and it happened.

D: *You were having problems in your personal life?*

P: Yes, I was very sad. I was in between places to stay. I stayed with a friend, I wasn't really happy there. I don't know, I was just looking for something more fulfilling in my life. And then that happened. Soon after that a lot of really interesting things started to happen for me. It was like a turning point, in a way. I had to ask first before it could occur.

D: *They didn't interfere then by doing this without your permission.*

P: No. It was my free will.

D: *But you didn't remember about that later, did you?*

P: I didn't really put the two together till now.

D: *Did you have any more physical contacts with them after that time when you were eight years old?*

P: (Long pause, as though thinking) No, not physically. But on other levels. Mental, astral, causal, spiritual.

D: *I was curious if you ever went back onto a craft like you did when you were eight years old.*

P: No, not with *these* particular beings.

D: *With any other ones?*

P: No. But some of the things I think you're inquiring about, are things that are *to* come ... and *are* to come. Actually some events are experienced on more of an astral level than the physical. But the other was physical.

D: *Then you think the others were astral, like in a dream state?*

P: Yes. But on the big wheel. The wheel. It *did* happen in that state, but it is to come. It's going to manifest more fully and there might be quite a few people that will experience it, when that descends on Earth.

D: *Can you explain what you mean by quite a few people?*

P: Well, in my astral vision there were a lot of people around. A lot of people. When the first sighting happens, whenever the craft, the big wheel, comes, many people from all over the world are going to see and know then, that there are extraterrestrials. This might be one of the craft that will land. It's a real strange one.

D: *Do you mean it looks different?*

P: Well, that wheel one, that's the picture that I get. (Voice very sleepy and sluggish. Difficult to transcribe.) I get the feeling it's not the only one that's going to land. That one is a more special craft, because it actually puts things out in the air to make people more conducive so they won't be frightened.

D: *Some kind of a chemical or something?*

P: It has green balls coming out from it. This ship might not be seen so much by the physical eye as some other craft. But it's going to come first to prepare people for the big arrival of the other ones. We're talking at least ... within thirty years.

D: *Why are they going to come? They've been so secretive all along.*

P: To trade technological advancements. If we give up war, fighting like animals here on this planet, they'll exchange technological and scientific advancements with us, so we can advance at a faster rate. To help us overcome sickness and other things at a much more rapid rate. But they aren't going to deal with us if we're going to continue acting like animals. So they're preparing us for their arrival in our dream states. Communicating with many. And there's more than one observer. I'm one. There are other ones out there. Because they can't always be here in the physical without alarming people. So they have to do it this way. It's one way they can study the information they need, of what's going on in the world and the news and the media and things. Seeing how they keep tabs on us, so to speak, so we won't blow ourselves up. They can bring the mental pictures up on the screen. And they can ask questions. It's almost like you do. The subconscious of the person hearing it, and having their questions answered almost automatically. The subconscious will just give it to them, if it's asked in a certain way.

D: *You mean they don't have to have physical contact with the person?*

P: No. But they usually are in the vicinity in a craft when they are doing this type of monitoring. They can get the pictures on the screen more easily that way.

D: *Does the person have to be asleep or in a trance state for them to get the information?*

P: Well, it helps if they're in a relaxed state of thinking. In a meditative state. If they are relaxed, they're not as alarmed by these events.

D: *You mean they can do this to anyone?*

P: No, if that person is at their level, an advanced one, then it would be difficult without that person's permission. Because they're so advanced, our world won't complain about it unless it feels violated. If it's something to help that being, and if it's not interfering with their regular lifestyle, if it's not conflicting with their inner goals, then there is no reason to complain. If it *is* conflicting, then it won't happen. They will only deal with individuals that have already given their permission before they took embodiment, so that won't be a problem. They can tune into the higher vibratory levels. Usually they like to choose beings that can deal with that type of energy.

D: *But you mean they can do it to anybody without that person knowing about it?*

P: Well, many people are aware to an extent that there's something in them. They know something's different, but they can't quite put their finger on it. It's very subtle. And in a way, their subconscious is aware.

D: *Yes, the subconscious knows everything.*

P: So it's not completely hidden.

D: *But do these people all have to have a device in their bodies before these beings can pick up their thoughts?*

P: Oh, no. They can mentally and telepathically communicate without a person having a device like that. But if they want it to be an "observer" for them, it's an honor, in a way. To be utilized in this way is almost an honor, because they're so advanced. We can learn a lot, and progress at a much more rapid rate, if you let yourself be an instrument in this way. It's like opening yourself up to universal energy in a positive way. So if they want to get certain information from you, then it's helpful if you have that implanted. And, too, they monitor different things about your body.

D: *You mean bodily functions?*

P: Bodily changes, yes, and see how the humans progress, at what kind of rate. Cellular structure changes. And they can keep a monitor on that also, besides events going on in the world. They're concerned with all of that, but world events seem to be drawing an extra amount of attention. At this time there is concern about the Earth tipping off its axis, partially due to nuclear testing going on inside the Earth that has upset the axis. And great shifts could cause many catastrophes on this planet. They're concerned about it. There are already other conditions because our ozone layer is messed up right now. We're already getting ourselves into an unpleasant atmosphere if we're not careful. But the shift in the axis would be a major problem to everyone on the planet.

At this time in 1987 I was accumulating my information from Nostradamus that resulted in my trilogy, *Conversations With Nostradamus.* No one else knew the extent and severity of the prophecies that were to be contained in that book. Yet here was a young girl verifying it by repeating the same information about the problem of nuclear testing and its effect on an Earth shift. The same information coming from another source.

D: *Then this would explain why they don't actually have to physically land so often. They're getting information from people's minds? They don't have to have physical contact?*

P: They don't. They *did*, for certain tests and everything. It was needed by them to study certain cellular structures. But they used gloves, they didn't actually touch me because of the fear of bacteria contamination.

D: *Is that when they took the skin samples?*

P: Yes. They had a type of gloves they wore because they can't take chances. They have to be careful not to insert bacteria on the craft or themselves. They say they will make a more physical contact, but it's usually only if that person has been attracting that situation to them. The person actually wants physical contact. And so the experience simply manifests when the two energies are brought together. Sometimes a being will kind of buzz into a person, or bounce off a person or something like that. It's just getting all this information by doing that. It's not a touching in a way we think of touching. It's a blending for information, and they can separate themselves from it very easily. They can find out so much just by absorbing things. It's hard to explain very well.

D: *Their minds must be much more advanced than ours.*

P: Yes. And so when a more physical interaction takes place, it's because a human being has wanted this experience. And there's an alien being that wanted an experience of being closer to a human. And so they exchange these thought patterns, structure manifests, and the experience happens. Thoughts are very powerful.

D: *Yes, I've heard that before. Does the human being have to be intelligent for the mind transfer ... thought transference or whatever it is, to take place?*

P: Well, for mental telepathy. You can have impressions in your dream state. When a being is near, you will pick up thought impressions from them. The more powerful the being the more mastery they have of projecting thought images. These thought images could project forth, and just about anybody can pick it up in their subconscious. It would be done automatically. But to be an observer, usually a certain thing must be implanted there, because that person is being studied over a long period of time.

D: *What about a native in the jungle, that was not highly evolved? Would it also work on them?*

P: Oh, yes. They would start to experience feelings and things, that they wouldn't describe very well. And it might come out in art. Many of these inexperienced people don't have words to express themselves, so it will come out through certain abstract type art. And music sometimes is an influence of these new ideas.

D: *But the being or the craft has to be in close proximity to the person that picks this up? It doesn't work over long distances.*

P: Unless that person is astrally projecting themselves to another planet or something. Then it could happen, but again you're in a close vicinity, but you'd be in an astral body. If not, the craft would have to be close to you.

D: *The craft would have to be somewhere around the house, or around where the person was?*

P: Well, it doesn't have to be that close. People have a ... (Softly) I must find the right words now. People have a tube of light around them. Right?

D: *Like an aura?*

P: There's a *tube* of light. (Used hand motions) There's an aura around a person, but there's also a tube of light. And the craft must be in a vicinity that can tune in to this tube of light. Tune in to the higher self. It communicates with the higher self first. It is at the top of the tube. And the higher self can project itself to many parts of the universe. But the space craft must be in a certain span of this tube, your particular tube, I guess you could call it. It's almost like a circle within a circle of the space. The tube is like a smaller circle, but then you have a larger circle around that. It doesn't have to be in close vicinity of that person's *house* or anything, by any means. It can be much further up. Not visible to and beyond airplanes. Beyond the clouds. It can be way up there and still be able to do that.

D: *Then they just beam in on certain people?*

P: Yes, they tune in to that. See, every being has a frequency, like a tone. A sound tone. And space beings discover what that person's tone is. And they tune in with the frequency, which is another way to describe a tone. They have it on their ... I guess records or something. I don't know what it is. But they'll know that being is that frequency. And when they're in that vicinity they sound a tone that's at a frequency that the physical ear can't hear very well. But the subconscious immediately will respond to it. The higher self responds to it. Higher self sends down the message to the lower self, and then the message is sort of absorbed.

D: *And then it just releases the information, you mean, without the physical conscious person knowing about it?*

P: Yes. But if that wasn't in that person's makeup, so to speak, or if that person did not want that experience, if they weren't willing to have that experience, if the will was in the way, then it wouldn't happen. Very rarely will an alien being of that nature try to conflict with the person's free will. In fact, it's a law of the universe not to. There have been a few aliens that are ... colder. We think of it as a colder nature, because they look at human beings like we look at cattle. And so they aren't as sensitive to our feelings and our needs. They're so advanced that they see us as very stupid, I guess. Some beings like that are not so concerned with the freedom of our will. The beings that really try to help and that are in association with the interstellar space group, are concerned. They care about us, these little beings here. But some other beings that aren't within that council are able to force their energies into our dimension. But they don't do it very often. We're just a curiosity for them. We can't really help them in any way. We're just data to them. But the older beings really want to help us advance, because they see our consciousnesses. We're all projecting mental thoughts out to them all the time, but we are all very protected. And there's a reason for all of this. There's a wonderful plan for man.

D: *Then if someone didn't want to experience this, they would just have to put their free will ...*

P: Yes. Just start thinking about higher, positive beings of an alien form, and show an attraction to them like you'd be attracted to a friend.

D: *I mean if some people felt this was an invasion of their privacy, could they just put up a ....*

P: They'd block it. They'll mentally block it from happening.

D: *Because most people don't know they can stop it, if they feel it is an invasion of their private life. That would make you feel a little bit like being in a goldfish bowl.*

P: It does, but the benefits are well worth it. Or I would never have made a decision like this.

D: *But they can only gain whatever knowledge you have. If you don't have a certain type of knowledge they can't get that.*

P: Yes. But as a monitor, we are exposed to so many types of knowledge. We're just a big data bank, in a way. (Laugh)

D: *I was thinking that scientists and people in the government would have a different type of information than we would have.*

P: Yes. And they've been contacted by some beings. People in the highest states of office are being monitored. Things are controlled to a degree here. This is a planet of limitations. And we embody here on Earth to learn how to overcome these limitations.

D: *Do these people in the government know they're being contacted?*

P: Some do. But they can't say that to the general public or they'd lose their office. But yes, some have been contacted, even in physical form, some on the telephone. But much of it will come in their dream state. They will be very influenced by dreams and it affects many people. Mass consciousness is very affected by this sort of thing.

D: *I see. They would just get ideas and not know where they came from. Do those beings understand what I want to use this information for?*

P: Research.

D: *Yes. But if I write about these things that I discover, would they have any objection to that?*

P: No. The fear is that it might alarm some. But they don't see it as a harmful thing, or they wouldn't do it. You must understand, things are implanted in us all the time: energies, ideas, thoughts, words. We implant them in ourselves from our environment. We are absorbing things all the time too. We're influenced by things constantly.

D: *We never really know where they come from.*

P: That's right! So it's humorous to them almost, because if we understood ourselves better, it would not be any big deal. There's so little we understand about ourselves. They did think it's important that it is written that they will not conflict with the person's free will. They can understand what people get upset about sometimes. There have been many people that have had a broken bone and had a piece of metal inserted, and continue to lead a very fine life. It never really messed up the rest of their life ... too seriously. And this implant is something that interferes a lot less. It doesn't really cause any physical discomfort ... usually.

D: *I guess human beings don't like to think other people are running their lives, so to speak.*

P: Well, it's not that way, because I still have a free will. I do whatever I want to do whenever I want to do it. They just tune in to what I'm doing. They don't tell me what to do. I'm not a robot. God has blessed me with free will and they will not interfere with that. It's important that this is *stressed* in what you write.

D: *Yes. But do you feel like it's an invasion of privacy?*

P: No, I really don't. Because it makes me feel good to know that someone is interested in me. It makes me feel different, but I'm interested in them too. I mean, they give me an exchange. By doing this for them they fulfill other needs for me.

Penny was then brought forward and oriented to the present day. Needless to say, she and I were both very surprised by this information. Before this session neither of us had any knowledge of implanting devices and monitoring by aliens. She certainly had no indication that such things were going on within her own body. But the subconscious is the guardian of the body, and nothing is kept hidden from it. As I began my UFO investigations I was to hear this repeated many times, but at this time in 1987 the idea of implants and monitoring was a totally new concept to me.

Later Penny said the information wasn't bothering her. She said as long as the device wasn't affecting her in any way, why worry about it? And she returned to her normal life.

CHAPTER FIVE

A WRONG TURN IN EVOLUTION

This case occurred while I was staying with a young couple in San Francisco in the summer of 1993. I was doing a whirlwind speaking tour and would be lecturing and doing book-signings in several cities. They had volunteered to let me stay at their house instead of going to a hotel. My books on Nostradamus had been in print since 1989, and I had received many letters and phone calls from people who were convinced they had been alive during that time. Several thought they had been associated in some way with the great psychic, and a few even thought they were his reincarnation. I have had the same response from all of my books. I can only surmise that they strike a familiar chord in the readers, and they are identifying with the time period or country rather than the characters. Who knows? In some cases I hypnotically regressed the people who had these convictions. I was not really surprised to find that when they entered the trance state they went instead to an entirely different time period than those connected with my books. This added validity to their regressions, because they did not find what they were convinced they would.

I had a feeling this case would be similar when Chris said he wanted to be regressed because he was positive he had a past life associated with Nostradamus. Chris was a young successful businessman who had no problems and did not need therapy. He wanted to have the regression to verify his suspicions and find out about his connection. It surprised us both and gave this case more credibility when he not only did not go to the Middle Ages time period, but he did not even go to a life on this planet.

He settled down on a comfortable couch in his living room with his pet cat curled up at his feet, and immediately entered the deep trance state when I performed my induction. He soon began to describe his first impressions. He was looking down on an alien landscape that appeared strangely desolate and lifeless.

C: There is a city. Dark buildings that seem to be made from a material similar to granite. They are shaped like domes and cubes. I'm going over them. It's like a city in a valley that doesn't have any inhabitants.

D: *What do the surroundings look like?*

C: They look like barren hills. Like the Valley of the Kings in Egypt, but no tombs. It's very out-of-place. There are no trees. There is no water. (Puzzled.) And ... it doesn't appear that there are any people. The city has tall skyscrapers with intermittent semi-circular domed buildings. And now I see windows on the roofs of the ... they look like *plazas.* (A revelation.) Everybody's underground. That's what it is.

D: *What do you mean?*

C: You can see in these ... skylights. They look like solar panels or power panels for the complex. Now it's changing. Everything has turned bright white.

D: *The buildings?*

C: The whole complex. And the panels are turning. It looks like something out of a science fiction movie.

D: *You mean the panels are moving?*

C: Yes, it is like they are tracking. I don't know how to describe it.

D: *Just do the best you can.*

C: It's like the sun all of a sudden came up on this complex that was dark. (With certainty.) We're not on Earth.

D: *You don't think so?*

C: No. I'm going to go up real high to get a better look. (Pause) It looks like the surface of the planet has been scorched. It looks like there are circles *etched* on the surface of the planet. Like marble ... like fudge on ice cream. It looks like the whole planet's covered with unusual valleys. And in these valleys there are these complexes. Everything is underground.

D: *You said the surface looked as though it was scorched? What do you mean by that?*

C: It looks like desert. It looks dry. It looks devoid of life, vegetation, in forms that *we* know them. And now everything's underground.

D: *You said when the sun came out these panels began to move?*

C: It appears as though it was a type of solared night. And then the sun appeared, and the panels on the roofs reacted to the light, and tracked to the light. Like solar panels with automatic tracking systems.

D: *Do you want to come down and stand on the surface?*

C: Yes. We'll go down. I'm gonna hold on. We have to land in an old area. There used to be surface activity in this *old* part of the planet, when people lived on the surface.

D: *Why do you have to land in that part?*

C: I don't know. It seems that it's a different material than the rest of the buildings. The rest of the buildings look like they were synthetically made, like molded plastic, but very large. There are some old pyramids in this area. They're unusually shaped. This is an old area on the planet that is as it was before they built the other complexes.

D: *What does the ground look like that you're standing on?*

C: It's scorched and ... or bleached huge stone blocks. They're very worn and scorched and have ... like Death Valley has salt crystal residue all over them. As though from some sort of blast. There is a rise, and on top of this rise it overlooks a really large valley. In the valley ... (Pause) it's really unusual. There is what would look like a lake, but it actually looks like a residue pond.

D: *Residue pond?*

C: Like there is a crater there, and at the bottom of the crater there are colors ... red ... and the residue at the bottom of it is multi-colored. I'm getting that there was a big blast right here. Because my whole body feels like something came over the ridge. It feels like when you walk in front of a sunlamp. It's hot.

D: *Does this pond have water in it?*

C: No. Just residue of some sort. And when you back away from the ridge, you can't feel the emanations of whatever is coming out of that hole. (Startled.) Oh! There are two suns. It's a binary system.

D: *Tell me what you're seeing.*

C: There are two suns in the sky.

D: *Are they both in the sky at the same time?*

C: Right. It's a binary star system. The two suns triggered something ... a memory. That would explain why everybody's underground.

At this point he shifted from the objective reporter to experiencing the scene.

C: (Becoming upset) We blew up our planet! And we're underground now. We can't come out. The radiation's too strong to live on the surface. (A deep, deep sigh.) That's what happened. (Pause.) It's cool now.

D: *Why is it cool?*

C: I'm underneath this shell now.

D: *Did you go inside?*

C: I was *brought* inside.

D: *Who brought you?*

C: The people that live underground. I'm living underground now too.

He began to exhibit physical reactions, as though something was disturbing him. I thought it was the sight of the alien creatures.

D: *That's not going to bother you.*
C: (He was breathing in short breaths.) No. It's the energy that is so different.
D: *All right. But remember you're protected.*
C: I'm experiencing this from memory.

His body was quivering and displaying physical sensations.

D: *Yes, the body remembers also. But it will not bother you physically at all. You can tell me how it feels, but you don't have to experience it. But it's a different kind of energy? Is that what you mean?*
C: Yes. I *wanted* to experience this. It's a memory. There's no problem with any danger.
D: *I don't want you to be uncomfortable. That's what I mean.*
C: They're showing me something. They're backing off, and I'm going down a hallway now.
D: *What do these people look like that brought you underground?*
C: They're ... shorter. (Mumbled some words) They're gray. They have large-skulls, black cat-like eyes. Their skin color varies from light blue-gray to some other ones that look very different.
D: *There are different kinds?*
C: No. They look like their skin's been bleached or something. Maybe they've had radiation poisoning.
D: *Do they wear any clothes?*
C: No.
D: *What about yourself? What does your body look like? You can look down at it.*
C: It looks ... (Pause) it looks like them, but I'm *pink*. And my body now is ... real tingly. It's adjusting. There are lights coming through this unusual and interesting transparent ... like plexiglass-stone and roofs. I'm just looking around where I am, and it's like a big *mall*. It's very interesting

because there are ramps that go down into tunnels adjunct to the mall.

D: *Look at your hands. What do your hands look like?*

C: I have four fingers. Thumb. Big hands, short fingers. Like the ratio of palm to fingers is two palms to a finger.

D: *What about your feet? What do they look like?*

C: The same, but more shaped like Vees. Like I am wearing diving flippers. (Surprised.) There are marks on the chest. It looks like scratch marks. They're sharks' gills type marks.

D: *On* your *chest, you mean?*

C: Yes. I'm viewing my body from outside. I'm looking back at myself. It's really unusual looking. I'm changing colors. It's from being outside.

D: *You were pink because you were on the surface?*

C: It seems that this happens. I don't know if I was returning ... (A big breath) Hold on!

The energy may have been affecting him again.

D: *Are you a sexual creature?*

C: There doesn't appear to be any apparent sexual differentiation between beings at this time.

D: *Can you see if you have any ears or nose?*

C: Very little. Nobody does.

D: *What about a mouth?*

C: Yes. A mouth. Whenever I try to look at the other creatures, they seem to shift in and out of physicality. It's getting dark now.

D: *It's all right if they shift around. Just tell me what you can. That's the only thing you can do. But do you have teeth?*

C: No.

D: *What do you use for sustenance? How does the body live?*

C: Let's go down the ramps and see. I'm in a corridor. It's almost square, and it has like lime-green tile on the walls. It's fairly bright. And we're coming around a turn, and it opened up into a ... (Thinking how to define it.) it's part of the city. It's like an auditorium. And then ... (Confused) I'm not in the same place.

D: *Why do you think that?*

C: Because there are *humans* all over now. (Laugh)

D: *There are humans now instead of the others?*

C: Yeah. (Confused) I went through a tunnel, and now I'm in an auditorium.

D: *These are people that look like humans, you mean?* (No answer.) *Do you still look the same?*

C: No. Now I'm me again. It's almost like I walked into a different world, into an opera house, from this other complex. And it's like it's frozen in time. There are people standing around, and lights are on. It's like I stepped into the middle of a preparation for a performance of some sort. And it's *very* different. It's very strange. They are not moving.

D: *Do you want to go back down the corridor to the other place again?*

C: Let me go back.

D: *Can you do that?*

C: Yes, I can. I'm going back up the corridor, and then we go around. And then the corridor ... there's no ceiling on the corridor this time. It's black. Dark. I don't understand. It's like when we came to the first place, I was not on Earth. Then I stepped out into an Earth-like auditorium, but everything was frozen in time. And now the corridor seems to go back towards where I was. But it looks different. It's coming out of the ground, and it's nighttime, or there's no sun. And there are stars out. And it's back on the surface where I was originally. Nearby, but it's more of a canyony-desert place than being on the ridge. It's all black and scorched also, but my body doesn't feel any tingling or heat as it did before. I'm just confused about what I'm doing there.

Did he inadvertently enter a doorway between two dimensions? Each vibrating at a different speed, so that one appeared to stand still? This occurred once in my work with Nostradamus (Volume III), and has occurred in my investigation of UFO cases, where time appeared to stand still. If these were parallel dimensions, then one was on Earth (past or present) and one on the alien world. It could also be parallel universes existing side by side. This type of complexity will be further explored in my book *Convoluted Universe.*

D: *All right. Let's return again to the place where you were. It looked like a mall, and you said you were underground. You saw all the other creatures.*

C: That's down the tunnel.

D: *Let's return to that again, and explore that area. You can do this. Do you want me to count you, or can you find it by yourself?*

C: Oh, I can get back in. There's an access way right here. And we go in, and up something like an escalator-type thing. And now I'm overlooking the area where I was standing before. It's like a mezzanine. That walk goes around it. And there is an indoor type of garden. It looks like an algae pond of some sort. They are growing algae. And it's illuminated from above by the plexiglass-like granite that is translucent. And inside the translucent material are large flecks, like it's made out of alabaster with big flecks of some kind of material. It's an unusual stuff. It shields the radiation and provides light and warmth for the building, and the algae. There appears to be a type of garden, but it's harvestable. It's very unusual. So I'm going around the mezzanine.

D: *If this was harvested, what would it be used for?*

C: Food.

D: *How would you take it into your body?*

C: It's smeared on their skin. It looks like a lotion. It's absorbed.

D: *They make it into a lotion, and then this is absorbed?*

C: Food. It looks like people are taking it, like you would scrape mold off a rock. And then they rub it on their chest where the shark-like slots are.

D: *If you were to do that, what would it feel like?*
C: I can't get down there from here to try it. But it probably would feel like rubbing ... putty. I don't know. The consistency looks a little more like snot. A mucousy-type of material. It's greeny-purpley-blacky-looking stuff. And it has a bit of its own luminosity. It looks almost like the stuff in a glowing watch. Something that emanates light. It's stuff like an electrolyte. I believe it has something to do with the water or the growth process. It's like there's light on the bottom of the pond. The energy of creating these molds or spores or funguses or lichens, or whatever they are. And if I was going to say it in context of Earth-based stuff, it looks like it would be a cafeteria.
D: *So this is how you take food, by smearing that on the body.*
C: It's definitely some sort of nourishment. Nobody's chewing anything.
D: *All right. What is your job? What do you do in that place? Do you have an occupation or something that takes up your time? See yourself doing whatever it is?*
C: I'm going into a small area. There are little rooms that look like giant test tubes. Almost like telephone booths that are round, that you can get in and out of. They almost look like a whole bunch of steam tubes. That's a good analogy. They're upright. But they look more ice cream cone shaped.
D: *With a point at the top?*
C: The bottom. (He had difficulty describing.) It looks like a bee nursery where ... there's a gestation process going on here.
D: *Do these little -- what should I call them? -- containers? Do they have anything inside them?*
C: Pods. They're bodies. They're bodies to be insouled.
D: (I didn't understand.) *In-what?*
C: Insouled. It's a genetic birthing center. There are three walls ...more than three walls. It's like the containers grow with the gestating body inside. Starting small, and then they grow larger. And they grow in squares. Like specific numbers are produced in series. They are arranged in tiers. I'm looking

at it through a containment material, not glass, but it's transparent. And I'm going down the hall next to it, checking them for failure rate.

D: *What do you mean?*

C: Sometimes there's a defect and the (he didn't know what to call them) ... bodies don't survive the process. Like producing. It's very strange.

D: *Is this how your race is reproduced?*

C: Yes. This is where the process is done. Where these beings that want to insoul choose the vehicle for the experience.

D: *Can you see the ones that are just beginning? How do they look?*

C: That's where I am right now. It almost looks like a bee hive, where ... (frustrated) it looks ... they start small in little containers. And then the container and the bodies grow with the process, and it moves along to the next level of the tiered facility. It's not moved by a conveyor belt. It moves more like something you'd see in a canning plant. It's a mass production. As far as I can see there's probably ... let's see ... hundreds ... maybe twelve hundred and something units in the process at this point. They're nurtured through the bottom of the pod. They're held like an egg, like a melon scooper with tubes connected to the bottom where the fluids enter into the process. So I'm walking by that, and now I'm going to another facility.

D: *There is fluid in these containers?*

C: There's fluid surrounding the bodies being developed.

D: *And the container expands with the being. Is that correct?*

C: Correct. Right.

D: *Can you see what it first starts out as?*

C: They come from a bunch of office-looking facilities at the beginning of the conveyor process, where the real small ones are. And they're coming up out of a room. The beginning process is in the rooms. When they first come out they look like a petri dish with a flat bottom connected to a base with a tube. Then there's a bump on the top. It's like a mucous expandable gelatin shell that holds the embryo, and grows with it. And we can go down at the other end and see what happens.

D: *When the process is finished?*

C: Yes.

D: *Does this take a long time for it to grow to the proper size?*

C: My understanding is that they grow them as fast or as slow as is required to provide the vessel for the insouling being. There are different rates, for there's not a large death rate here. But people can come and go. Entire families can come and go for other experiences, and do so, for accessing incarnational probabilities in other realities. Group pods of beings ... I'm seeing families, memories of my family being born all at once. I see the insouling ... ah, ha! that's at the other end. The fully gestated vehicles wait for a decision for the bodies to be insouled. And then they're brought into like a plexiglass (Surprised) shower!

D: *Shower?*

C: The containers are washed or treated, and then they dissolve. And the vehicles are animated, and checked, and are ready for a life cycle. It's like a human hatchery.

D: *Are they full size whenever they come out of this?*

C: No. Almost. There is some growth process.

D: *Then if the soul doesn't enter, what would happen to the vehicle?*

C: It would perish.

D: *So a soul has to enter at that one point.*

C: This is where the choice of vehicles is made. This duplicating process is done because the radiation has affected the genetic pool.

D: *So in other words they can create life up to a certain point, but the soul is the final deciding factor? Would that be correct?*

C: The DNA genetic processes are like duplicating processes. There's no way that these vehicles have sentience* prior to the choice of insoulment. *(Capable of feeling or perception, conscious.)

D: *And there is a little growth that occurs after they exit the shower part?*

C: There is growth to the extent of the amount of genetic variation that's been applied to the particular batch of vessels produced. That's done down at the other end, where we were before. That's where I work. We're going back down past the conveyor belts. I am going to the laboratory. Going in, it has an unusual door to keep contamination out. We're going inside. It's a spinning-like thing, almost like a department store. (Like a revolving door?) I feel very comfortable in here. There are some ... it looks like mixing boards of .... Hold on while I figure out how to explain it. (Pause) There are tables that are perforated. They have holes in them that are about three inches around. And it looks like a giant ... I don't know how to describe it. It's like a table that's six or eight inches thick, of solid material that is perforated with holes. The whole thing emanates light. It is like a light refrigeration system for the DNA materials. And these materials are brought out. And there is a device that reads the DNA coding onto the ... it's hard to describe ... it's a wand of some sort. And it goes to predesignated containers. It appears that the light emanation from the different holes is coded so that the DNA material information is in a frequency of light. This goes onto the rod. Then the rod is used to encode the physical material in the ...egg. There's another name. I can't find the word. There are no words for the technology in English.

D: *Why have they had to resort to this method of reproducing?*

C: This wasn't decided to do this. There was a decision made by all regarding these matters. And when these things were lost in the destruction on the surface ... I'm having memories of what happened.

D: *Can you tell me what you're remembering?*

C: Large auras of radiation. It's like bombing in the night, with saturation bombing going on on the surface of the earth. It's chain reaction now. It's all being destroyed. There are underground cities. There's a large panic. It's ... I'm confused between what I'm seeing and what I'm remembering. I'm outside now. It's fine and then there is the destruction on the surface. And now we're inside.

D: *You said it was like bombs. Where did they come from? Why were they detonated?* (Pause) *Can you find that information?*

C: The information is shielded. Right now it's more important to understand what happened.

D: *Why did the destruction come about? Do you have that memory or that knowledge.*

C: I don't know. There are bits and pieces. It has to do with the reason why we're reproducing in laboratories. I'm in two places at once, and I have to consolidate myself.

D: *Yes, we're just curious to know why the destruction occurred. What caused the radiation?*

C: All I see is this large door shielding me from this. Your accessing of the information is something that is another experience on the planet, from another time. That was long ago, and there's been much shifting of the understanding of the past. It's hidden. It's hidden. It's not something that's discussed. It needs to be healed. It's not remembered.

D: *Do you mean the* reasons *why it happened are something that nobody talks about? They keep it hidden?*

C: It's something that's gone.

D: *I thought you meant they didn't want anyone to know.*

C: It is a denial of error made. The ability to go back to the past is closed.

D: *So that information has been destroyed. It's gone, in other words?*

C: It's known, but it's not acknowledged, as to the significance of it. And how it affects the civilization and its inability to understand how they got to this point. And why it seems that there's no place to go.

D: *They just don't consider it important? Is that what you mean? Or they just don't want to talk about it.*

C: It's known by all, but in this reality this experience is not part of that. (Sadly) It's the end result of a wrong turn in evolution. There were some processes that continued the race. There is a sense of hopelessness, but life is there. This is one area. There are others, but there is sense of aloneness. There is a sense of being just contained, and being (Big sigh) ... it's just there. I just have no variations of consciousness. There is great group understanding of beingness, but not any capacity to create life existences and experiences above and beyond the containment in these underground facilities.

D: *Is that what you meant by the feeling of hopelessness?*

C: (Sadly) There is no place to go.

D: *As though there is nothing beyond that? Is that what you mean?*

C: There are groups who moved off the planet. They can come and go in certain cycles. They have a different agenda.

His following answers were confusing. Did he mean they were coming and going [cycles] by reincarnation?

D: *Where do they go when they go off the planet?*

C: They don't come and go. They are just there. They have their own existences in space, as we do underground in our own space.

D: *You mean a different part of the planet?*

C: They live in their spaceships. They don't come.

D: *They just travel in spaceships, you mean?*

C: Yes. There's a situation with the evolutionary processes that give us *hope,* if that can exist. A feeling of *desire* for something, not "hope" as humans know it. It's a *desire* to survive. A desire to investigate the potentials from what we have, and go forward. We are so limited *here,* and ... alone.

D: *But you are able to reproduce, you are surviving.*

C: It's an aloneness. It's like working in a factory that makes the same product over and over and over and over and over and over. And it's very interesting stuff. But there's nothing really new going on. I guess that's the best way to put it from a human standpoint.

D: *But if they're in the spaceships, where do they go? Just fly around the planet or what?*

C: The planet is dead. There's nothing here. They go out, and they're working on new possibilities of recreating the potential of the civilization, through reworking of the genetic coding with diversity.

D: *In other words, they want to get back to what they were before, or just get back to something that's different?*

C: Heal the past. There are other members of the family on different planets that are doing other projects, but they do work with the earth, with ... I can't pronounce the name of the planet. It sounds like Luther, but ... (He made attempts to pronounce it, but the best he could do was make the first syllable "Luth".) Some other. They also operate .... (He was taking deep breaths.)

D: *Operate what?*

C: ... need space. I'm back on the planet. It seems to be the focus of the life experience. The feelings of ... well, the feelings ....

D: *But you are not one of the people that go back and forth in the space craft.*

C: We're here. We go nowhere. Civilization exists. It's very interesting how it is done.

D: *Well, these bodies, do they have the ability to die?*

C: Definitely. And by choice. It's much akin to willing oneself into the death of the vehicle.

D: *So they don't grow old?*

C: No.

D: *Do they suffer disease?*

C: Radiation poisoning causing genetic dysfunctions.

D: *What is the radiation poisoning caused by?*

C: Radiation poisoning from the past has affected the genetic pool in ways where some of the codes have changed, rendering them unpredictable. They're more random than specific, and that causes, what would you call it? A genetic defect. This is about as close to disease as I can relate to.

D: *So this radiation poisoning is still passed through the genes, and they never know for sure if it will come out in the vehicle. Is that what you mean?*

C: That's why there is a failure rate. It's nothing that we can't deal with, but it is limiting the possibilities of diversity.

D: *So that is something that can act as a disease. Can it also kill the vehicle?*

C: Yes. But it's not as if that insouling entity can't acquire another vehicle in a modality that doesn't involve emotions or death. And the replacement vehicle is ready in no time, as it were. There's also a room where some of the more unusual defects or variations are kept. There are some very hideous-looking creatures, not insouled, just defective.

D: *Do they keep them alive?*

C: No. It's more of a museum than it is a specimen.

D: *To show what can go wrong? Is that what you mean?*

C: Yes. Case histories type of thing. There are some that are very, very tall, and almost look scorched. It's like burnt toast. And they're old. Very odd.

D: *Do you think these were some of the first ones, when they were first trying this process?*

C: It would appear to be a combination of that and defects in the experiments.

D: *But the bodies you have at this time, is that what the bodies looked like when they were living on the surface?*

C: No. (A deep breath.)

D: *Or do you have that information?*

C: Just memories in cellular level. Memories. We could go outside in a past life. We could go out to the place where the bricks, the huge stone buildings were. The old part.

D: *Do you think you were alive at that time?*

C: This was many, many, many millennia ago. But the memories are kept. The old stone place antedates the newer cities. They antedate the apex of the civilizations. They were brought by the seed groups.

D: *Seed groups?*

C: Seed groups. The original beings.

D: *That was where they were living before the destruction.*

C: It was a cultural center that survived the rise of many political and, what you would call, theological systems. I'm getting an image ... a real fast moving movie of what happened. It was a lush planet. There were large populations. I can only see certain areas of it. It's in bits and pieces.

D: *But the people looked different?*

C: They had gender. They had lighter skin. Their bodies were of greater bulk. They had greater frequency modulation in the emotional level. There were greater beings of more, even human nature, in a way. There were very different ones too that were there then. They had ... I'm seeing images of ...apparently helmets or head gear. They were very unusual, like winged.

D: *Winged?*

C: They had winged head gear. And there are diplomats of some sort. Then there are treaties being signed. And there's ... I'm in another space. It's shifted my perception.

D: *As you're looking at it like that, accessing your cellular memory, can you see what happened to make this explosion occur?*

C: Technological disagreements with colonists. And separation, which is against the nature of the consciousness of the civilization.

D: *Was it different groups of the people or what?*

C: Various groups. More warlike attitudes creating political upheavals. Doing colonization without authorization. There was an overreaction to a political decision that created a chain reaction of destruction, that tore the fabric of the planet's biosphere. The life support systems of the planet were rendered useless, in regards to exposure to the radiations of the binary. Forcing the people to go underground. Making a descending of consciousness involving decisions. There's blaming going on. Everybody wants to place the blame on the experience. And the splitting of factions caused so much disruption to the group line, it tore apart our civilization.

D: *These underground cities, were they already built before this happened?*

C: The cities were built. The underground complexes were dug, expanded upon after the surface failure.

D: *So they didn't have to start from scratch. They did have some cities.*

C: It was known, because of the radical shift in light and dark on the planet, of exposure to the binary. And the binary is on the polar opposite side of the planet. They also knew that this light had certain affects, and they could use this light. The buildings have a capacity to utilize light more efficiently for their photosynthesis process, directly to the body as nourishment. They took these buildings as protection, then expanded on them as the colonies no longer had the surface to utilize for activities.

This sounded as though they built the buildings originally for the growing of their type of food. Then they were put into service as living quarters because they could shield out the radiation.

C: There's a lot of pain. There's a lot of doubts and reflections on things that had happened. And this is what I've had memories of as I work in the nursery. Of what was, and what now is an interesting project with no interested people.

D: *But you said they also had a different frequency. They had more emotions. Do you mean after they lived underground for a long period of time many of these emotions are no longer there?*

C: They were removed through genetic technologies, as by the initial process.

D: *Why were the emotions removed by this process?*

C: Because the group mind felt that they posed a threat that could possibly completely annihilate the underground cities also, if they were retained. There is a part of this that I am being shielded from right now. I can't talk about that.

D: *But it seems as though they thought they should genetically remove much of these emotions so this wouldn't happen again?*

C: So that they wouldn't completely destroy themselves.

D: *As though the emotions were the blame?*

C: That is where the blame was placed. That is where the reflection of the causal and then group mind was born into that area. Not fully understood as the group mind over matter, matter being emotion. In this case, it was thought by consensus the way to survive, without thinking of the consequence.

D: *So they were turned into a group mind rather than individuals. Is that what you mean?*

C: It's always been group mind.

D: *But the emotions created problems.*

C: Within the group mind, but as a fracturing of the mind of the entire groups. This is the .... (He began to show signs of being disturbed.) I'm real hot! Right now where I am. I better go down these stairs. They move by themselves, like a corkscrew. And I'm going down levels.

D: *Where are you going?*

C: It looks like different levels of places that are habitats. And it's still light. As we go through the layers, the material looks like a layer cake. And the light parts of the layers emit a light. It's very unusual. And it goes down like a corkscrew to these different layers. Then it's like a large beehive complex, as if you're looking at a wasp's nest. Layers, and there's like a large panel on the other side, which is shielded from the outside. It's like the complex is built into the side of a cliff. We enter from the top, and now we're down near the bottom of this. It's very interesting. Everything is like you would see in a transparent insect or bee makeup.

D: *What is this part used for?*

C: This is the housing. It's like a communal existence where we all live together. Group pods within the larger groups that family, soul families, inhabit.

D: *You mean each one has an individual cubicle, so to speak?*

C: No, and yes. They're like bee hives. They have a central common room with smaller rooms going off to the sides. And they're connected by no doors, they're connected by walls running like partition wall setups in office complexes.

D: *Well, do you sleep?*

C: Yes.

D: *So those would be places you would sleep in?*

C: This is the place.

D: *I see. That helps me to understand. All right. Now backtracking to what you mentioned before. You said some of these beings had entered spaceships and were going back and forth to other places. And they were looking for variety. If the emotions had been removed as a safety factor, why would they want to get those back? They run a risk if they're looking for variety.*

C: It was a mistake, and not all believe that the emotions were the cause of the destruction. It was a long time ago. It's known that there were alternatives to the route that was taken by genetic means to proceed. This is an area that is like a large empty cavity for me. It's not understood by so many of us exactly the reasoning behind it, because of the confusion at the time to deal with the situation. Perhaps vestige emotions remained in some that saw that the destruction of the emotions would be advantageous for all their agendas in the future also. This is not understood. There are also other agendas being pursued by various groups of the other race, to aid in understanding the best way to heal this. For the future. There is a connection to other ships and civilizations, in regard to what's to come from the remainder of the civilization.

I felt we had learned all we could about this strange lifetime, and our time was running out. So I moved Chris forward in time to the present day and oriented him before awakening him. We discussed what he had described afterwards, and more insight came from Chris' conscious reasoning.

It is difficult for people in our society to understand the concept of group soul. One of the blessings and rewards for living a life on Earth is that we can experience individualization. In many other civilizations on other planets and in other dimensions they do not have this privilege. The best example of group soul on our planet is the insect world, particularly ants and bees. It has been proven through various scientific tests that they are in complete communication and function as a cohesive unit.

In my book *Between Death and Life* we explored the various levels of existence that the soul must experience before it reaches the human level. Earth is a school, a learning place, and all lessons must be learned before the soul can move on or graduate to the next level or class. The levels are: gas, matter, plants, animals, human, spirit, divine. The gaseous state will be explored in Chapter 9: "The Earliest Forms of Life on Earth." Plants and animals are classified as group souls. This can be observed in the herd instinct of many animals. Before the animal can take the next step up the ladder and reincarnate as a human, it must individualize or separate from the group. Once it has separated and entered the human incarnation, it cannot return to the animal state, despite what various Asiatic religions preach. One way to help an animal separate and become an individual is to make it a pet and show it love. Love is always the magic key.

With this understanding of what group soul is, I offer the following explanation for the lifetime that Chris related. When some of the "old" race began to journey out into space they separated from group soul and began to individualize. This eventually led to dissension and war, because there was no longer total agreement. Thus the return to group soul underground and the removal of emotions via DNA manipulation. They blamed their troubles on the individualization and the subsequent development and strengthening of emotions. Before this time emotions were felt simultaneously by everyone, and they existed together as a unit, as a whole. When emotions were individually expressed and the group was no longer acting as a cohesive unit it caused severe problems and their planet was destroyed. Because of radiation contamination their only hope for the survival of the species was to produce genetically compatible clones. In their attempts to perfect the race, their solution was to eliminate the factor that they agreed had caused the problem: emotions, and return to the safer existence of group soul. They did not realize how terrible this would be several generations down the road. Without emotions everything became monotonous, with nothing really to live for. As he said, there was a desire to have something more. The people in the spaceships were searching for new genetic material to help them perhaps breed back the thing they had lost. They must have wanted this very badly to risk having the same catastrophe happen again.

Emotions do cause problems, but the control of these emotions is also part of the learning process. In our race, emotions are a vital part of us and is what makes us human. How sad that a race felt the only way they could keep such a terrible event from happening again, was to destroy such an integral part. They must have felt great guilt and desperation to take such a critical step. As Chris said, it was a wrong turn in evolution.

This also explains why Chris chose to have a life on Earth. To experience the very emotions he lacked in that mundane, hopeless and depressing lifetime. A world where emotions were eliminated as a mistaken method of survival. What a terrible price to pay.

CHAPTER SIX

THE UNWILLING RECRUIT

This case is a perfect example of how unusual information can come even when working with a difficult subject. Steve was a businessman who traveled extensively in his work. He had a strong control-oriented personality. This type have to maintain control of all situations. This usually originates from the type of work they are involved in. It is normally a successful businessman who subconsciously believes he cannot be hypnotized because this would be giving up control to someone else. I often wonder why this type of personality wishes to have regression, if they have these strong suspicions about hypnosis. During the discussion at the beginning of the session I try to determine what type of personality I am dealing with, and what preconceived notions they have about hypnosis. If they are this control type of personality, then I try to explain that hypnosis is not the giving up of control. When a person is hypnotized they are more in control than ever. All their senses are heightened, and they are sensitive to all that is going on around them, even things they would not be aware of in the conscious state. If anything were to occur during the session that they did not approve of, they would awaken immediately. The same way we awaken from a nightmare. This demonstrates how much control the subject has. I can never really make the subject do or say anything they do not wish to. My results in obtaining these unusual stories is accomplished by establishing rapport with the subject's subconscious mind, and developing a mutual trust. When this occurs the subject does not feel they are losing control, but that it is a cooperation effort. Still, this type of subject is more difficult to work with, and is always a challenge to the hypnotist. This was the situation I knew I would be facing in 1990 when Steve asked to be regressed to a former life.

In the beginning he resisted hypnosis and did not become a good subject until we had two or three sessions. Even then he maintained enough contact with his conscious mind to be suspicious and question what was coming forth. In the first session he could not describe things in as much detail as he did later. By the last session his subconscious was comfortable enough to allow the information through in a more detailed form.

This first session was held at Steve's small apartment in Fayetteville near the college, as were all the others. It was the middle of summer and the weather was hot and sticky. There was no air conditioning, so the oscillating fan made noise that often made transcription of the tapes difficult.

After much work I was able to induce a comfortable state of trance, and Steve regressed to a simple and mundane lifetime of a native living in a jungle. It was very nondescript and he had difficulty adding any details. Often the first session will be this way, almost as though the subconscious is testing the waters, so to speak, before allowing more important information to come forth. After several minutes the lifetime seemed to be going nowhere, and I decided to move him to something that would be more relevant to this lifetime. I asked the subconscious if there was something else it thought Steve should explore.

Steve left the native lifetime, and began to see scenes that were snatches that would not hold together. Some of the scenes were pieced together and all mixed up. For instance, he saw Indians and tepees, and a big machine like a tank. His conscious mind knew the two didn't belong together, and was causing him to doubt the session. His mind was doing what I call "leap-frogging". Jumping from scene to scene without seeming importance or continuity. The subconscious often does this when it is first asked for information. It is almost as though it thinks it will not get another chance, and tries to release as much information as it can. Thus it releases scenes that seem to have no relation to each other. It will also do this by switching from one lifetime to another. It always seems to be a desperate attempt to get something out. There is also the feeling that it is reluctant to release too much, because it doesn't know how the conscious mind will handle it. Later, when it sees that no harm is done, and the person can accept past-lives, it will start releasing more pertinent scenes. When this happens the best technique is to continue in hopes that it will settle down and stay with a lifetime that will have relevance. In these cases I have to keep pursuing whatever the subject talks about, even if it doesn't seem (to me) to make sense. It may have some importance to the subject, even though it seems unimportant to me. My questions would have to be aimed at trying to get Steve to stick to a lifetime we could explore.

I decided to ask about a strange framed drawing that Steve had hanging in his living room. The drawing was a stylized version from his imagination (he thought). It gave the appearance of looking out through the cockpit of a plane. There was a control panel with dials, knobs, etc. in the foreground. And through curved windows above the panel could be seen a brightly colored strange alien-looking landscape. It was an orange and yellow barren desert-looking scene with unusual-shaped rocks and cliffs on both sides. It gave the appearance that the plane was flying down a corridor between the tall cliffs. Whatever it was, it did not look earthly. Steve said he had a compulsion to draw it, but he did not know what it represented.

D: *I want you to visualize the drawing that you made that hangs on the wall in the front room of your house here. Can you see that in your mind?* (Yes) *And all the little details that you put into it. I'm going to ask your subconscious, is that a fantasized scene? Or is it something you are familiar with?*

S: It's a symbolic scene. And I'm quite familiar with it. It's a symbolism of a situation that looks just patently impossible to navigate, among all the junk and between the two halves, the rocks, and through the crack and that landscape. But it is quite possible to navigate between it. It's just a matter of acuity and patience.

D: *So it is a symbolic scene, like dream symbols?*

S: Probably.

D: *Does that feel right?*

S: No, it's not a dream. It symbolizes the way things are. It symbolizes the subjectivity of our perceptions of what we live in. But they're not necessarily accurate.

D: *So it's not a place that you have actually been to or seen. Because the subconscious has the answers.*

S: It's this place right now in this time. Any place. It's my situation.

D: *Because it looks like the interior of a vehicle of some kind.*

S: I'm not sure why it came out that way. Except that ... well, I am. It's the interior of ... it's *me.* I'm the vehicle. My body is the vehicle, and I'm guiding it through all this mess. This mess we call life.

D: *That makes a lot of sense. All right. I'm going to ask the subconscious, is there anything in Steve' past lives that he needs to be aware of at this time?*

S: Absolutely! That's doubtlessly why we're here.

D: *Can it show you something that is important for you to see?*

S: (Pause) It's having great difficulty getting through, because my conscious is not letting go.

D: *I think much of that has to do with all of the emotional problems you're having too, at this time. That can do it.*

S: No, I don't think that's it. My conscious has always been very tenacious. It might help if we can get my consciousness temporarily out of the way.

D: *Very often it has a hard time letting go. But it has to realize this is something important that you want to know and find out about. So as you relax, just let your mind drift.* (I gave deepening suggestions.) *I'm asking the subconscious to show you a scene or a picture that is important for you to know at this time. I will count to three and a scene will form, and you can recognize what it is showing you.*

S: Make it five.

D: *Five? All right. I will count to five and on the count of five you will see a scene that has importance for you. 1, 2, 3, it's beginning to form. It's coming. You know it's there. 4, 5.*

He responded immediately, before I had a chance to ask him what he was seeing.

S: It's a desert. It's a yellow desert.

He seemed excited that he had finally broken through and was seeing a scene. His doubts disappeared.

D: *All right. Tell me about it.*

S: There's an explosion over on the horizon.

D: *An explosion?*

S: Yeah. It's a completely foreign landscape. I've never seen anything like this. And there's a red and white and yellow explosion over toward the horizon. There are some hills off to the right. Everything's barren.

D: *Do you want to go over there?*

S: Circumspectly. I want to kind of skirt it. I feel like I need to be real careful, because there are some dangers.

D: *What is dangerous?*

S: There must be some kind of a war. I don't know.

D: *All right. Look at your body now.*

S: (Softly) Jesus Christ!

D: *What?*

S: I can't seem to look at my body. I can't tell you what my body looks like.

His conscious mind was again interfering and preventing him from seeing something he might not understand.

D: *That's all right. If it comes later, then you can tell me. You have the feeling of some kind of war? And the feeling of danger?*

S: I can handle it.

D: *All right. What are you going to do?*

S: I am going to investigate. I'm going to find out ... I know what it is, but I don't ... it doesn't come, but I know that I know. I don't have any means of saying it. There's some kind of a conflict between groups or something, and it's a long, long, long way off.

D: *Are you going to go over there and investigate?*

S: I think so.

D: *All right. Let's go ahead, if you feel comfortable doing that.*

S: I don't know how to transport myself.

D: *Oh, you can do it very quickly. The mind is very miraculous. If you were going to go, would you walk or how would you do it?*

S: I'd fly.

D: *You would fly? Do you have a vehicle of some kind?*

S: I can't tell.

D: *All right, then let's go. You can do it very quickly. Let's go to the site that you saw the explosion coming from.*

S: I feel like I'm kind of flying, floating along. Kind of sticking toward these yellow hills that are over on the right. And the thing keeps being a little further over the horizon. And as I come on it ... there's been a big explosion. I don't see anything alive.

D: *What do you see?*

S: I feel like it's got to do with some kind of ... I don't want to say "space travel". (Confused) But I don't ... maybe I'm ....

D: *That's all right. Just trust whatever you're getting.*

S: I can't.

D: *What does the scene look like?*

S: Well, now it's starting to look like cartoons. But it *was* real.

This occasionally occurs when the conscious mind doesn't like what is happening, and is still aware enough to cause interference. In an effort to regain control it will turn into what Dick Sutphen calls the "babbler." It will interject that this whole session is silly. That you probably saw it in a movie or read it in a book, that the things you are seeing are definitely not real. If that ruse doesn't work, it will occasionally change the subject's perception of the scenes by turning them into cartoon images. It is a further suggestion that the scenes are not real, in an effort to make the session stop. My job then is to get the subject's mind and focus back onto the real scenes, and to ignore any cartoon images. As the subject goes deeper and deeper into trance the "leap-frogging", cartoons and other distracting images and thoughts stop, because the conscious mind interference is removed. These things no longer present a problem once the subject has several sessions and becomes accustomed to the trance state. He may still question the reality of it, but will be able to stay objective during the session.

D: *All right. You said it looked like an explosion, but you didn't see any people?*

S: No. I felt there was a danger from some people or something that was a lot different from me.

D: *But you can look at that scene again.*

S: (Chuckle) This is a little far out. I guess it was some kind of spacecraft that crashed, or was shot down or .... I have the sense that there's some kind of conflict. A war or something like that. And that it might be completely somewhere else, not on Earth. I'm analyzing it and denying it.

D: *Well, that happens. But do you feel like you had anything to do with the explosion?*

S: Yes. I don't think I caused it. I'm not sure. Maybe I did. I feel like ... "By God, they're after me."

D: *Why are they after you?*

S: I don't know. They're not like me. (He unexpectedly opened his eyes.) I think we've just been rollicking through a swamp of paranoia.

D: *(Chuckle) Who knows? That's all right. Close your eyes again.*

S: Sure.

D: *You know, anything can come out, no matter how strange it is. Just go with what you feel. Who knows? All right. But you said the scene seemed very real.*

S: Yes, it did. It was a yellow desert-like landscape. I can remember. And I was flying. Not fast, just ....

D: *All right. I want you to see that scene again. Concentrate on your flying, and your subconscious will tell you. How are you flying? How are you able to do that? Your subconscious knows, trust it.*

S: As nearly as I can tell, I can just do it. I can't tell that I have any kind of craft involved. I want to say that it's a machine, but I'm not *in* it. I'm part of it.

D: *Part of it. Just elaborate a little more and let's see what you mean. The answers will come.*

S: I'm hooked up to a machine. I'm inside it and hooked up to it, so that I operate it. But I don't use any controls or anything like that.

In the investigation of UFO cases I have found that spacecraft are often propelled by thought. Sometimes it is the united combined mind power of all the beings on the craft. But this incident sounded different.

D: *Is anything surrounding you?*

S: The machine's skin is my skin. The only thing surrounding me is whatever atmosphere there is.

D: *You were hesitant to look at your body, but what does it feel like?*

S: I don't have one.

D: *You don't have a body? What do you mean?*

S: I'm some kind of a craft.

D: *I'm trying to understand. Let's get it a little clearer. You mean instead of having a flesh and blood body, it's like a machine body? Is that what you mean?*

S: (Pause) If I have a body, it's inside this machine, and I'm not conscious of it at all. I don't have any idea what it's like or anything about it. My entire mental capacity relates to the machine itself, with the craft, what I'm flying. And I'm *it.* And I *know* that I have a body or something like that. But it's either out of the picture or gone or I'm just not dealing with it.

D: *Okay. Now I'm still talking to your subconscious, because these are answers that apparently you need to find out. Can your body exist without the machine?*

S: No. Not here.

D: *Not where you're at there?*

S: No, no, no way, no. I'm entirely dependent on the machine. I don't know where I came from, but wherever it was, I'd be able to exist there probably. But no, here I can't even think about being outside the machine.

D: *So you are totally dependent on it.*

S: I *am* it.

D: *You* are *the machine where you are here. But if you went back to where you came from, you wouldn't need it.*

S: No. They'd disengage me from it.

D: *Who would disengage you?*

S: My people. (Surprised) I think I'm a soldier.

D: *But where you're seeing the scene, you need this machine to exist.*

S: Yes, absolutely. I'm in a war, and I'm a soldier of some kind. And I'm bonded with this craft. It seems to me there are a bunch of these crafts and they're specialized. I'm not one that engages in the actual war. I don't shoot anybody or do whatever that is. I gather information.

D: *That's why you didn't really have anything to do with that explosion?*

S: No. I'm reconnaissance.

D: *You just gather information about the area?*

S: About what's going on. I want to say "enemy".

D: *This place where this war is going on, is that near where you're from?*

S: No, no, no, no. I don't have any idea where it is.

D: *I was wondering why you would be* there *if the war wasn't threatening your own land.*

S: I'm a soldier.

D: *You've got to go where the war is? Is that what you mean?*

S: Yeah. I don't give a damn about the war, but I've got to do what I'm supposed to do. (Surprised) Dolores, this has got to be where that picture came from!

D: *Do you think so?*

S: I don't know, but it might be.

D: *What feels right?*

S: Well, this feels awfully real. And it's not like that picture. That picture has controls. And I don't feel ... the experience that I was just describing -- and I seem separated from it now -- but in the experience I was just describing there weren't any manual controls or gauges or dials or anything like that.

D: *Otherwise it's like that picture?*

S: Either I'm *in* some kind of a spacecraft, and operating an observer craft remotely ... that must be it! Yeah, that's it! And I'm not sure how much of this is really subconscious, but it seems right that, yeah, I'm in a craft of some kind. And I'm hooked up to some kind of a transmitter, and I'm operating this machine remotely. And it's involved in the conflict where this yellow place is.

D: *So you're not actually flying around, but you're doing it through your ....*

S: It feels like I am, because the hookup is so good. I have to be making this up, but it just doesn't seem like I am. It sure seems real. (Laugh) (He again opened his eyes unexpectedly.)

D: (Laugh) *That's all right. You can close your eyes again. Okay. But it's interesting to speculate where that scene would come from.*

S: That's what I had. I'm away from that now.

D: *Well, think again about it. You said you thought you had a body there somewhere. Try to imagine what that body feels like. Does it feel like it has a personality? A sex?*

S: (Pause) My body. I'm a human being. (It sounded as though he was trying to convince himself.) I believe so.

D: *I was wondering if you felt machine-like, or robot-like, or if it did feel more like a physical person.*

S: I feel ... like a person. That machine is a remote control, fast, and it's my job to operate it. At least that's what I'm experiencing.

It sounded as though he was trying to justify the experience and put it into terms he could understand.

S: It's exciting!

D: (Laugh) *It's different anyway. I'm going to ask you to go to the last day of your life in that life, and see what happened to you. But it won't bother you at all. You can look at it as an observer if you want. And you can see what happened to you in that lifetime. I will count to three and we will be there. 1, 2, 3, we've gone to that time.*

S: That explosion killed me. Something about it. I saw it happen.

D: *But you weren't* in *the explosion, were you?*

S: No. But it was the radiation.

D: *When you went over there to look at it?*

S: I think it had killed me before I did that. I can't visualize dying.

D: *But you don't think you were inside of that machine?*

S: Maybe I was. Maybe that's it. Maybe I was in that. I'm not sure now.

D: *That's all right. It's very strange, but interesting anyway. Let me make a suggestion. If you want, tonight while you're sleeping you can have some dreams that will offer more scenes, and bring more clarification. Would that be a good idea?*

S: (Softly) I think I'm probably going to, whether it's a good idea or not.

D: *Once you've opened the door you can let some more scenes come in to help clarify.*

S: Yes, I'm going to have to find out something about that.

Before I brought Steve out of the deep trance I conditioned him with a keyword to make induction easier and faster the next time we worked. I usually ask the subject to give me a word (or words) that I might say. I believe if they choose the word it will be more effective because it will be personal. It doesn't matter what the word is because once the subject is conditioned to accept the word, the instructions will last for an incredible length of time. I have used this method of saying keywords to subjects a year or longer after the instructions were given, and it is just as effective as if it were given the day before.

I was taken offguard because the word Steve chose was strange. The word he came up with was "Thermo-Docular." He kept repeating, "Thermo-Docular," to make sure we got it correct. Then when he woke up, he said he had no idea where that word came from, what it meant, or why he had chosen to use it.

In the weeks that followed the word was effective in inducting immediate trance state, and I never had any more trouble with Steve resisting hypnosis. He had proven to himself that he did have control over the session when he opened his eyes twice, and then was able to return to the scene he had been watching. This knowledge allowed him to relax and cooperate with me.

In the following sessions Steve relived in great detail the lifetime of a Negro saxophone player in Chicago during the 20s and 30s. It helped explain many of the problems in his life. Further information about the alien lifetime came through unexpectedly a few weeks later. This was to be our last session, because Steve was moving away from Fayetteville to live and work in Seattle. By now he was more accustomed to the trance state and was able to ignore conscious mind disruption.

His request to use "Thermo-docular" for a keyword intrigued us, and we decided to track down the meaning or origin.

D: *I would like for you to drift and float and find a time and place when you were associated with those words: Thermo-docular.* (I gave more instructions.) *What are you doing? What do you see?*

S: I'm in a building. Not a building, a structure. I'm in some kind of a structure, and it's dark inside.

D: *Tell me about it.*

S: It's *very* large. I can see the structural members, and they look like they're off in the distance. I think that's what they are. I'm inside something. For some reason I don't seem to need very much light. Maybe I'm in the Thermal-Docular. I don't know.

D: *What's around you?*

S: It's ... I'm in some kind of fluid.

D: *Fluid?*

This was a surprise. Yet in this work you learn to not allow anything to throw you offguard. The unusual becomes normal. You accept it and continue questioning.

S: Yes, I'm suspended in some kind of fluid. That's it.

D: *You mean you're not standing or sitting?*

S: No, there isn't any standing. There's just ... I'm suspended in this fluid. I have hands.

D: *Can you see them?*

S: No, but I can feel them. And as nearly as I can tell, I have a human body.

D: *What does the fluid feel like on your skin?*

S: Just exactly right. It's some kind of support system.

D: *What do you mean?*

S: I'm not in a spacecraft ... exactly. I'm in *some* kind of a craft. A vessel that's made for some kind of travel. I don't know what kind. And I'm inside it. And instead of it being filled with air, it's filled with fluid.

D: *The entire inside?*

S: Yes. It's a fluid atmosphere evidentially.

D: *But you feel comfortable with it though.*

S: Yes. There's not much light in it. And I can't tell whether I'm actually operating anything, or maybe I'm just a passenger. I think there may be some other people there too. I think everybody's kind of sleeping.

D: *Why? Do you know?*

S: A very, very long voyage. And there's no need to be awake.

D: *Do you think that's what you are doing too?*

S: Evidentially. Whoever is running this show probably would be upset if they knew I was thinking. I guess there's no way for them to know. I don't know. Maybe there is. But I don't think any of the people around me are having conscious thoughts. I don't know where I'm going or where I came from. I know it's a long, long way. I don't know why, but I have a feeling it's not what *I* want to do.

D: *It's something you don't want to be a part of?*

S: Maybe I've been inducted. Inducted may not be the right word. They're taking me somewhere to do something for them, but I'm not going to get anything out of it. But there's not much to do except go along with them, I guess.

D: *What about the rest of the people with you? Do you think it's the same or are you picking up anything?*

S: I think we're all supposed to be unconscious. That's probably why it was so hard for me to sort this out. And I still don't have it sorted out very well.

D: *But we know the subconscious is always awake. And that's the part we're talking to. So you're not disobeying any rules or anything.*

S: I don't care if I am.

D: *I wonder how the ship is being operated.*

S: Well, whoever or whatever is operating it is ... I'm not sure if there is any way for me to directly communicate with it through them. Because of where I am, and because of what it is. I don't know that there's any correlation for me to conceptualize them or it very well.

D: *Well, do you want to find out how you got there?*

S: I think that might be a good idea.

D: *We can drift back to the event, when you were first getting into this situation. You can see what happened. You're able to do that because your subconscious has all the answers. Just trust whatever it shows you. Let's drift back to the beginning of this episode, and you can see how you came to be there. Are you seeing anything, or do I have to count you?*

S: I think that I was recruited some way. I'm not sure I was recruited voluntarily.

D: *What are you seeing?*

S: I guess I'm seeing pyramids, but they're not Egyptian pyramids. They're a lot smoother, more polished.

D: *Any certain color?*

S: No particular color. Just like a very slick black would look if it had lots of light shining on it.

D: *Can you see where they are?*

S: There's not much light here.

D: *But you're able to make them out, even if there isn't much light.*

S: Yeah. There are just pyramids, and I guess there are quite a number of them. I'm trying to see the ground. I don't know whether they're on some kind of manufactured surface or on soil or dirt or what.

D: *Can you feel it beneath your feet?*

S: (Pause) It feels like it's dirt, but it's been processed and compacted. It's almost like pavement. It's nothing I like very well.

D: *Are you outside or inside?*

S: I'm outside. I'm standing on this surface. And there are lots of these pyramid shaped objects, that are as big as good size buildings. Several stories tall.

D: *All right. What does the sky look like?*

S: Black, and it has stars in it. It's not necessarily familiar to me. I don't know the constellations. And I don't see any that are familiar. I don't think this is Earth.

D: *Why isn't it very light? Is this the normal condition?*

S: I believe it's on a small planet or a moon, and there's just not much light. It's pretty weak.

D: *Can you make out anything about your body?*

S: (Pause) My body is totally encased in a very, very thin membrane of some kind. Maybe a force field. I don't know what it is. But it's too dark, I can't see my hands. I'm very thin.

D: *Is it covering* all *the parts of your body?*

S: Everything. Entirely.

This strange idea of a membrane covering is repeated in the story of the future being (Chapter 12.)

D: *What does your head and face feel like? Is it covered also?*

S: Yes. I'm trying to figure out how I'm respiring.

D: Are *you respiring?*

S: I'd have to be. I don't know whether I am or not. I guess I'm not. I don't know.

D: *What feels right?*

S: I don't like it. Oh, it's not that bad, I guess. It's just ... different. I'm very thin. My arms are too long. I guess my legs are too. And thin. I've always wanted to be thin, but this is *very* thin.

D: *How many fingers do you have?*

S: If I hold a hand up in front of me? (Pause, as though examining.) I've got five fingers counting my thumb. But my little finger's not right. Not on either hand. I don't use it. It's weak.

D: *You mean it's there, but it's not used?*

S: I think that's it. It's not as developed as the rest of my hand.

D: *Is it the same size?*

S: No, no, no. I have long fingers and thumbs, except for my little fingers. Neither of those are very developed. It's not much more than a bud. It's just not functional.

D: *Can you determine what your feet are like?*

S: My feet are ... very thin. *Very* thin. My weight is on the balls of my feet, on my toes. And the little toes are like my little fingers. They don't do much.

D: *What about the rest of the toes?*

S: They're not very big. They're thin. They're strong.

D: *What about your face? Can you tell anything by feeling? Or just by knowing?*

S: (Startled) Jesus Christ!! I'm a monkey!!

D: *A monkey?* (He laughed.) *What do you mean?* (He laughed loudly.) *Is that what your face looks like?*

S: Not exactly. Kind of. (He found this amusing.)

D: *What do you mean?*

S: Well, if you ... my head ....

He was smiling, obviously amused but also embarrassed by what he was reporting.

D: *That's all right. Just tell me about it. Are you seeing it or are you feeling it?*

S: I guess I'm imaging it. My head is not shaped like a human head. It's shaped more like a monkey's head, except it has more of a cranial capacity than a monkey would have. A lot more. But it's not a monkey, it just kind of ... looks like a monkey. (Chuckle) And my skin's black.

D: *This membrane, you mean?*

S: No, I feel like my skin's black underneath the membrane. You can't see the membrane. It doesn't have any color. It just has a little bit of a sheen.

D: *Do you have any hair?*

S: (Pause) I can't tell that I do, no. I'm black-skinned.

D: *What do your eyes look like?*

S: Well, they sure don't look like eyes.

D: *Why not?*

S: The eyelids are more elaborate, more developed. There's more skin, more wrinkled skin. I guess it's for protection. But not protection like an animal is protected from fighting other animals. It's not like that. It's protection against some kind of an atmosphere, or element or light or whatever. I don't know.

D: *What does the actual eye look like inside of that? Can you make that out?*

S: (Long pause as he examined it, then mumbling.) I think it's black.

D: *No pupils?*

S: I don't ... I can't tell if there's any pupil. There might be. Aw, I can't tell.

D: *What about your nose and mouth? Can you see them?*

S: My nose isn't very developed. That's the part that looks more like a monkey. The nose and the mouth. I don't think it has any teeth. I don't think this gentleman has very much fun. (Chuckle)

D: *Do you have any ears?*

S: Ears, but not like a monkey. I can't tell about the ears.

D: *Okay. Can you tell if you have a heart and blood systems? I was thinking you might feel it beating.*

S: (Pause) Yeah. Whatever this thing is, it's got a heart and circulation of some kind. I guess the circulation isn't quite as centralized as in a human.

D: *What do you mean?*

S: The circulatory system pumps itself without so much of a centralized heart.

D: *Does the body have blood?*

S: It has fluid. It's not a human body, so it doesn't have human blood. It has some kind of fluid that circulates in it. And I don't know what kind of fluid that might be, but I would imagine that it's comparable in its function.

D: *Do you feel like this body consumes anything?*

S: It has to have something.

D: *What comes to mind?*

S: Nothing.

D: *What does the body use to supply fuel? Because every body has to have something to create energy. What comes to mind?*

S: Liquid. Nothing but fruit and liquid. But it's not the kind of fruit you would recognize. I guess there's some kind of plant life evidently, although I don't see any plants. Everything's black.

D: *Why do you think you have that extra membrane covering your body?*

S: (A revelation.) Because there's no atmosphere.

D: *Do you think you have that membrane when you're somewhere else? Or do you always have it?*

S: Everything has it.

D: *Everything?*

S: (Surprised) Yeah!

D: *What else do you see that has it?*

S: I don't see any plants, but I'm imagining ... mosses, small dry bushes. And fruits that grow like mushrooms. Maybe they are mushrooms. I don't know. I know that mushrooms dissipate....

D: *You said everything has a membrane?*

S: Yes, that's what bothers me, because I know that mushrooms reproduce by sending out spores. And there's no way that could happen here. Everything travels underneath this membrane.

D: *This may be something different that you're unfamiliar with.*

S: I don't have any idea really. Maybe I do. I don't know. I don't like this. It's not uncomfortable. It's just ... this gentleman surely doesn't have any fun. (Chuckle) I don't see any women around. (Laugh) (I laughed.) He just stood there in the same place all the time I was talking about him. And I don't know whether it is me or not.

D: *All right. But let's see what happens to him. How he gets on board that vessel or that craft that had the fluid. You can see it happening.*

S: (Pause) He goes inside. Some way or another he gets inside a pyramid, but I don't know how he gets inside it. (Surprised) All those pyramids are spacecraft, or some kind of craft. I don't know whether they travel through space or travel some other way. But they're some kind of travel mechanism. I can't tell if *I'm* inside of it, but I know that whatever that creature was that we were talking about went inside one. I don't know how he got inside it. They don't have any doors.

D: *Are there any objects or furniture or anything?*

S: (Slowly) I don't see any. It's just a pyramid, and the space inside that pyramid. These aren't stone pyramids. I'm not sure they're even matter.

D: *Why do you say that?*

S: They don't have any thickness. And they're not the same size inside that they are on the outside.

D: *What do you mean?*

S: They're huge inside.

D: *You mean they're larger inside than they looked from the outside?*

S: That's the sense I get. Or maybe the person, or whatever it was, that went inside, just got a lot smaller. (Chuckle)

D: *What do the walls look like?*

S: You can't touch it.

D: *Why not?*

S: It's not there.

D: *What do you mean, it's not there?*

S: (Pause, as though studying it.) If you reach out and try to touch it, you can't reach it.

D: *You mean it moves away from you?*

S: Not exactly. It's just not there. No matter how long you would walk or travel, when you're inside this thing, you couldn't ever get to the wall.

D: *Do you have any idea how that is possible?*

S: Well, the word "concept," "conceptual" is in my mind, but I don't know how it applies. It's not logical.

I have come across this idea of the distortion of space and time in my work on UFO abduction cases. There have been times when the person entered what they thought was a small craft, only to find that it was as much as five times larger on the inside. Time has also been condensed or distorted, and events occur in a shorter period of time than would be normal. A great deal of investigation has been done with cases involving missing time. I have encountered these, but I have also found those with condensed time, which I find much more puzzling. A person will be driving and will arrive at their destination in a shorter length of time than would be normally possible. For example, an hour's journey would only take ten or fifteen minutes. In each of these cases a UFO sighting was involved in some way. Even though I have heard of these concepts, I cannot explain them.

D: *Are there any other people with you?*
S: Not with me. There are other people. They're not people. I'm not a person. Whatever they are or we are, there are other ones. I know they're there and I can't see them. I can't touch them, but they're there.
D: *Do you know what they're doing?*
S: They're being transported.
D: *All right. Let's move ahead and see how you got in the fluid.(Pause) How did that happen?*
S: As this thing travels it reaches such high velocity that the ... not the atmosphere. There isn't any atmosphere. The magma -- no, that's not it. There's a word. The -- whatever it is that's in it. It's not atmosphere. You can't even feel it, but as they travel very, very much more rapidly, that increases a *mass* until it's just a very, very syrupy consistency. It surrounds you. It limits your movement, but it doesn't feel like liquid.
D: *At first you thought it was a liquid?*
S: But it's not. It's not ... there's a word that I know. It's a word that I know.
D: *Maybe you will think of it. If it's not an atmosphere, it sounds as though the space inside that craft changes consistency?*
S: Yes, yes. The space itself almost congeals.
D: *Except that if it completely congealed it would be solid. But it is in a fluid stage. Is that right?*

S: It's in a fluid stage, but it's not fluid. It's more fluid than liquid, if that makes any sense.

D: *But this is something that happens when the craft goes at a very high rate of speed.*

S: Yes.

D: *And it doesn't bother this being whose body you are in. It can take this.*

S: Evidentially. No discomfort. Extreme boredom.

D: *But he is also made to go to sleep?*

S: Extreme boredom. This *long, long* time. Time isn't ... it just doesn't ... it exists, but there's no way to conceive it. It's just *so* long. And the speed is inconceivable.

D: *So the easiest thing to do would be just to shut down and rest. Does that make sense?*

S: Yeah.

D: *All right. Then let's move ahead. I can count you there ....*

S: Oh, I'm for that. Let's do that. (Chuckle)

D: *That's what I was thinking. We can get out of that situation. I was just curious how you got into it. Let's move ahead till this craft gets to wherever it's going. And you'll be able to go outside of it, and see what happens there. Should I count you, or can you see it?*

S: Till it gets where it's going.

D: *Yes. You said it was going somewhere on a long journey. (Pause) What are you seeing?*

S: Where this *thing* came from, space travel isn't possible. The concept isn't possible. Travel, as we would conceive it, isn't even possible. Only the kind I've just described, and it's not a very good description. And where it's going is to some destination where space travel *is* possible. And when it reaches that destination, then I disembark from it and get into some kind of a spacecraft. Not entirely under my own volition. And go on somewhere else.

D: *Do you think that pyramid-shaped object was actually traveling through space?*

S: Not space the way you think about it. I don't have anything in my experience to name that.

D: *Did it leave the surface of the planet, moon, whatever it was that he saw? Did it* actually *move?*

S: It doesn't have to leave there to go someplace else. It can exist in more than one place. It travels so fast.

D: *Then it doesn't have to physically move anywhere. Is that what you mean?*

S: Well, those words, that question, just doesn't apply.

D: *I was afraid of that. Much of our language is insufficient. But when he got where he was going, he got into a normal spaceship -- if we can consider a spaceship normal?*

S: Yeah. He got into some kind of traveling vessel that travels from one place to another. And uses real time and real space. That much of it's rational, logical, although I don't really understand it. The first ... the pyramid wasn't rational.

D: *Well, can you see what this little craft looks like?*

S: It's plastic.

D: *What do you mean?*

S: It's made out of some kind of plastic.

D: *Why do you think "plastic".*

S: It's not metal. And everything's got to be something.

D: *That's true. Well, where does this little craft go?*

S: (Long pause) I'm still this skinny, thin black monkey-kind of character. And it's going somewhere. And while it's en route I'm being ... several of us are being taught to operate it, or to operate something.

D: *Is it hard to operate?*

S: No. We're being taught ... all of us are being indoctrinated. (Pause) I've got to do something for these people, and I'm worried that they might be having a war, and I'm getting into a war of some kind. And that doesn't make sense. It's like being in an army. And I don't know whether there's any war or conflict. I suppose there must be. That might just be a fact of life.

D: *And you don't like the idea?*

S: It's not profiting *me* anything. I don't care about these, whatever they are, whoever they are. All I can do is just whatever is necessary to survive. And build my relationships with my peers. I can't tell really for sure whether I have any peers that I'm acquainted with. But I have a sense of regimentation. I don't like it. I guess I need to tell you that whatever I was doing, if that's a past existence for me, I disliked the regimentation, disliked servitude or whatever you might call it. Enough that ... I didn't end my own life, but I didn't try to keep from ending it either. I didn't really care.

D: *All right. Can you see what it is you're operating? What you have to do to operate it?*

S: (Long pause) When you finish learning how to do it you have a control fastened to both hands and both feet, and to your knees. The further you get into your training, the more the controls encompass you, until when you've completed your training the controls are like a skin. And operating whatever kind of vehicle or vessel this is, or craft, is a matter of conceptualizing what you want it to do, and making the movements with your muscles, that you would ordinarily do to make that kind of movement. And the craft responds back by moving that way, or traveling that way.

D: *By conceptualizing, you mean you can use your thoughts?*

S: It's not operated by thought. It's operated by electrical impulses and muscular tensions, *minute* electrical impulses and muscular tensions in the surface of your skin. And of course your major muscles too. As you move your body, it moves the controls that encompass your body almost like a skin. And those controls move the craft.

D: *That's why you have to learn which muscles and which movements to make.*

S: To an extent you have to learn, but it's not something you study. You don't study it like memorizing in books. You practice it. And you're doing it, it's like riding a bicycle. It's natural. And I can't escape the notion that it has to have this kind of sensitive response and maneuverability because it's some kind of combat-related craft.

D: *What does the craft look like that you operate? Is it large or small or what?*

S: It's nearly impossible for me to tell you. I can't tell what the outside of it looks like. I have never seen the outside of it. And when you're operating it, it feels like you're operating your own body. You don't use your eyes. It's all electronic. What you see is what the ship sees with its sensors, and they're fed in through your eyes. (Disturbed) I don't like this.

D: *Yes, you would just be a part of it. But it won't bother you.*

S: No, it's not that way.

D: *You just don't like having to do it. Is that what you mean?*

S: Yes. Whatever it was that I had to do then, I didn't like it. I'm not sure how I felt about the other side of the conflict. It wasn't my conflict. I'm interested in saving my butt if I can. But I don't care about it *all* that much. I'm wondering ....

D: *What?*

S: What the other side of the conflict was.

D: *Maybe you were never told.*

S: Oh, of course I wouldn't be.

D: *Is there anyway to find out what it was all about?*

S: I don't know.

D: *You only saw a very small portion.* (Pause) *Does anything come to mind?*

S: Yes. The concept of horrible conflict. It's the same ... the same. Still the same. I mean, they've taken me and put me in a situation. And I'm occupying a space with this vehicle. And they know that I'm going to try to protect myself. They know that I don't give a damn about them. And by protecting myself I occupy this space, so that whatever the other side is can't occupy it. It's the same thing they do to soldiers *now.*

D: *It's a situation where you* have *to fight then.*

S: Yeah. I don't like that. If I can make any kind of a contact with the other side, I probably will. I'm interested in knowing whether or not I did. I don't know.

D: *Well, if this is some kind of combat, what could you do with that craft that would cause harm?*

S: If anything threatens me, all I have to know is if it's threatening me. And it's destroyed. I don't know how.

D: *How is it destroyed? Can you see?*

S: Well, if the craft does it, it's just not there anymore.

D: *So by putting you in a situation where they feel you'll be threatened, you would automatically destroy whatever it was.*

S: Yes. I think this is a spacecraft. And there's probably some kind of a planetary system that ... that's the object of the conflict. There's probably another ship. I don't know. I don't like that.

D: *You don't like the whole idea. Well, you're in a very uncomfortable situation there. I can see that. But you had no choice, did you? No way you could get out of that?*

S: Not that I know of. Unless I default to the other side. And that idea keeps occurring to me. I wonder if I did. I might of. I had no reason not to.

D: *That would be a choice you would like to make, wouldn't it?*

S: Well, not necessarily. I imagine the other side is the same. I guess my instinct is to just take the thing and escape *both* sides.

D: *Is there a way to do that?*

S: Just do it. I think that's where that existence ended.

D: *Well, the superiors that put you in that machine, were they beings like you?*

S: I don't know. I can't tell. I don't think so though. But I think that's probably how that existence ended.

D: *Do you want to move ahead and find out?*

S: There isn't any *ahead*.

D: *What do you see?*

S: I just went in the direction that I wasn't supposed to go. And the idea I get expresses itself most easily by saying that they exploded it. That's not exactly accurate, but for practical purposes, it'll do.

D: *So you wouldn't have been able to defect, even if you wanted to. Is that what you mean?*

S: I'm sure that I wouldn't have been able to. I would have been seen as a threat by the other side. And the other side wouldn't have been any more to my liking than the side that I was in. I didn't want anything to do with either side. And I just lit out.

D: *But you didn't get away doing that either.*

S: No. Well, I got away in a way.

D: *That's one way of getting out. But do you have any concept of what the beings were like that connected you to all of this? And trained you?*

S: Any time I try to conceptualize them I get the idea of a ....

D: *Of what?*

S: (He was having difficulty finding the words.) Of kind of an insect-like intelligence. Just alien, completely alien.

D: *You mean, alien from anything that you are familiar with? Or anything the being was familiar with?*

S: Yes. The being, that black whatever it was, didn't have any more idea how to describe his captors, or whatever you'd call them, than I do. He just knew that they were powerful, or it was powerful, or whatever.

D: *Did he ever see them, do you think?*

S: That wouldn't be possible.

D: *Then they trained him without him seeing them, or having any contact with them. Does that sound right?* (He nodded.) *It does. But you said an insect-type intelligence. What do you mean by that?*

S: I don't mean that they were insects. I mean that they ... it was or they were -- I don't even know if it's a plural. I don't know its purposes. I don't know what it was even made of. I don't even know for sure if it was protoplasmic.

He might have been trying to describe a group mind concept, which his subconscious equated with an insect-type intelligence. Similar to the manner in which bees and ants operate.

S: Plasma is the word I was trying to remember earlier to describe the inside of that pyramid. The *plasma* inside it congealed.

D: *That makes sense. We use the best word we can to describe things. But I was curious as to why you called it an insect-type intelligence.*

S: Because it had absolutely no concern for my well-being, other than for its own purposes. It had an understanding of my habits, values, life systems -- which were extensive -- but that understanding was only in so far as it served its purposes, their purposes. And I have no idea what those purposes were.

D: *So in that way it was alien or insect-like. Well, what happened to you after the explosion? When you said the being was destroyed?*

S: Well, I'm not sure that was me. I guess it was, if there's any kind of continuity. I feel an identification with that black being. And I don't know what the connection could be. It may just be conceptual.

D: *Okay. Is this the life where the term that you used, Thermo-docular, came from?*

S: (Long pause) It was supposed to have been. That's what we set out for.

D: *But nothing comes to mind?* (No) *Then let's get Steve's conscious mind pushed out of the way, and talk to his sub conscious. What was the reason for showing Steve that existence?*

S: That was his first existence in this reality.

D: *He seemed like an innocent type of being in that life. Is there any way of knowing where that existence occurred? Or is that possible?*

S: It's not relevant.

D: *Was it in our ... shall I say "our galaxy"?*

S: Sure. In terms of space, it was not far away.

D: *Do you know anything about what was going on with this war? He was curious about the other side.*

S: There wasn't any other side.

D: *What do you mean?*

S: Both sides were the same.

D: *I'm trying to understand. Why were they fighting then?* (Long pause) *Is there any way to explain what you're trying to say?*

S: Explaining and answering that question always instills ideas of ... no matter how I answer that question, and it's been answered over and over and over, people always take the answers and twist them and bend them into human form. They put human faces on them, and give them human values, and human motivations. And if they're very, very powerful they make them deities. I suppose it's not harmful ultimately, but it just doesn't have much co-relation to the real answers to the questions you ask.

D: *Still, we have to put human values on it, because that's the way we think as human beings. But I'm still trying to understand how one side could be both, and* why *it would have to fight.*

S: The deity that .... Well, the being or the ... I might as well jump into it and just start putting names on things, because it's not going to be right any how. But the being that you're talking about that put this whole little show on, that this fellow was involved in. That being, you'd call a deity, you'd call it *the* deity. And that being invented both sides of the conflict. It is, and was both sides of the conflict. And asking whys ... there isn't any why.

D: *Just for its own entertainment?*

S: That's as good an answer as anything.

D: *I know it's impossible to have an answer for some of these things. At least, an answer that we can comprehend anyway. But you said that was his first existence in this reality.*

S: That's true.

D: *And we went through other lifetimes he had where he was on Earth. Did those happen soon after the other one? I'm thinking in a linear sense.*

S: Well, in a non-linear sense everything happens simultaneously.

D: *Yes, I've heard that theory. But were there other experiences besides the ones we've covered?*

S: Yes. Countless. You're calling him "he" or "it", and it's just....

D: *It's not either one of those names?*

S: What you'd call a "soul", or what you would almost erroneously call a "soul", has very little to do with the way you conceive it. You're putting a name on something that is too complicated to have a name. Picture this: if you have a lot of material and you mix it all up, so this time it comes up to be red, and the next time it comes up maybe to be green or blue or orange. And you mix it up over and over and over. All the times it comes up to be red, then you'd say all those existences were this same person. They had something in common. They had a particular attitude. All those times had a way of *making* themselves, but they're not all the same times though. The person lying here on this little blanket is not the same person that lived the other lives, or was flying some kind of a craft.

D: *Yes, I can understand that.*

S: The only thing really that there is in common is that the set of characteristics -- and not even characteristics, not physical characteristics, but conceptual (had difficulty explaining) ....

D: *I was thinking of spiritual, is that what you mean?*

S: (Interrupted) No, no, no, no, no, no, no, no. There are conceptual propensities. A set of conceptual propensities is the linear that you're talking about.

D: *All right then. I think we're running out of time, and we've gotten into some complicated ideas. But I want to thank you for sharing that with me, even though it is complicated. All right, then I want that entity to depart, and I want all of the consciousness and personality of Steve to once again return to the body of Steve.*

Upon awakening and discussing the session, one of Steve's first remarks was, "Well, he sure didn't care a damn about their damn war."

"Yes," I said, as we laughed about his observation. "He was *really* drafted."

CHAPTER SEVEN

STRANDED ON EARTH

This strange case occurred on my first trip to England in 1992, and the session was performed at the subject's house in London. It shows that these bizarre occurrences are not limited to Americans. I have encountered them all over the world.

The subject in this unusual case was Mona, a young dark haired divorced woman in her thirties. Her time was spent raising a young boy, and being involved in the unusual occupation of trying to teach others how to develop their latent psychic abilities. She had devised a simple method, and was much in demand to teach people, such as security guards and policemen, how to recognize potentially dangerous people by utilizing natural telepathic abilities they didn't even know they possessed. Her life was full and interesting, and her only complaint was that she had been trying to lose weight. She was having no success although she had tried several methods. She was looking for the answer in a possible past life that might be influencing this.

Weight loss is a very common reason for requesting past-life therapy. Often the cause can be traced to starvation in other lifetimes. This is probably the most obvious answer, but there can be causes that are unexpected. In one of my cases the woman subject was the male leader of a powerful clan in Scotland. The responsibilities were great, and they did not cease upon the death of the individual. While the man lay dying his subconscious leaked a very important and crucial clue to the carrying forward of excess weight, when he said, "I will never be rid of the weight of my responsibilities." The subconscious is very literal and responds to what it is told to do. It does not understand the concept of time, and carries out unconscious instructions, no matter which body the person is wearing at the time. In its primary job as protector it feels it is required to guard the body, no matter what the insignificant conscious mind wills it to do. This is why it is so important to recognize the subconscious' power and to deal directly with the subconscious in therapy. If this crucial part of the mind does not understand it is really harming the body, and agree to work on reconciling the problem, then no amount of therapy will work. The therapist has to convince the subconscious that, although it is only doing its job as protector, this is a different body that does not need the disruptive type of protection. It has to be given a different set of instructions that will be more helpful and beneficial to the subject. It has to be spoken to as one would speak to a child, and startling results can occur when it agrees to cooperate. Out of all the various reasons for obesity, this case had to be my strangest. And the suggestion that the subconscious gave to obtain release from the overweight problem was equally strange. In my type of work you have to be prepared for the unusual and be able to adapt yourself to the unexpected.

When Mona was in a deep state of trance I used my cloud method to take her backward to search for the lifetime that would hold the answer to her problem. In this method the subject drifts slowly off the cloud until they are standing on the ground. The suggestion is always given that it will feel as if they are a leaf drifting out of a tree, a slow and floating sensation, in order to create a peaceful atmosphere. This was the normal reaction I had experienced in hundreds of cases of using this method. So I was surprised when Mona's descent was radically different. She came down from the cloud experiencing a spinning motion, as though she was falling.

M: I see mountains against a white sky. It's coming fast now. Almost as though I'm sliding down a mountain side.

I tried to reassure her that she was perfectly safe, even though the effects she was experiencing were unexpected.

M: Oh, yes. It feels very dangerous, but I'm not worried about it. I'm moving very fast.

She was trying to gain control of the dizzying spinning motion. Her words were interrupted by cries of dismay. Every time I asked her to observe her surroundings she couldn't comply. Raising her head to look around only caused her to spin more radically.

M: I have this feeling now, of going faster and faster and faster, *down* at an angle. But a free slide of the angle *down.* Sliding, sliding. And I'm aware if I look up -- it is hard because I'm moving so fast down -- I'm aware of blue sky and some white clouds, and mountains. Almost like I'm sliding down the middle of a glacier. It's really weird. A chasm. It's strange. And I'm spinning a bit now. I physically feel as if I'm spinning. I have no idea why I'm falling. And now I'm dropping in a straight line down. I'm actually... I seem to be surrounded by something very heavy. It's the weight. And I'm definitely *it,* you know. And I'm just dropping like a stone. It's not scary. I'm just aware.

D: *Usually I ask you to drop like a leaf, so it won't feel so sudden.*

M: Isn't that strange that I'm dropping like a stone?

D: *Yes, instead of like a leaf from a tree.*

She gave the impression of someone hanging on during a gyrating amusement park ride. It was the feeling of being totally out of control. I was helpless to stop her descent until she was able to control the slide on her own.

M: (Suddenly) I've stopped. I've landed.

D: *Are you on your feet or what?*

M: Well ... it's just white. And ... this will sound weird (Chuckle) ... I'm in a sort of tear-dropped pyramid-shaped ... that's interesting. (Surprised) It's a spaceship!

D: *A spaceship?*

M: It's spinning. The base is spinning. And it's white all around me. It's not scary. It's not frightening. It's a spaceship. (Surprised) I *am* the spaceship! Does that make sense?

D: *Yes, it does. It does to me.*

M: Oops! I'm spinning. There we are. I'm spinning. I can physically feel my body literally turning now.

D: *Have you landed on the ground?*

M: Snow.

D: *That's why it's white. Tell me what you mean about* being *the spaceship. Why do you think that?*

M: Because I *am*. I'm aware that I have a mind, and I'm aware that I'm separate. But I'm also aware that I am the ship ... because my mind controls it. That's why.

D: *Your mind controls?* (Yeah) *It can't fly without you?* (No) *All right. Look down at yourself. Do you have any clothes on?*

M: No. I'm very white too. Whoa! I'm spinning even more. And I'm managing to slow myself down. Whoa! (Laughing) Whoa, whoa, whoa! And now I'm taking off. Whoa!

D: *We don't want you to do that. Let's make it stop and hold still.*

M: Whoa! Sorry! Hang on! Whoa! (Laugh) This is like being on a Helter-Skelter. It's very, very disconcerting.

D: *If you're controlling it, then you can make it slow down.*

M: Yes. It was just that when you said to look at myself, the whole thing took off. Whoa! Wait a minute.

D: *Tell it to stop. It's stopped, and turn it off, so it'll stay still.*

I knew I wouldn't be able to get any answers until the distracting movement stopped.

M: Okay. Well, whoa! I know I should stop spinning. Whew! The speed! The speed!

D: *Listen a minute.* (I didn't want her to go off without me.)

M: I am listening. It's okay. I've got you. Listen! I'm spinning two ways at once. Literally. The center part of me is spinning in a clock-wise direction, and my extremities are spinning in an anti-clockwise direction. And that's how the spaceship moves. Okay?

D: *Is this a big spaceship?*

M: No. A small one.

D: *Can you look at your body without getting dizzy?*

M: I can look at my hands. It's quite difficult because ... it's almost as if I'm transparent, but I'm not. I'm white to light, light. I'm luminescent. And ... I can't tell you whether they're big hands or small hands, but I can tell you that the tips of the fingers are bulbous. They're slightly swollen, almost as if they would have suckers on them, but they don't. Does that make sense?

D: *Kind of like the bulb on a thermometer, you mean?*

M: (With certainty.) Yes! And quite knuckley, as well.

D: *How many fingers do you have.*

M: (Counting) One, two, three, four, like a human hand. Five with a thumb. I have a thumb. But the tips are different. And they're also bonier and fleshier. They're more contoured. Actually it's quite stabilizing to look at my hands. I'm less aware of the spinning of the vehicle.

D: *Tell me what your facial characteristics feel like.*

M: Oh, okay. A pointed chin, a round egg-shaped head, small eyes -- well, not so small, but they slant up like almonds. A very small long sculptured nose with just two holes. And a small mouth.

D: *Do you have any hair?*

M: No, nothing. No hair. Nowhere, anywhere. I have a big brain.

D: *You know that?* (Uh-huh) *Do you think that's why the head is shaped that way?* (Uh-huh) *Why are you in that ship?*

M: (Pause) What I want to say is that it's actually my job. And I crashed, you know. I *crashed.* This is like I'm stuck. And I'm very confused right now.

D: *Why did the ship crash?*

M: Something happened to the gravitational ... I don't know. It dropped. It just dropped, bang! It shouldn't have done that.

D: *Is that what was causing the spinning and the disorientation?*

M: It's very strange, because I am confused here. I am surrounded by cold ice. I'm definitely in the mountains somewhere. And ... I'm a scout ship. That's what it is, but I crashed. It was very sudden. It was like hitting a wall, and then the whole thing went out of control. But I didn't hit anything.

D: *Are you going to be able to repair it?*

M: Right now I haven't had time to check things out, but I'm very aware that ... I banged my head.

D: *Do you bleed?*

M: Not like you mean. But there is a disturbance. There is a leakage.

D: *Of fluid or what?*

M: It's ... (difficult to explain) it is tangible. But it doesn't ... it's not dripping, it's floating. Like plasma almost.

D: *What color is it?*

M: It's white. It's luminescent also. Slightly darker than my skin.

D: *It's coming out of your head?*

M: It's leaking up. It's up. It's completely staying up.

D: *Floating up? Because it's inside the craft?*

M: I've never been outside this. I don't know what would happen if I stepped outside of this.

D: *I see. Well, do you have a way to summon help, if you were a scout ship?*

M: I have a panel in front of me that I can control. But the lights are the wrong colors. Something's happened. The frequencies have all gone crazy. It's yellow and green, and it shouldn't be that color. No reds.

D: *It's supposed to be red?*

M: Yes. It's very confusing.

D: *Are there many little lights or what?*

M: Yes, like tiny light bulbs. I am very aware that the left side of my head is actually quite damaged. My ear also, internally, is quite damaged, and I'm very confused.

D: *What kind of ears do you have? What do they look like?*

M: Just sort of ... how can I explain? It's like a raised protuberance with just a hole. Not like your ears would be. Different. Like a mushroom really with a hole in the middle.

D: *I see. But you think you have damaged that side of the head and the ear also.*

M: Yeah. It hurts. It hurts! But it sort of feels .... There is one point that actually does hurt quite a lot.

I immediately gave suggestions to relieve any actual sensation of pain.

D: *I don't want you to experience any physical discomfort. -- Do you know, were you supposed to come to this part of the Earth?*

M: I was mapping magnetic lines. That's what I was doing. I was recording magnetic lines. And then something happened.

D: *Well, what are you going to do?*

M: At this moment I feel I should get out, and just check out where I am. Because my head hurts and I can't control this. The spinning must have been why I banged my head. Because it got out of control for a few seconds, and it shouldn't have done that. I am very experienced, and that was out of control.

D: *So you can't operate it or summon help, or take off again, as long as something is wrong with your head?*

M: Yes ... I have to repair. I have to mend.

D: *Can you do that?*

M: I hope so. I don't want to be stuck here. It's very strange because I ... (Sigh) I'm experiencing almost like a grief, a howling inside my body. I think I'm marooned.

D: *Is it like fear, or do you know what that is?*

M: Fear? No, it's like mourning. It's grief.

D: *Why would it feel that way?*

M: I don't know.

D: *Well, where did your ship come from?*

M: (Chuckle) If I said "straight up and to the right" .... (Laugh) A long way. (Sigh) I'm hearing a language. It's sounds almost like a guttural, throaty ... I can't even do it. My voice box can't do this, Dolores. I can hear it in my head, but I can't ....

D: *Well, translate. Tell me what it's saying. Don't try to imitate it.* (Long pause, as she listened.) *Is it trying to tell you where you came from?*

M: Yes. But it sounds .... (She was frustrated because she couldn't make the sounds.) Not from this universe.

D: *Did it come directly?*

M: No. Two stops. Two stops. Long, long journey.

D: *Do you know where the other two stops were?*

M: Sirius one.

D: *What was the other one?*

M: Outskirts of solar system. On the ring of Saturn.

D: *I thought you might have come from a bigger craft.*

M: No. Thought, thought is faster.

D: *This craft is capable of going that far then.*

M: We don't eat like you.

D: *Oh? How do you get your nourishment?*

M: Lights.

D: *Light? How do you get light onboard a craft?*

M: Radiation.

D: *Where does that come from?*

M: Everywhere.

D: *I was thinking if you were enclosed on a craft there wouldn't be any kind of light inside it.*

M: No, it's not like you think. Not like you think. They divert ... it is not like .... One, explain things. Radiation is not harmful. It is nourishment. Vehicles are for ease of travel, rather than necessity. It's strange.

D: *Then the light, the radiation, is coming from inside the craft?*

M: Inside and outside.

D: *Outside in space, or what?*

M: Yes. I just absorb it. It's everywhere. My skin ... moisture. That's the reason. The craft keeps the moisture.

D: *All right. You said you think you have to go outside to orient yourself, to see where you are. But didn't you say you have never been outside the craft?*

M: Not for a long time. I've been traveling.

D: *So you're able to exist as long as you're in the craft. It doesn't make any difference how long or far the distance is.*

M: I know how long until I crashed.

D: *Were you communicating with anybody before that?*

M: I am always linked to every thought ... to all the others, to everybody.

D: *Won't they be able to pick up that something's wrong?*

M: I feel totally disconnected. Something bad happened.

D: *If they could still connect with you, they might come and get you.*

M: I feel totally disconnected. I'm very sad.

D: *Well, let's move ahead and see what you do. What are you going to do next?*

M: Now I'm ... some*one*, some*thing* has given me fur.

D: *Fur?*

M: I'm sitting in a cave with fur around my body, and a fire. And it feels strange, but it seems necessary. I lost a toe. It froze. It's gone.

D: *Then you went outside of the spacecraft. Is that what you mean?* (Yes) *What did it feel like when you did that?*

M: Shock!

D: *In what way?*

M: Like breathing for air. Flames searing inside me. It's cold, but it feels of fire.

D: *Breathing the cold air was a shock?* (Yes.) *Do you breathe with a respiratory system?*

M: I have a system for adapting to the environment. I can breathe if need be. Mostly through skin, but can breathe should the intake of gases be more needed.

D: *I see. So you adapt to wherever you find yourself.*

M: Almost. Not all places. Some could be hostile. Acid would be. Sulphur's no good. Sulphur's acidic.

D: *But the gases that you're in now are not harmful? They were just burning at first, or was that the cold that was burning?*

M: Both. One needs time to adjust. Can adjust, but it's ... hurts something.

D: *Were you walking in the cold? Is that when you lost your toe?*

M: I remember little. Just falling, and waking in this place with furs, and ... everybody has furs.

D: *There are other people?*

M: One, at present. I know, but I believe more.

D: *Are you comfortable there?*

M: I'm stranded. How can you be comfortable when you're stranded?

D: *I mean, you're no longer cold, are you?*

M: I'm numb.

D: *Then the fire is not helping?*

M: I think ... (Chuckle) you would term the situation "depressed". I think I am very depressed and despondent. I'm still stranded.

D: *Yes. Well, what does this person look like who is with you?*

M: Furry. Hair everywhere. Hair.

D: *On his skin?* (Yes) *I thought you meant fur like they had over you.*

M: No. I am wearing fur ... but this is fur on the skin. He is big, tall. Much, much bigger than me. I come to chest high. Four to ... Wait please. Five heaval (?) tall. (Had difficulty finding words) Tele .... *You* say "telepathic". Works, speaks with the mind. It is a most compassionate being. Most intelligent.

D: *He must be compassionate if he took care of you.*

M: There is a bonding occurring. A friendship. I am very lonely. I can't reach my people. (Sigh) I need the craft to do that. It is damaged. My head is damaged. I can't connect myself back in.

D: *Are you able to communicate with this other being?*

M: Yes, yes and no. Sort of ... we understand each other, but there's no detail in the speech pattern. It's from mind to mind. You think "hunger, warmth, company, friendship." Those things occur. No possibility for conversation.

D: *I see. Simple concepts?*

M: Yes. (Had difficulty explaining.) There is a great sharing, and yet no .... There *is* a great sharing. I understand much of this friend, and he tries to understand me. He understood my need for protection, and gave me furs. I don't know where they came from, because he can't understand the question.

D: *So it seems like he can only understand basic, simple things.*

M: No. But they are concepts, there are no .... How can you communicate about star maps and space travel, when this being, with all his compassion and wisdom, has never been anywhere else but this mountain?

D: *Yes. But it is a human type? It's not an animal? Is that correct?*

M: I don't understand "human".

D: *Is it more like you than an animal? Or do you know what an animal is?*

M: No. (Pause, as though trying to understand.) Five heaval (?), tall, hairy, kind, wise, telepathic.

D: *With lots of fur.*

M: Thick. Ah! More than one. One white, one black.

D: *Did another one come in?*

M: Yes. One is slightly shorter. They seem concerned about my head. They are attempting to do some healing with their minds, jointly. Now another and another. Five now have come.

D: *Do they all have different colored fur?*

M: Mostly black and white. Some brown, but not all over.

D: *Like spotted?*

M: No, just patches. Mostly black and white.

D: *And they are communicating with your mind and trying to heal you. Is it working?*

M: There's less pain. (Softly) I think I sleep now.

D: *But you'll be able to hear me. That's good, isn't it, that they were able to help you?* (Uh-huh) *That's very good.* (It was obvious that she was going to sleep.) *All right. I want you to move forward again. Let's move forward till something else important is happening. Tell me what you are seeing.*

M: Humans! Now I understand what they are. People, people. Bald skins like mine.

D: *Do you see somebody different?*

M: Yes, yes. I still have my fur, but now I am down lower, from the mountains. *They* chatter like monkeys.

D: *Who does?*

M: The humans. Noisy, noisy, noisy. They're so noisy. No silent telepathic. The others were silent, different, soft, compassionate. These are noisy.

D: *They don't have fur?*

M: No. -- On the head! They have on the head.

D: *And this is what you think I meant by humans?*

M: Oh, yes!

D: *So they look more like you?*

M: They're so ugly. (Laugh) So ugly.

D: *Why are they ugly?*

M: They have such big noses.

D: *What color is their hair? Or fur?*

M: Black.

D: *Black fur on their heads? And big noses. Are they wearing anything?*

M: They have ... around the top of their legs and their bodies, fabric, woven.

D: *How did you get down there with them?*

M: The others sent me, in the dream.

D: *In the dream? How do you mean?*

M: After the healing I woke up in this place. They sent me in the dream.

D: *Do you think maybe they carried you down there?*

M: In the dream I floated.

D: *So you don't really know? You just woke up with these chattering beings?*

M: (Laugh) And the noses. So ugly.

D: *But the people with the fur are gone?*

M: Just in my mind.

D: *They're not with you now.* (No) *Well, what are these people doing? The chattering ones?*

M: They're praying. They're kneeling and praying. Down ... hands, heads down to the ground. Ummm.

D: *Why are they praying?*

M: They think I'm a god or something. I glow. I'm luminescent. They are not that way.

D: *This is your natural way?*

M: Oh, yes.

D: *So it's something they've never seen, I suppose. How is your head? Is it better?*

M: It feels as if a part is missing, but there's no pain.

D: *It was probably caused by the damage. Well, at least they're not harmful to you, are they?*

M: No, like children. Like young children.

D: *Before you felt depressed and stranded. How do you feel now?*

M: I ... I have an empty space. And the sadness comes and goes.

D: *Do you think there is any way you could contact your people, and let them know where you are?*

M: I can build a satellite with time. (Sigh) But they know nothing of how to smelt metal.

D: *I see. I would think that your people would come looking for you.*

M: Rubbed out. Rubbed out. When you leave the ship it's like the light goes off.

D: *Oh. So they won't be able to contact you, or trace you?*

M: Not unless they're very close. And I was a long way from home.

D: *I see. Well, what do you think you're going to do?*

M: (Pause) I can't think.

D: *You can't go anywhere anyway, can you?*

M: (Sadly) No.

D: *You have to stay there.*

M: I don't want to. But I have no choice.

D: *Let's move ahead again and find out what you do. Move ahead in time.*

M: (Her mood changed abruptly. She no longer sounded sad.) We are building things.

D: *You are?*

M: Oh, yes, they learn fast.

D: *What kind of things are you building?*

M: Bridges. Houses.

D: *Did they have that before?*

M: No, I showed them with sticks and twine. They use a bark, and they rub it with stones to make rope. They showed me, and I showed them.

D: *Where did you get the ideas? It this something you have where you come from?*

M: I've seen these things. And we have structures that are ... (She had difficulty with the words.) that are ... structures, but not like this.

D: *That you live in?*

M: Fields, connections, energy points that can be used. ... Geometry is important. Yes, I need to be busy.

D: *Yes, you need to have something to do. That makes sense.*

M: There is a gorge, a *big* gorge. And we, me, I, intend to build a bridge.

D: *You're going to show them how to do it?*

M: Oh, yes!

D: *That would be helpful to them, wouldn't it?*

M: Well, I don't know. They seem happy enough. I'm bored. And *I* need to do this.

D: *Did they have any structures before?*

M: A few. No, very few. Caves, trees. They sleep in trees sometimes, these ones. (Chuckle)

D: *So you're trying to show them a better way?*

M: No. I'm bored.

D: *So you're teaching them. How are you doing it? With telepathy, like you said you communicated with the other people?*

M: No, with showing them. By taking sticks and twine, and showing them. And drawing on the ground. The others are still in my mind; they can communicate better with me. I have a language with my hands now. They do too. They speak a lot with their hands.

D: *That way they can understand you?*

M: Enough.

D: *Well, that's very good. Even though you're bored, you're doing some good things for them.*

M: Well, selfishly.

D: *They are treating you well. That's the main thing. Do you still wear the fur?* (Yes) *Because it's cold?*

M: No, because it hides the difference, the luminescence. Except I can't hide my head. So they pray sometimes. They think I'm more than I am, because I can be different to them. If I take off my robe, I float. (Chuckle) So I keep it on.

D: *Does it frighten them?*

M: They tend to pray a lot. (Laugh) If I float. And they chant if I float. It's a pleasant sound.

D: *Well, at least they're not threatening.*

M: They're very simple.

D: *That's good. All right. Let's move ahead further in time and see what other important thing you're doing.*

M: There is a structure. I seem to spend most of my time building. This is stone. (Sadly.) I'm worried. I don't glow anymore.

D: *Why not?*

M: I don't know.

D: *Do you think because you're getting used to that place?*

M: No. I think I'm sick.

D: *Well, what is the stone structure? (Pause) Did you make it?*

M: Assisted.

D: *What does it look like?*

M: It is a cuboid type with steps. The front is the entrance to an opening in the mountain. But it is very big and it has carvings and steps.

D: *How did you make it? It sounds like it would be much more difficult than the wooden structures.*

M: Yes. I feel that the others assisted also. Like moving the blocks with the minds. (Was she referring to the furry creatures?)

D: *To get them into place.*

M: Yes. And we have a way of making the surface shine.

D: *How do you do that?*

M: You use the straw and another rock, and you just rub and rub and rub. And it happens in time.

D: *How did you get the carvings on it?*

M: We have a furnace now.

D: *You made that?*

M: Oh, yes. We have tools.

D: *Did you show them how to do that? (Yes) Did they make the carvings then?*

M: Yes. (Chuckle) They have one of me. Very strange. Different to them, so big. The head is so large. Some of the children make woven heads like mine and put them on their own. (Laugh)

D: *Do you think the carving looks like you?*

M: Well, I see my shadow, and my hands. But it is not the same.

D: *It's the best they can do, I guess.*

M: I guess.

D: *Why are you teaching them all these things? Are you still bored?*

M: Well, I feel cared for. I'm lonely. But there is so much to teach. (Chuckle) Even ovens for baking bread. About grains and how to sow them and grow and harvest. Because before they were all wild. So we have a way of splicing, of altering the grains to make them more substantial.

D: *You know how to do that?*

M: Oh, yes. You just use two fingers.

D: *Oh? And you can change the structure of something. Is that what you mean?* (Uh-huh) *I see. That's like magic, really.*

M: For them, yes. For me, no.

D: *To you it's very natural.* (Yes) *Then you've done much good for them.*

M: I think they've done much good for me.

D: *If you hadn't had that, it would have been really lonely, wouldn't it? And boring.*

M: Well, it is lonely. (Sigh) I've been here a long time. Many of them have come and gone and died. Many generations.

D: *Did you say you thought you might be sick, because you weren't glowing anymore?* (Yes) *What do you think's going to happen? Can you heal yourself?*

M: I don't know. No one else ever told me about this.

D: *But nobody else of your kind has ever been in a situation like this before.*

M: No. But I have a feeling that ones will come soon. I can feel something. I hope it will be soon enough. They are getting much closer.

D: *Do you think that?*

M: I feel it.

D: *All right. Let's move ahead again and see what happens to you.*

M: Oh, dear!

D: *What happened?*

M: (Sigh) Well, some others came. And they *don't* like me.

D: *They don't?*

M: Oh, no.

D: *Are these others like you?*

M: No. No.

D: *How are they different?*

M: Well, they feel different. And they look more like the people that I live with. (Sigh) But they are ... (Sigh) Well ... (had difficulty explaining) they have problems, because they ... they fall through things.

D: *Fall* through *things?*

M: (Emphatic) Yes! They want to sit down and they fall through the chair.

D: *How come?*

M: I don't know. It can't hold them. They can fall through it, and it can be part ... in their body.

D: *In their body?*

M: That's how they're different. They're not so solid. They said I interfered. And they don't like me. I'm going away.

D: *Well, do these people belong there?*

M: They have come before.

D: *They have come from somewhere else?*

M: Oh, yes. They have a rocket.

D: *A rocket?*

M: Oh, yes.

D: *But they're more like these people than your people?*

M: Oh, yes. They say I have interfered. So I'm leaving.

D: *Can the other people see them?*

M: Oh, yes. They think they are gods too. Masters. Masters more than gods.

D: *Are you going to go with them, or how are you going to leave?*

M: I am just going to walk.

D: *You're not going with them in their ship?*

M: They don't like me. I interfered. I don't like them. They have no respect for anything.

D: *Do you think they came from a different place than you did?*

M: Oh! (Chuckle) This is a different place.

D: *I see. Maybe you're two different types or something.*

M: Well, monkeys look different. There are many monkeys here.

D: *Well, what do you do? Do you just start walking?*

M: I'm going back to the others in the caves.

D: *What about the people you were helping and showing how to do things? Do they want you to go away?*

M: They say nothing.

D: *Okay. So you're going to the ones in the caves. What happens then?*

M: I stay there. I'm welcome.

D: *Well, let's move ahead to the last day of your life in that lifetime. You may want to look at it objectively. It won't bother you at all. You will just see it and tell me what happened. What happens on the last day of your life in that lifetime?*

M: I'm just lying down in a cave, listening to the wind. And I just disintegrate.

D: *Disintegrate?*

M: Like dust.

D: *Was part of it because you weren't glowing anymore?*

M: Ah, yes. I can just see myself being blown away.

D: *There's no body left anymore?*

M: No body, but *I'm* here.

D: *All right. Let's look at that life and examine it. What do you think you learned from that?*

M: Well ... emotion.

D: *Is that something you didn't know before?*

M: No. I didn't know.

D: *Where you were from, you didn't have those feelings?*

M: No. Everything was ... (Chuckle) *dull.*

D: (Laugh) So you learned feelings. Did you learn any other lessons from that lifetime?

M: There are many abuses, and many manipulators. And I don't think exploration should be allowed.

D: *Why not?*

M: Because it messes up the natural order of things.

D: *You mean exploration like you were doing?*

M: Oh, yes. And others too.

D: *The other people that came?*

M: Oh, they came. And they stole and they took and they ... (Sigh) no respect.

D: *So you don't think that should be allowed. But in your case it wasn't a matter of allowing. You just couldn't get back. You didn't do it on purpose.*

M: I had a job to do. I was making maps of this place.

D: *Yes, but whenever you were stranded there, it wasn't your fault. You had to find something to occupy your time.*

M: Well, yes. But it should not have happened. I should not have been there in the first place.

D: *That still wasn't your fault.*

M: No. That is just my opinion. This place is strange. The pull here is very unusual. It is a dense, dense place.

D: *Maybe that had something to do with why the accident happened.*

N: I think so. It doesn't matter anyway. I'm stuck. I can't go home.

D: *Even now? Even after the body has disintegrated?*

M: Even now. Now I have to find a way of *merging* with something if I wish to be physical.

D: *I see. Well, I want to thank you for telling me these things and sharing it with me. I want you to move away from that scene.*

M: To where?

D: *Oh, just to move forward in time, away from that scene.*

When Mona went forward she began to describe a lifetime of an Incan priest with a feather headdress. We were running out of time for the session, so I was trying to end it. I didn't have time to explore another lifetime. But at least we established that the pull of the Earth was so great that she continued with more lifetimes on this planet, instead of returning to her own. I think she probably incurred karma with the people of Earth because she had "interfered" by teaching them cultures before it was the proper time for them to learn. Through her own boredom she had done no apparent damage, but would have to remain in a physical body in order to repay the karma.

I also had not explored the cause for her obesity, and that would have to be done before the session was completed. Personally I could not see any connection with the lifetime she had described, but I had not counted on the strange logic of the subconscious.

D: *I want you to leave all those scenes you are looking at. And I want you to move forward in time.*

M: Forward in time.

D: *And I want all of the consciousness and personality of Mona to once again return to this body. And I want the little creature that we were speaking to to recede to wherever he belongs. And I want to thank him for sharing his story with me. I loved talking with him.*

M: (She interrupted me.) No!

D: *What?*

This was unusual. Normally by this stage of the regression the subject does not talk. They merely obey the commands to return to the present.

M: Because you don't understand. It's not *gone!*

D: *All right. But I still want it to recede into the background, into the subconscious.* (A deep sigh.) *And I thank it, because I have loved speaking with it. I am very happy it did speak to me. And I want all of the consciousness and personality of Mona to once again return to the foreground of the subconscious. I would like to speak to Mona's subconscious. Would I be allowed to ask your subconscious some questions?* (Yes)

The story had been very interesting and different, but what did it have to do with her present problem of being overweight?

D: *Did this life that she was exploring have anything to do with her weight problem she's been worried about? Is there any connection with that life?*

M: She doesn't want to float away.

D: *Oh! She's afraid of that?*

M: Of being different.

D: *I see. She's making her body denser and heavier. She's afraid if she loses weight that she will float away like the other little being? Is that correct?*

M: (Sigh) She's different.

D: *But she's a good person. She's happy in this body. The problem is she wants to take-off some of that extra weight. She doesn't need it anymore now, does she?*

M: Well, no.

D: *Can you make her realize that in this lifetime, in this body, she doesn't need to have that extra weight?*

M: Well, we don't think so, maybe. (Big sigh) We'll have to see.

D: *Do you think you can work with her and make her understand that was a different body altogether? She doesn't have to be afraid now, and she doesn't need that extra weight anymore.*

M: She can take off the coat.

D: *Yes, she can take off that fur coat. Within the next six months of our time, she would like to shed that coat. She would like to take off about fifty, sixty pounds, and look very nice. Do you think you could help her realize that this is a human body like all the other humans, and it is attached to the ground with gravity. This body won't float away.*

M: Well, the problem seems to be that ... (big sigh) the consciousness is not that of the human, but of the being.

The subconscious continued to argue with me using its own unique form of logic. I continued to attempt to persuade it by appealing to its concern for Mona's body, and its protective monitoring of its systems. The following is a greatly condensed transcript of the amount of cajoling and coaxing I had to do before the subconscious finally came up with an unusual solution.

D: *She feels she'll be happier and more comfortable if she doesn't have so much weight. It's hard on her body.*

M: Yes, this is true. The joints.

D: *The joints, the functioning of the body. That's why she would like to take off about fifty, sixty pounds.*

M: Yes, this is true! Yes.

D: *So why don't we separate the consciousness of the being, its influences, and make it understand that this is a different body.*

M: Well, we have a problem. For the being ... is her. This is Mona. And the being can finally go home. And there are connections now to others like herself. And she talks with him. And she ...Ummm, we will have to think about this. ...Well, we could modify the energy system.

D: *Of the body?*

M: No, of the being.

D: *Okay. Because we don't want it to go away if it doesn't need to go away. But just help it to understand and work with her.*

M: It cannot go away. It is an aspect. It is a part. It is genetic. The gift comes from the unusual history.

The gift referred to her amazing psychic ability, and that she was teaching others how to utilize their own latent psychic abilities.

M: So we will rebuild the body.

D: *Tell it it doesn't have to worry anymore. It's time to shed the coat. We don't need that heavy coat anymore.*

M: It would make her very happy. But I must say that the picture is thus: when the coat is removed, the body floats.

D: *Yes, but not in this life. It won't, because it is attached to the ground by gravity. It really is.*

M: The picture won't go away.

D: *I see. Well, maybe you can help her work on that picture.*

M: Well ... we'll try boots instead.

D: *Boots? Have her wear boots?*

M: (Very satisfied.) Yes. That's best. That's much better. We can also work on the body, make it lighter. This can be done, yes, it can be. Molting. Yes, this can be done.

D: *And if you want her to put boots on to hold her to the ground, that's a good idea.*

What a wonderfully unique and novel idea. This is one that I would have never thought of to suggest as a solution for weight loss. Since it was supplied directly from the subconscious it would work, no matter how strange it seemed. This was the picture the subconscious needed, so it would have something to work with. The extra weight was being equated to the heavy coat. In the other lifetime the coat kept the being from floating, and also hid his glowing appearance. The subconscious felt that if the coat (the excess weight) was removed the body would float, and people would once again see she was different, and thus fear her. What strange logic? The substitution of the boots would give her something else to hold her to the ground, and it would not affect her health as much as obesity. The subconscious had supplied the perfect solution that would protect the body. How clever!

M: We will use this until she feels safe without the boots.
D: *That's a good idea. That way she'll know she's not going to float, because they will hold her to the ground.*
M: We will also take the time to expand the brain. Yes. We have started molting already.
D: *Oh, that's very good. I know she will be happy to hear that. And I really thank you for cooperating with me.*
M: Well ... we have enjoyed you.
D: *And you realize I have her welfare at heart.*
M: Well, we do too.
D: *We always want what's best for her.*
M: She is very stubborn. (chuckle)
D: *She is stubborn, isn't she? That's why I am glad you were able to talk to me so we could work it out. Thank you.*
M: No, thank you.

I was then able to have the personality of the little being recede, and the personality and consciousness of Mona to integrate fully back into the body before I awakened her. There was no more protesting now that the subconscious had agreed to work on this in its own unique way.

In these last two chapters I had uncovered cases where the subject was literally part of a space craft in alien lifetimes. Strange as it may seem, the concept began to disturb me because I wondered if we are on the doorstep of introducing such a possibility into our own future. Could the new computer games called "Virtual Reality" be the first step by putting the player into a situation where he is controlling the environment of the game with his own mind and muscle reactions?

I came across another example of this while conducting a regression on another young woman, whom I shall call "Laura", in London. Since it was short I will include the relevant portion of it here. Everything was proceeding normally in the session until she moved from the mundane lifetime she was observing into one with an alien atmosphere. She reported seeing a huge spaceship. Then she physically felt a great restriction in her body. A very tight encapsulated feeling.

After I gave instructions to alleviate the uncomfortable sensation she was able to describe what she saw as she looked down at herself. She saw that she was in an elongated body wearing a very tight-fitting suit of a silvery fabric. Her long and narrow hands were holding what appeared at first glance to be an open book. It had two parts and was open like a book, but she soon discovered it was actually a machine. She was then told she was in a "time meld" capsule, and the piece of machinery in her hands allowed her to move through time and space.

L: It's almost like I'm not just an individual, but part of a whole system.

D: *Of other individuals or what?*

L: No. It's more like a large machine of some sort. This ship that I mentioned before, I'm in this ship. I'm a part of this ship. I and it are one. There is a dark walkway, a corridor, lit by some type of silvery light. I am walking along carrying and am also a part of this contraption in my hand.

D: *What do your features look like?*

L: I have these very long, long hands. These long fingers are a lightish color, but are differentiated from the silver garment that I'm wearing.

D: *What about your facial features?*

L: My facial features are ... it's a bit difficult, because I'm aware of my own nose. But I think my nose is longer. My face is a bit like a human face, but it's more elongated. I don't know whether I have any hair or not, because I'm wearing a helmet, which is the same color as my clothing. I am aware that we are very close to human beings.

D: *Do you have a sex?*

L: We are one and the same. Androgynous people.

D: *You don't have one distinguishable sex.*

L: We do not differentiate between the two. We are one and the same.

D: *How do you reproduce then?*

L: Our beings reproduce by osmosis. If we choose to reproduce, we share a thought and it is done. It is not difficult for us to perceive it, but difficult in your time frame to understand how it is accomplished. It is difficult for us to convey to your time that which we are. Only that by thought it is accomplished.

D: *The new being, is it as a baby? Or how does it develop?*

L: The being develops its own characteristics by sharing with its parents in thought. Remember it is by osmosis, transference of thought. Physical communication is not necessary. By thought alone. Then the child will choose the personal characteristics it wishes to carry in its thought forms. Now we realize it is difficult for you to understand that which we are.

D: *But does it start as a baby and grow? Or is it already a fully developed adult size when it is first created?*

L: It is already fully developed. There is no need for childhood and birth as you know it.

D: *Do you have to eat? To consume any kind of food or anything?*

L: It is not necessary. We can, if we choose, experience an eating concept. To reconnect with the life forms, as you know them, by thought we can do this. And choose to experience eating, as you know it. But for our own part it is not necessary or desirable to consume food. It is not necessary at all. We grow and develop without the necessity of food, as you would know it.

D: *What kind of nourishment do you need to keep you alive then?*

L: The life force, as you know it. Think of it as light that encapsulates your body and permeates your being. It is around us always when we need it. To consume anything would be totally unnecessary.

D: *You also spoke of being as one with the ship?*

L: That is correct.

D: *Does that mean that you cannot exist separate from the ship?*

L: No, it does not. But when we travel to distant galaxies, it is necessary to be a part of that system. While I am in the ship, then I am encapsulated.

D: *I see. Then the ship cannot operate without you.*

L: That is correct.

D: *I understand now. But you can come and go without it. You can go wherever you wish.*

L: That is true.

D: *Are there others on the ship besides you?*

L: Indeed there are many of us present at this time on this ship. Some of us integrate directly with the mechanism that moves our ship from place to place. That is my job to integrate with the machinery, to move it from place to place.

D: *Where do you go on your travels?*

L: We visit many galaxies. From time to time we interact directly with the people in the different time frames. You must understand, we move in dimensions of thought. The thoughts move then into time frames. Then we can interact with the different people that we meet on our journeys.

D: *Is there a purpose for meeting with these people and interacting with them?*

L: Yes, there is. The thoughts they have will interact with ours. The developments then take place as we interact in dimensions of thought. This opens up channels of communication so we can assist their developments. That is part of our task, to assist in development throughout the galaxies we visit. Our job is to help and assist directly with those thoughtforms that require our assistance and development.

D: *Have you ever interacted with the people of Earth?*

L: (Seriously and purposely) Indeed we have! The thoughtforms that emanate from Earth are directly related to the work we do onboard our ship.

D: *Have you reacted with Earth -- you personally -- in the past?*

L: Indeed we have. The time frames have varied, but the communications we have has .... (She stopped abruptly and showed signs that something was occurring.) (Softly) I am moving now.

D: *Where are you moving to?*

L: To a different time frame. My body is tingling, particularly on my left side. My left hand is tingling, all the way down the left side. I'm peaceful. Relaxed.

D: *Why is it tingling?*

L: Because the time frame I am in now does not require the energy frequency that I last spoke of. When the transition is complete I will no longer be able to speak to you.

D: *Do you know what happened to you when you were in that lifetime on that spacecraft? What happened to that body at the end of that lifetime?*

L: It has not ended yet.

D: *What do you mean? Is it going on at the same time that the present one of Laura is going on?*

L: That is correct.

D: *Is it possible to do that, live two lives at once?*

L: Without a doubt it is possible.

D: *Without the one being aware of the other?*

L: That is correct. I am aware that while I am Laura lying here in this body, that I am also the other entity. That is my true beingness.

D: *Do you think that is the one that has been continuing through time?*

L: That is correct.

D: *Is that part aware of Laura?*

L: Indeed.

D: *But Laura doesn't know about it. Is that correct?*

L: On another level, yes, Laura is aware. Not the conscious one. And yet that is not entirely true. I am aware that I am Laura in this earthly form, but as the other being I traverse time and space, and move in a different frequency. The time capsule, that we spoke of, is a part of this energy frequency system. Each person will become aware of their own particular frequency in their bodies. As Laura I am interacting more and more with this other frequency, the alien one. When I meditate I integrate with this frequency, and I learn and develop. I am understanding more and more of who I really am. My job and where I really come from. This has a purpose which will unfold gradually within the subconscious, and more directly in Laura's conscious mind. She will understand more of this as she grows older in her physical form. She needs to know, which is why we have shared with her today. She has asked many times to know more about herself, who she is and her task in this lifetime. It started so long ago. Now she will know that we are part of each other, the alien being and herself. We can never be separated, because we are one. -- Now I must cut off this transmission because our craft is entering another time dimension, a different energy frequency, and we can no longer communicate.

When I played this tape back later for transcription all the words after this remark were strangely garbled and impossible to transcribe. This has occurred on other occasions when static was so strong on the tape that it overshadowed the words. I have also had tapes blank with no recording, and had the voices slowed down to a deep guttural sound, or speeded up to produce the "chipmunk" effect. In every case there was no malfunction with the tape recorder. It is almost as though different energies are often present during the sessions, and these can interfere with the recording equipment.

It is interesting that these were three cases where the subject was connected to and a functioning part of machinery needed to operate a space craft. Another interesting aspect is the repetition of the physical description and bodily functions (eating and sexual reproduction). Can these be coincidence, similar reports by accident? Or are the people in this book actually describing a real, functioning society in other realms and dimensions?

CHAPTER EIGHT

INTERFERENCE CREATES ENTRAPMENT

I returned to London several times after Mona's session. I began to make regular trips in connection with my book, *Jesus and the Essenes.* I became firmly associated with the Essene Network in England, and spoke each year at their Essene summer convention. On one of these trips in 1994 I met Caroline.

This young woman wanted to have a session, and it was another case of trying to find the cause of being overweight. Caroline was an attractive blond on the heavy side, but not obese. As a sideline, she mentioned she was interested in ancient Egypt, and thought she might have lived during that time. She also wanted to find out about karmic relationships in her life. It turned out that the bizarre reason for being overweight was the only one that came forward during the session. The other interests may have been present in her other past lives, but for whatever reason, her subconscious chose to focus on the weight problem. Maybe it was because that was primary in her life, even though she did not realize it.

The session was held in my small hotel room in London. During this entire regression the traffic noises outside of the hotel were very loud. At times this made it difficult to hear her soft-spoken words. London hotels are notorious for not having air conditioning (they don't need it over there), so I had to leave the window partially open for air circulation. There was no way to block the noise without cutting off the air.

I used my normal cloud method, and asked her to go to the lifetime that would be the most relevant to this lifetime. She came off the cloud into a strange scene. She had not yet reached the ground, but appeared to be hovering, and could see a pair of hands handing her a baby up into the air.

D: *Why are they handing you this baby?*
C: They can't look after it.
D: *What do they think you will do with it?*
C: They think I will look after it.
D: *What do* you *think?*
C: I wonder how I will be able to. There's not much food around. I don't know how I'm going to feed it.
D: *Why isn't there much food around? Is there a reason?*
C: The ground is hard and dry. I think we're in a field. I see stalks of crops that are withered.
D: *Do you get the impression the people are hungry?* (Yes) *Do you feel that you belong there?*
C: No. I've come from somewhere else. That's why they're giving me the baby. They think I will be able to look after it, because I've come from somewhere else, which is possibly better able to care for it. They're so desperate. If it means helping the baby, they would like me to take it.
D: *Were you going on to another place?*
C: I don't feel I'm there for very long.
D: *Do you think you're traveling alone?*
C: There may be other people behind me. But where I am, at this minute, I'm on my own.

She became aware of her body, and said she seemed to be a male wearing very loose clothes like a short toga, and laced lattice boots. Her hair was gold colored and her skin was very white.

D: *What are you going to do?*

C: I want to help them. If I don't help them, the baby will die. But I don't know how to look after the baby. Oh! But I'm connected to .... (Pause) They're taking soil samples, or they're looking at the land to teach them what is causing the problem. And to take a baby ... not only do we not know how to look after such, but we have work to do.

D: *Are there many in your group?*

C: No. About six.

D: *And you think it's your job to show them how they can grow food, so they can live? Is that right?*

C: Not at this stage. We are there to find out why the crops aren't growing.

D: *Why have you come to do this? Are you associated with these people in some way?*

C: No. We don't know them. It's just a job.

D: *Why have you come there if you don't know these people?*

C: It's a problem throughout this place. We are not the only team that is sent to try and understand what is killing the crops. And the wildlife.

D: *The wildlife too are dying? That means the people can't hunt either. Is that correct?*

C: It's getting more difficult by the day. We won't be there long. Enough time to do some tests, take some samples, analyze, and return to our base.

D: *How did you come to this place?* (Pause) *Did you walk or what?* (No) *Can you see how you arrived there?*

C: I want to say "in a bubble."

D: *A bubble? Can you see it, so you can describe what you mean?* (Pause. She was having difficulty.) *Can you see what it looks like?*

C: It seems to change shape.

D: *Well, tell me what you see.*

C: It's a multi-purpose vehicle. (Pause) It ... it changes shape in different dimensions. It moves.

D: *You mean it's not like a bubble all the time?*

C: No.

She was making hand motions to demonstrate a round shape and then a flattening. It was confusing to watch.

D: *I'm trying to understand from your hand motions. Is it round sometimes? And then what?*
C: It's round when it's down on the ground. And when it moves off the ground, it changes shape.
D: *Into what kind of a shape?*
C: In order to move ....

Hand motions. She put her hands with the palms facing each other sideways a few inches apart. A squashing effect.

D: *I'm trying to understand your hand motions. What? It flattens?*
C: It seems to ... flatten. That bubble seems to twist and flatten (hand motions).
D: *Kind of compress like that?*
C: Compress! (That apparently was the word she was looking for.)
D: *Does this bother the people when they're inside of it?*

It seemed like such a strange motion. From her hand motions, it would twist and compress down to a flat shape that was much shorter [top-wise] than the original bubble shape. It was a drastic change.

C: No, because they can do the same with their energy.
D: *What do you mean?*
C: They can change the shape of the bodies they're in.
D: *So they don't always look the same, you mean?*
C: They don't always need bodies.
D: *You mean they need the bodies when they come to see these people?*
C: Yes, because otherwise they couldn't communicate with them.

D: *Would the other people be able to see them the way they normally are?*

C: No. They would .... (Pause, had difficulty.) I want to say ... they are *there*, but it's like there is another dimension. Almost like a doorway. So they *could* see them if they were on the right frequency of vibration.

D: *Then unless you "made" this body appear, they couldn't see you?*

C: That's right.

D: *Are all of your people the same way?*

C: Oh, yes.

D: *When you look at each other, in your natural form, what do you see?*

C: Oh, it's just energy.

D: *Could you see the energy?*

C: It's like ... (had difficulty). It's like a space in the air. Not like light. It's like the molecules of air are dispersed where this energy is. So there's a hole in the air.

D: *This is how you know there is another being like yourself there. So you don't have to really* see *each other.*

C: No. But we can communicate.

D: *Where do you come from when you make these journeys to this area? (Pause) Did you say something a while ago about a base or something?*

C: A base.

An ambulance was going by on the street below with its siren screeching, and it was difficult to hear her. There was a hospital about a block away. The noise did not disturb her at all. When the subject is in deep trance they completely shut out their surroundings. I picked the conversation up again when the siren stopped.

D: *A base? Is that near here?*

C: It doesn't take long to get there, if you travel the way we travel.

D: *How do* you *travel?*

C: We move the bubble into this .... (Difficulty). We twist it into this other dimension. (Hand motions again, of twisting and compressing.)

D: *And you compress it, you mean, and change the shape. Then you're able to move it into another dimension?* (Yes) *And that dimension is where your base is?* (Yes) *Is the base on a physical place?* (Yes) *Is it a different physical place than the one that you are visiting now?* (Yes) *So you're saying, you, yourself, in your natural form are* not *physical, but you live on this other physical world?*

C: (Confidently) Yes.

Although the concept seemed unusual to me, it seemed very natural to her. She just had difficulty explaining it in a way I could understand.

C: We can choose to be physical or non-physical.

D: *But do you live in cities and things like that in your natural place?* (Pause) *Or do you know what I mean?*

C: There are constructions. They have frequencies. So much is like ... we have the bubble to travel .... (Pause) How we live is much an extension of the travel bubble. We can make the constructions the way we want them.

D: *Do you take any kind of sustenance, or any kind of food, to live?*

C: No. We get energy from the source. So we just tap into the source.

D: *Do you know what the source is that you get your energy from?*

She had difficulty explaining, and had to start and stop several times.

C: It's a place, but it's an energy. It's like a stream of energy, a stream of light. Like a spotlight ... a spotlight.

D: *How do you get energy from that?*

C: We can stand in the spotlight. So we can revitalize and get energy and sustenance from this source.

D: *Do you have to be there with it all the time?*

C: No. The source has its own knowledge. We revere this energy.

D: *Then you can go on this ship you described and be away from it, and it won't harm you?*

C: No. We just need to tap into it at regular intervals.

D: *So when you go to these other places, you can make yourself look like the people there, so they will see you? And that's what you're doing at this time?*

C: Yes. We are trying to help, but we are also trying to learn.

D: *What are you trying to learn from these people?*

C: We are questers after knowledge. We do not need the crops to survive. We are curious and compassionate.

D: *Have you been doing this for a long time?*

C: Oh, yes.

D: *This place where these people are, does that have a name? Do you call it anything?*

C: It used to be called something. I don't know where it is. There aren't many people left. They haven't been able to survive. A famine. It is affecting their spirit. And they're dying from starvation.

D: *Who told you to come here and do this?*

C: The source.

D: *Does the source speak to you, or how do you know it?*

C: When you're in the light you get the communication. So it enters your mind, and you know what you're supposed to do.

D: *Have you done this before at this place?* (No) *So what kind of tests are you and the others doing?*

C: We have to put things into the soil, and bring out samples to test in our labs. We have to see whether there's a poison as well as a drought. We think the ground has been poisoned.

D: *Where are the labs that you take these samples to?*

C: We can work in the bubble.

D: *You have the equipment inside the bubble.*

C: Oh, yes.

D: *What will you do if you discover what it is?*

C: We will try to find a way to cure the problem, to help the people, and to further our knowledge. I am not the person that makes the assessments. I am a person that communicates with the people.

D: *That is your job. But you said there were not many left alive at this place?*

C: Not very many. We don't know how many in other communities are still surviving.

D: *Can you see what these people look like?*

C: Ragged. Dusty, very dusty. Their hair is very dusty.

D: *What about their features? Do they look human?*

C: Yes. They have brown eyes. They all have brown eyes.

D: *Can you see what kind of structures they live in?*

C: They have had to build them themselves. (Was she referring to the fact that her people created structures by mind power, rather than physically?) They build them out of hard baked earth.

D: *So they were existing all right before this happened. But now something has gone wrong.*

C: Something has gone very wrong.

D: *All right. I want you to move ahead, and tell me what you discovered. Did they take the testings of the soil?*

C: Yes. It's not a poison. Things are eating away at the roots of all the crops. It is some kind of insect.

D: *Is it the same thing that is killing the animals?*

C: No. The animals are dying from starvation and from lack of water. Just like the people.

D: *What do your people propose to do? Can they help?*

C: We believe that it would be very difficult to rid the country of the infestation. There are too many of these insects. We are in a dilemma.

D: *Do you have someone you can consult, or ask for advice?*

C: We can go back to the source.

D: *What are you going to do?*

C: We can take the people with us. They would find it very uncomfortable. They would not be used to what they would have to do.

D: *Is there any other solution?*

C: Even if we managed to do something about the insect infestation, they need the rain to make the crops grow. Until the rain comes ... they have a problem.

D: *Yes, it sounds like they have several problems. What are you going to do?*

C: We have to talk about it, and make a decision. And in the morning, based on the majority, we will make a plan.

D: *Then let's move ahead until the morning, and you're discussing this. Tell me what's happening.*

C: We have decided to offer them the chance to come with us. It is possible to ferry them in small groups. They are naturally alarmed about the possibly shifting dimension.

D: *Of course, they don't understand it. Is that the only decision you can come up with?*

C: They will all be dead if they stay.

D: *What happens when you offer them that decision?*

C: Only two come with us. The rest decide to await their fate. They were afraid to come.

D: *But you did everything you could, didn't you?*

C: We did.

D: *So it's their decision. You said there were two who decided to go?*

C: Mother and child.

D: *Was it the same baby that was offered to you?*

C: The baby.

D: *Have they entered into the craft with you, or what?*

C: We are preparing them. They will need to be able to change their shape. It will not be comfortable for them. And we have to do it soon. We can't wait too long. I am worried for their sakes. It is possible for it not to work.

D: *What would happen if it didn't work?*

C: They will die.

D: *What kind of procedure is needed to help them change their shapes?*

C: They need to feel disconnected from their bodies. So they see everything happening at a distance. Once they have stepped out of their bodies, 'tis no problem. But it is getting them to step out in the first place. That is the major problem.

D: *How can you make them leave their bodies?*

C: We teach them.

D: *But you said you didn't have much time.*

C: No. We could do it, if they are receptive to it, like I am.

D: *Tell me what happens.*

C: They're frightened of what they're going to do. They know there is no chance for them in any other way.

D: *I think they're very brave. They are the only ones that wanted to take the chance. Then you said you are able to make them go out of their bodies, even though they are afraid?*

C: That's right. So ... one of them's being really silly.

D: *What do you mean?*

C: Because ... I thought it was a woman, but it's a man. And he is flying around. He thinks it's very clever. I am cross, because we must get on, and he's fooling around.

D: *Do you do something to his body?*

C: We compress it. This will not be comfortable. Just till he gets used to it a few times. It's difficult to find the words, but ... it feels that the ship compresses and twists (hand motions again), and lifts into another dimension. So that's what the people have to do too. I take the baby. It is possible to help the other person do it.

D: *What about the baby? Is the baby able to do it?*

C: The baby's fine. I'm more concerned with the adult. I've had several years of getting used to being the way I live. So does the adult.

I think he meant it was more difficult for the adult because he was set in his physical ways, while the baby was more flexible to change.

D: *That's natural. Maybe they won't have to do it very long. Let's move ahead to when you get to your place. What happens then? Were they able to make the journey?*
C: Yes. And everybody is really tired.
D: *Of all the working with them?* (Yes) *But can these people exist in your world?* (Yes) *Won't it be difficult for them with a physical body?* (Yes) *What happened when you got there? Did the body return to normal?* (Yes) *What about their spirits? You said they had to step outside the body?* (Yes) *What happened when they got to your place?*
C: They all wanted to have a bath, because they hadn't had one.
D: *Did they enter back into their body again?*
C: Emotionally they did.
D: *But how will they be able to live in your world? Will they be able to breathe and to eat, and things like that?*
C: I hope so.
D: *Then you really don't know what's going to happen to them?*
C: We've never taken people like this with us.
D: *And all the other people that were left behind, will they all die?* (Yes) *Well, let's move ahead in time, if you recognize time. And tell me, did these people adjust? Were they able to live?*
C: With difficulty. They felt a sense of disloyalty.
D: *Disloyalty? What do you mean by that?*

Caroline seemed to be getting sleepier, and her answers were coming slowly.

D: *How did they get the food?*
C: They ate what was unpolluted in the river, and they made bread from the seeds.

D: *You mean on your world things could grow?* (Yes) *So they could make food on that world?* (Yes) *Did you help them to learn what to do?*

C: Yes. To love too.

D: *Well, then do you ever go back to that world where they came from?*

C: I think I must go back.

D: *Why do you feel you must go back there?*

C: Something's pulling me back.

D: *What do you mean?*

C: I can see other people in caves, and in other dwellings. And I wasn't aware that so many people were around. If we leave them, they will die.

D: *What are you going to do?*

C: I'm going to stay and help them.

D: *Can you do that?*

C: I shouldn't be doing it. My first duty is to the ship, and to the planet.

D: *But you feel you must stay there and help them?*

C: If I can.

D: *But can you stay away from the source that long?*

C: I can leave it for as long as I dare.

D: *What will happen if you stay away from the source too long?*

C: My energy will diminish until ... there's nothing left.

D: *Are you willing to take that chance?*

C: I don't have a choice.

D: *Why don't you have a choice?*

C: These people have awakened some feelings in me, which we are not emoted (?) for. Although I see the mistakes, a mess I have made. I would like a chance to help it, back in their community.

D: *So they've made a difference in you, you mean. Well, what are you going to do?*

C: (Long pause) I shall not change shape again. I shall stay in the body.

D: *If you do that, how can you maintain your energy? How can you live?*

C: The way I lived before.

D: *How was that?* (No answer) *How did you live before?* (No answer) *Can you tell me what you mean?*

C: Not at this moment.

D: *Why not?*

C: I can't seem to put the information together.

D: *All right. Do you mean that at another time you had a body?* (Yes) *And you are going to remember the way it was in those times?* (Yes) *But if you do that you won't be able to go back to your other place, will you?* (No) *Are you willing to take that chance, to help these people?* (Yes) *I think that is very good.*

C: There is a feeling in them that I want to experience. A feeling that we do not have. Some kind of a ... an emotion. We have compassion, but we don't have attachment.

D: *Attachment? Is that the feeling you want to experience?* (Yes) *So that is why you want to live with them.* (Yes) *And you think it will be worth it?*

C: This is my belief.

D: *All right. Then let's move ahead in time, and find out what happened to you. Did you stay in that body?* (Yes) *Did you live among these people?* (Yes) *Then what happened?*

C: We lived as best we could, but not for long.

D: *Did others also try this?*

C: Others may have tried it, but not from my group.

D: *What happened then, if you didn't do it very long?*

C: People just fell onto the ground, and never got up again.

D: *What happened to* you?

C: My body seemed to lose its substance. It seems to shrink.

D: *Then what happened to* you?

C: I perished with them.

D: *After you perished, did you decide to go back to your place, or what?*

C: I see ... enormous light. Like being in a hammock filled with light.

D: *Do you know where you are?*

C: This is ... getting ready to come into another body. I'm perfectly happy where I am.

D: *Do you think you* have *to go back to another body?*

C: There is a finite time I am allowed in this place, before I can be pushed into the next experience.

D: *But do you* have *to enter another body? Couldn't you go back to the type of existence you had before?*

C: I lost the chance by staying with the other. I had my choice, and I chose to stay with those others. And I was told that I would not be allowed back.

D: *You were told this when you made your decision?* (Yes) *So that was a very important decision.* (Yes) *And now you have* to *enter another body in a physical world or what?*

C: It's a physical world. And a physical body.

D: *How do you feel about it? Do you think you made the right choice?*

C: (Emphatic) No!

D: *Why not?*

C: It's hard work. I haven't the gifts that I had before. Everything happens so slowly.

D: *Is there any chance that you could go back to the other way in another lifetime?*

C: Not to *that* way.

D: *Why? Because you made the decision?*

C: Yes. It was once and for all.

D: *So you were never allowed to return then, because of that?*

C: That's right.

D: *Then did you have to keep making physical reincarnations each time? Do you understand the word?*

C: For the present.

D: *All right. I want you to leave that scene, move away from it, so you can look at that lifetime objectively. Look at it and observe it. What do you think was the purpose of that lifetime?*

C: To feel strong emotion, attachment, connectedness. The other life had no emotion attached to it.

D: *But you said at one time you had a body back before that type of energy lifetime. Did that other body have emotions?* (Yes) *So you've gone through cycles? Would that be correct?* (Yes) *As you look at that lifetime, you've brought it forth for a reason, to apply it to the lifetime now as Caroline. What were the lessons to be learned from a lifetime like that?*

C: I'm trying to put the thoughts into my mind.

D: *Because now you can look at it objectively, and be removed from it.*

C: I chose to be in a place with no food, in order to feel the strong connectedness and emotion of the people trying to survive under impossible conditions.

D: *Do you think that was a lesson you were trying to learn?*

C: I think so, because there could be no other reason for leaving the well-constructed, well-ordered life that I left behind.

D: *How does that experience apply to the life you're living now as Caroline? Allow your subconscious to help you find the answer. Why were you shown that lifetime, in connection with your present lifetime?*

C: I seem to be thinking that I equate feeling deep emotions with lack of physical sustenance. But I came into that experience from another dimension unconcerned with food. So I'm having difficulty correlating.

D: *Do you think this is connected to your weight problem?*

C: I think there is a link.

D: *Because of the strong emotion associated with these people dying from lack of food?* (Yes) *But can you see now that it has nothing to do with you in this body?* (Yes) *Put that together. This is a different body. And this body does not need those same feelings connected with the other lifetime. Does that make sense to you?* (Yes) *You were trying very hard to help them, but that was another people in another lifetime. And you're now in* this *body, that is very healthy, and where there is plenty of food. So there is no danger of starving. Can you see that connection? Does that make sense to you?* (Yes) *Then what do you think the solution will be, so that you will be able to lose the weight that you desire?* (Pause) *Allow your subconscious to help you with the answer.*

C: I suppose I am still thinking that if I allowed myself to lose excess weight, I would starve.

It took quite a bit of talking and repetition of suggestions to convince Caroline's subconscious that there was no danger of the present body starving to death in the present world. It finally agreed to help her to lose weight, and I knew the therapy was being accepted.

When Caroline returned to full consciousness she wanted to describe the bubble. That scene remained in her memory.

D: *You said it was very difficult to describe.*

C: It's like the bubble could move in and out of space and time at will. At the will of whoever was in control of the bubble. Bubble is not quite the right word. I can't find the word to describe it. But it could just change ... it's almost like ... in the molecules of air or whatever, the air particles. (Hand motions) Like you could slip in between them ... some way.

D: (Chuckle) *Some way. Because you kept making motions like it was round, and then it would compress some way and twist, is what you said.*

C: Yes. It felt as if it had to twist in order to go into the other dimension.

D: *To slide through or something.* (Yes) *But that's one part you remember?*

C: Yeah. Because I saw that over and over again. And I remember the field. And the baby being held up. That was the first image. Everything else is quite hazy.

D: *But that's because you were very deep. That was a very strange story. And it apparently ties with what you were asking about losing weight.*

C: Isn't that strange.

D: (Laugh) *That's what we were going after. It's not exactly what you would normally consider to be the source of weight gain.*

I then described the lifetime to her, and how she felt she had to stay with the people. Her interference into their lives apparently created karma, and she became trapped by becoming human herself in subsequent lifetimes.

C: Yes. It felt like a step backwards. And yet I needed to connect the emotions. Everything in the other dimension was so easy. There was no struggle. This was the way things happened. There was a constant flow. But there was no vitality.

D: *It was as if you lost something when you came into that part.* (Yeah) *But to get it back you had to also make a sacrifice.* (Yes) *To come back into living in a body. It's as though once you did that, then you were more or less trapped, and you had to come back into a body again time after time. So it was a big price to pay.*

C: Very.

D: *And that was the reason for the weight gain, you were associating that with starvation.*

C: I had preconceived ideas of what would logically come up in the session, and I must say this was nothing like I expected. It was bizarre.

Two separate cases, each woman looking for the cause of being overweight. And in each case it was traced back to an alien becoming entrapped and thus involved with our Earth, and having to pay the karmic price of returning again and again into a physical body. I think the odds of two such cases appearing at random must be astronomical. Thus I do not consider either of these to be fantasy. There was too much similarity, and also they followed the pattern of all the other stories in this book. Caroline was correct when she said it was bizarre.

CHAPTER NINE

THE EARLIEST FORMS OF LIFE ON EARTH

This case occurred in the autumn of 1986. Fred got my name from someone and spent several days trying to locate me. My mother was in the hospital in the nearby city, so he even went to the hospital trying to find me there, but ended up missing me. In his persistence, he rode his motorcycle to the small town where I live. But even in this type of environment where everyone knows everybody he still couldn't get in touch with me. After leaving several notes at different places we were finally able to talk by phone and set up an appointment.

Fred was a college student at the University, yet because of spending time in the Army he was older than the majority of his classmates. His main ambition was to become a psychologist and practice it from the metaphysical angle. But he had so many emotional and physical problems he was having a hard time even completing a semester. Every time he would get close to finishing and getting credits he would get sick. It was usually his stomach that gave him trouble, but he had been known to pass out in class. He would often be unable to eat or many days at a time. He had difficulty finding a doctor that was sympathetic to his problems. They all thought it was psychosomatic in origin, even though he was experiencing real physical symptoms. I suspected from the conversation that his troubles might be coming from something emotional, probably stress related, but until I got to know him better it would be difficult to say.

He had a definite defeatist attitude, as though it wasn't worth the effort because no one could help him anyway. He was interested in metaphysics and wanted to explore that route, hoping to find the solution in past life regression. He doubted that he could be hypnotized, and was even more skeptical that he could be regressed. He said whenever he tried meditation all he would see was what he called his "cartoon show", a series of cartoon characters or sketched scenes with no life or substance behind them. When I asked if there was anything specific he wanted to look for, he said he was interested in possible past life reasons for his physical troubles. He thought they were possibly being caused by some kind of karma. Also, he had always wondered what his very first life on Earth had been. At the time we did not know if he would get his wish to find out, and we certainly had no idea how far *back* that first lifetime was.

While I was conducting this first session I was unaware that my tape recorder and microphone were malfunctioning. It had already messed up a couple of other tapes, but I did not know this because I had no reason to play them back. The wheels were sticking, and caused missing gaps on the tape. When I discovered the problem after this session, I had to buy another recorder and microphone. I had simply worn out the other ones. Thus there were many gaps on this tape, especially toward the end. I had to fill in those parts of the session from memory.

When I began my induction it was obvious Fred was fighting me and resisting relaxing and letting go. After much work I was able to put him into a comfortable depth of trance, and I began to ask questions. In response he saw many varieties of cartoon type figures. This was what he had referred to as his cartoon channel. This has happened on rare occasions, and always indicates to me that the conscious mind is causing the resistance. It tries to convince the subject that the entire situation is silly, and should be stopped, usually because it is afraid of information being revealed that it cannot handle. By only allowing preposterous scenes to come through, it assumes that the subject will stop the session, or wake up voluntarily. When this interference occurs, I try to distract the subject by ignoring the protests and proceeding with the questioning until something significant comes through. Normally, with persistence, at this point the cartoons will change to identifiable scenes. Fred said normally his "channel" would move very fast from one frame to another, and not allow him to slow it down in order to focus on one creature or scene. This time there was a difference. For the *first* time it was slowing down, and pausing at one scene or a single frame (preposterous though that frame might seem), and allowing him to look at it. He saw a cartoon mouse dressed in a medieval Robin Hood style costume. Then a cartoon mule with a rainbow face.

He said, "They usually flip by so fast. It's interesting to really see them." This was entertaining for Fred, but it was not delving into the reasons for his problems, or helping us to find answers to his questions. I switched techniques to create different visualization effects, and his conscious mind kept fighting me by interjecting cartoon scenes. But now it was changing again. He said he had two channels running simultaneously. He was able to look through the cartoon state to the other scenes.

He said, "I am a cartoon person in this thing, and I am also perceiving the actual thing. My cartoon person is looking at a butterfly. But I am perceiving the butterfly in the physical way. Like looking through the cartoon with ESP. There is a triangular tunnel now, and I see the Earth at the end of it."

It was evident now that the cartoon interference was beginning to melt away as Fred drifted into a deeper state. He walked through the unusual tunnel, and saw just open space when he came to the other end. "Just open space, very few stars. I don't see any constellation or anything familiar. I think it's outer space."

D: *Well, you know you're free to go anywhere you want and to see anything you want.*

F: I see ... some more, too. It's a cartoon world also. Because somebody is standing there. His face is like a cloak. And I'm trying to see his face. (Softly) It's changed already. It is a holy person. Of blond hair, but cartoonish. A cartoon holy person.

D: *Do you know what he wants?*

F: He said he is my guide. He said, "It's all right. You can trust her. Relax. Don't try." He's reassuring me. He's telling me it is all right to be in outer space. I usually am afraid of outer space.

D: *Well, that would be natural. What feels right to you?*

F: To feel free while I am floating in outer space. Because in past dreams I've felt fear in floating. I have to go out to the planet or whatever and come back quickly. He says, "Don't be afraid."

D: *Because you know you're safe, and you can explore anything you want, and then you'll be able to come back. Is there somewhere you would like to see?*

F: Yes. I'm going already before you ... it's always that I *know* what you're saying ahead of time. I see a sun to the left. And I'm going through its corona.

D: *Is your guide going with you?*

F: He's off at a distance to the right. He's not entering the corona. It's a blue corona, with an orange glow down near the base of the flame. I'm flying sideways through the upper atmosphere, being totally encased in the flame. I'm flying sideways as a stiff board.

D: *Where are you going? Do you know?*

F: Going down. Closer to the surface.

D: *And nothing can harm you at all, mentally or physically. You are protected and you can tell what you see.*

F: I see a person looking at me. He has on ... almost like a rainbow. It looks like the hood of a viper, or a hood of a snake. Or maybe he is the deity in that area. He is an angel like an angel in the sun. His eyes are yellow. They're glowing. I'm looking directly into them. I feel to go into them.

I wasn't sure if this was a cartoon representation of something he could not understand, or if it was the actual appearance. It didn't matter. I would not stop to question, because he was obviously going deeper and leaving his cartoon channel behind.

D: *Is it a good feeling?* (Yes) *We want you to be comfortable at all times. Tell me about it.*

F: It's almost like the cartoon. It wanted to change to a negative thing. And I said, "Now this was negative." But it's ancient, not negative. I feel like I was that person. The lord of this area. I had the rule over this section of this solar sphere.

This statement did not shock me or surprise me, because I had encountered a similar situation in my book *Keepers of the Garden.* In that book Phil saw himself as a sovereign over an entire solar system before a serious mistake in judgment caused his fall to our physical planet Earth. Thus I knew a spirit or soul can experience any number of incarnations which we might assume are impossible.

D: *That would be a lot of power. Is that what you mean? Or was it considered in that way?*

F: It was considered an appointment. It's something I was chosen for. And I wanted to be free. I didn't want to stay there.

D: *Too much responsibility?*

F: No. It was a trapped feeling. I was trapped in my duty. I was fulfilling a certain time, a certain function. The duty of the place I was at. But it was not a feeling of wanting to be there on my own will. I wanted to be other ... other ....

D: *I can understand that. Sometimes you have duties you don't really enjoy.*

F: I was not ... I guess, human. I was more ... my body I see is changing. Gassiness. It radiates out from a central point, like an oval.

D: *As though it didn't have a form?*

F: Yes. That form oval was not a form.

D: *Apparently a form was not necessary to perform the duties, you mean?*

F: No. I see that what emanates out from my body is composing this atmosphere that I came through. It holds the atmosphere together. These tongues of flame. I was doing my duty.

D: *Sometimes that can become a burden, can't it? Is that what you mean?* (Yes) *Did you have control over a large area?*

F: This is coming straight through. I don't understand it. It was five miles. Five ... miles. I wouldn't say it was that. It seemed to be wanting to say a different word. Five something.

D: *It's a word you're not familiar with?* (Yes) *Did you have anyone that helped you with this?*

F: Someone watched over me, but not helped me.

D: *That can be very lonely trying to do that by yourself.*

F: Very ... lonely.

D: *Do you think that's why it became a burden?*

F: Just no one to communicate with. No one to talk to. Just radiating out. Just radiating out.

His wish had been fulfilled. He had gone back to find his first life. However, it was not as a physical human being. In fact, he did not even have a body that we would recognize. What was he?

D: *I can understand that. You would need one of your own kind to communicate with.*

F: They have other duties.

D: *Well, when did you decide you didn't want to do that anymore?*

F: I was not to give up. I could not give up until my time was up. Then I was freed. I was bound to it until then.

D: *Did you perform your duties admirably?*

F: I just *did* it. There was no judgment. I couldn't judge it. There was no thinking.

D: *Just performing the duties that you had to do.*

F: Just *being.* This stuff came out of me into the atmosphere. There was no judgment. I just radiated.

D: *Then when the time was up, where did you go?*

F: I'm out now. Away, looking at the planet from a distance. Feeling cold again, to be in space.

D: *What does the planet look like?*

F: It just looks like millions of colors. I'm going now. I'm in another place that has green lights.

D: *Do you have a choice of where you go, or does someone tell you?*

F: I just went from there to here. I wanted to get away from there as quickly as possible. This is a place where there are green lights.

D: *Tell me about it.*

F: It feels very peaceful. I'm talking to others.

D: *That's wonderful to be able to communicate again. What do the others look like? Can you see them?*

F: I'm back using cartoon figures as I still cannot see forms. I must create forms with my mind to know what a form is.

D: *I can understand that. And that's why your mind puts in cartoons, because it's something it can understand. But that's all right. What are you talking to the others about, now that you can finally communicate?*

F: They are saying, "Welcome back. Welcome back." And then something like "missed you", but not missed. They had their jobs to do, too. But they make me feel welcome.

D: *They are glad to see you again.*

F: Yes. Sort of glad.

D: *What are you going to do now?*

F: I'm going to another job.

D: *Does anyone assign these jobs, or do you just decide on your own?*

F: A ... power. I was going to say "a council" decides. "You go here. You go there. This is good for your development. This is for *you.* You are given this." Then it gives the assignment.

D: *Do you have anything to say about it?*

F: I don't feel I have any way to say anything about it. I do not feel physical as I do somewhere else. I don't know where else.

Fred was definitely detaching from the body lying on the bed in his apartment, and becoming the other entity.

D: *If you said, "Well, I don't know if I want to go there." It's not like that?*

F: No, no. No, you just *go*. It's a command. *They* decide. So I am able to perceive all these states at once.

D: *That's very good. And you said they have assigned you another job?*

F: Yes. I feel it's back on Earth.

D: *Did they tell you what they want you to do?*

This is where the machine, the tape recorder, began to malfunction and cutting out the sound. It was sporadic. I tried to fill in the blanks from memory when I transcribed the tape.

F: They're trying to get some work done.

D: *What do you mean?*

F: I go and do things. I know how to work.

D: *Was this what they told you?*

F: Go! Yes. It makes no sense.

D: *It must make sense to them.*

F: They've done it before.

D: *Can you tell me what happens then?*

F: I'm looking at the Earth. It looks like another ball like the other one. And I do not want to go there.

D: *Why not?*

F: Because I am afraid of being trapped again. I'm down on the Earth. But it is not at this time. It looks different. There is nothing but glowing liquid fire. The surface does not appear solid yet. I like the fire. It feels like the fire I was used to on that star.

D: *Oh, yes, it would be similar.*

F: It feels good to have a familiar feeling.

D: *What else can you see?*

F: Now I can see the mountains. Water. But only a little bit of water. Little pools of water on the ground. The ground is very hard and cracked.

D: *Do you see any creatures?*

F: I see nothing alive in that manner. This atmosphere is not conducive to life. The Earth is still cooling, and this smoke and fire are hazardous to life.

D: *What about trees or anything like that?*

F: Just steam and smoke. And this fire. All over the ground, too. Just coming out. Right at the base and the top of this mountain, this thing. I don't have words for it ... then. Volcano. That's what it is. I am going into the fire, the lava. It feels good to be inside this heat again. It's warm. It's fluid. It's heavy. It's dense. Denser. Now I'm back out.

D: *You just wanted to experience it.*

F: Yes, I can go into things. And come back out. Someone told me I could do this.

D: *A guide or what?*

F: The person that is afar off, that we saw.

D: *He is helping you with these experiences?*

F: Yes. He says I do not want to remain in any experience.

D: *What are you going to do now?*

F: Form the fires into air. Something to do with the smoke. To make it into a different substance.

D: *Like steam, you mean, or what?*

F: Make it into, I guess, what you would call ... I am able to know what it is. Back here ... it is air. That's what it will be in the future. In the future it is air.

D: *At that point then there is no air as we know it?*

F: It is just ... something else.

D: *Then one of your jobs is to work with this?*

F: I mold it. I actually transfigure, transform it into the other thing. Air. I have to get rid of the dirt, the blackness of it. I will act as a filter for it. My new job is to lure the blackness.

And pass the substance through me. I must get rid of the blackness. I have problems with this.

D: *Like a filter?*

F: Scraping. Pushing it off myself, whatever my self is.

D: *I can see why you didn't see any living creatures. This atmosphere* would *be poison to anything physical.*

This was difficult to visualize and to understand. We are so used to thinking of a spirit being encased in a physical body. This was something I had never encountered before, so it was difficult at times to think of the proper way to form questions. He seemed to be describing himself as some type of membrane that could filter, although he was not physical in that sense. Even though he was not solid he was intelligent and had a personality.

His job apparently was to help cleanse the impurities out of the atmosphere and transform it into air. This would have been a task occupying an enormous span of time. But of course he had absolutely no concept of time. Only of the job to be done. At this point he began talking about a form of life that was in the atmosphere. This was the only living thing he could see. It sounded to me like a microbe or germ of some kind. Perhaps one of the first forms of one-celled life. He described it as a little, tiny thing. It was moving around him in the developing atmosphere. He had instructions not to harm it, but to allow it to pass in and out of him like the smoke he was filtering.

F: They're real small. I'm observing one of them. They're just flying through the air, like a fly, I guess.

D: *Are they things that can live in this type of atmosphere?*

F: They live a short time. They feed on the ... I don't want to put in the wrong word. Ammonia? They feed on the ... gases? The language is difficult. It's hard to find the words.

D: *I've been told that before.*

F: They feed on the air. They float on the air. They're never on the ground. They're never down there. I am up in the air, myself.

D: *Do you think the ground is too hot to support life at this time, or is it the wrong kind of conditions?*

F: It would kill the little creatures if they went into that fluid that they call "lava". You would call "lava". It would kill them. I would cry. I would feel some sadness about their death.

D: *Then this is the only thing you can see that's alive. And you're supposed to leave those alone.*

F: They can go through me, yes.

D: *There's no other form of life, so to speak. Although I would think the fire is alive. But no other form of creature, as I perceive a germ to be.*

F: I don't .... Fire? I know what you're saying but, at this time, I do not know what that is. I perceive it. I see it. I feel it. There is no judgment in my mind about being alive or dead or anything. It is something I can pass into and pass out of.

D: *It's an element like the air then. Do you know how long you'll have to stay there changing the gases into air?*

F: I had to stay there for, what you would call "many years". (He grinned.) This is silly.

D: *The words do not apply. I know what you mean.*

F: Yes. I was there, I'd say ... thousands and thousands of years. Not a short time.

D: *Was that your only job that you had at that time?*

F: Yes.

D: *Did anyone help you with this?*

F: I see others working down at the ground. They are cooling the fire, the stuff, the fire into ... rock. They are helping to cool it. Almost like blowing on it. To create rock. (He made blowing sounds.) They're blowing on it. Forcing air over it.

D: *Then they all have different jobs to do, is that what you mean?*

F: Yes. I am doing mine. They are doing theirs. I don't feel as lonely as I did before. They are there. They are doing their job.

D: *At least you can see them, and communicate with them.*

F: I don't seem to communicate with them. I do my thing.

D: *How many would you guess are helping you with your job.*

F: I would say ... hundreds.

D: *I was thinking it would be a very difficult job to do all by yourself.*

F: No, there were others like me at that other place. They were coming also to help me. There was no talk. There's one I know. Another one I know.

D: *But some of the others are cooling the earth. Are there any other jobs that you see being done?*

F: Something to do with the water. Making the water ... making more water. Working it, expanding the water from within. I am above and watching this, perceiving this. And they are expanding like I am expanding on the other place. They are expanding, and making water out of elements. I guess the elements of this rock and earth. It's like little explosions and they're making water out of this ... rock. You see, there are all these atoms and then water is flowing out of them. Out of a central point, there is water flowing out of my companions on the ground.

D: *From the inside of the rocks?*

F: No. Out of this being. They are like *eating* the rock. Chewing it. Digesting it. And then shooting the water out as a new element, you would say.

He was grinning. Even in this trance state it seemed ridiculous, but he still had to report what he was seeing.

D: *It has something to do with chemicals and atoms, I suppose.*

F: I don't like that job. I see this person as if I was there helping him. And then I move back to my job.

D: *It seems as if the job that all of you are doing is trying to make this world habitable so that life can exist? Do you think that's what it is?*

F: I guess that's what they wanted us to do. We just do it. It makes no difference at all. I could not resist talking. Part of my mind feels like it has to explain. Time must have passed.

Things have changed. Now there are trees and more atmosphere.

D: *Things are beginning to grow?*

F: Yes, I am done with that now. That's why I am able to see this. I am released again.

D: *What do the trees look like?*

F: What I'd say a palm tree would look like. It's more of a bush though, a short bush. To me it looks short, fat, with thin, thin green leaves. But then they turn orange.

D: *They turn orange after a while?*

F: Yes. After their ... something cycle.

D: *What about the earth?*

F: It's now covered with these green things.

D: *Are there any other forms of life besides the plants?*

F: There are something like spiders underwater. They're on the bottom. I feel like I am one of the creatures. I look out of the water, but I do not ever venture out of the water.

D: *They must have to stay in the water then.*

F: I breathe in the water.

D: *Well, come back on the land. All right. I want to thank you for everything you've been telling me. It's been informative. Will it be all right if I come again and ask more questions?*

F: He is giving permission.

I then conditioned Fred with a keyword to make future induction faster, and brought him out of trance. I felt he had made significant improvement by progressing from his cartoon channel to being able to describe fascinating scenes. I felt we could continue to explore this in the next session.

It really upset me when I found out that I had lost so much of this very informative and unusual session. I thought I would attempt to regain some of it at the next session by taking him back to the time after the earth had cooled and some forms of life were developing. I could not fully understand what type of life form he was. A chemical? An element? A gas? Or just energy?

When the next week's session began I was going to try to recapture some of the missing and garbled parts near the end of the tape, that were deleted due to mechanical failure. I especially wanted to obtain more information about when the world had begun to produce life. I used Fred's keyword and counted him back to that scene. This time he went quickly without the interference of his "cartoon channel". We never had any trouble again getting him quickly into deep trance and into the scene.

D: *You had a job to do at that time, a very important job, taking care of the earth. I would like to return to that time period, and we can explore that some more. Let's go to the time when those first signs of life were beginning to appear on the earth. They seemed to be palm trees and little bushes. I will count to three and I want you to return again to that scene. 1, 2, 3, you have gone back in time again. What do you see? What are you doing?*

F: I'm back up in the air ... looking down. And I see these trees, short and squat.

D: *You said their leaves resembled palm trees or something like that?*

F: Yes. But I see another kind of tree. It looks like the bud or the middle of a dandelion. With spikes sticking out all around it.

D: *The same color as a dandelion?*

F: No. This is kind of a reddish color.

D: *Does it have any other foliage?*

F: It's like another one of these bushes. Short, it looks like a pineapple. It has little leaves sticking up around the sides of the trunk.

D: *This bud that you're talking about, is that on the ground or on the stalk?*

F: It's on a stalk, like a pineapple and then you put the dandelion on top. (He chuckled at the absurdity of this description.) And then it has these projections, and they have little fuzzy ends to them, which are gold in the middle. And coming soft on the ends.

D: *I'm trying to see what you are seeing. That's why I ask so many questions. That sounds different from the little palm trees.*

F: This is a different one. It's shorter than the other.

D: *Do you see any other type of plants?*

F: I see grass, like scrub. A real tough texture. It would hurt to walk on.

D: *Do you mean the blades are larger?*

F: Tougher, like sandpaper. I would feel sandpaper on my feet ... if I had feet. (He laughed.)

D: *Then it's a rougher texture. But it's the same color as grass?*

F: I see dark green.

D: *Are the blades very long?*

F: Hmm, no, short. Some scrub ... it's like crab grass, clump. But in sections. A lot of rocks, a lot of grass around, and these other bush-like trees. It's sort of sandy, or I guess the volcanic soil. Kind of crumbly. It's almost like a seashore. Sand and rocks.

D: *What does the horizon look like? Is it hilly or flat?*

F: I see the water. I'm near a shore. And the horizon is ... no rocks, no hills, kind of flat.

D: *Do you see any signs of life other than the vegetation?*

F: (Pause) I see birds.

D: *Can you describe them to me?*

F: They look almost like pelicans with pointed wings. The point is in the front part of the wing and then tapers backward, not like an airplane wing.

D: *Do they have feathers?*

F: No. These ones have long wings. I can see a V shape. With wings coming down off the top of the V. And then kind of a pelican neck with a long beak.

D: *How large is the bird?*

F: I could carry it in my arms. It's pretty big. I think there are three sizes of birds that I see. One that looks like the size of a bat and has kind of rounded wings. No feet. And it has this skull cap like the bone is stuck out in the back, then skin, then kind of a rounded beak, like a parrot. But no feathers on the top, just skin, black skin. And a bony, bony head. Really kind of a reptilian head. And leathery wings.

D: *And this was the smallest one of these three types of birds?*

F: Yes, I see some small insects. (Softly) Oooo, the bird just ate one. (Grinning) Just kind of "chomp".

D: *What do the insects look like?*

F: I can't tell you now, because he's gone.

D: *But any other ones. Are they big insects?*

F: Hmmm. Like a mosquito type. It has rounded wings. Rather shaped like a butterfly's rounded wings, on the edges. But it's sort of like a mosquito's head, with a long pointy thing. The driller, I don't know what you call it.

D: *Is it about as big as a mosquito?*

F: A little bit bigger. More like the size of a moth.

D: *Okay. You said there was another size bird between the small one and the larger one?*

F: No, a larger one.

D: *A larger one than the one that you mentioned earlier?*

F: Yes. It just looks like those, I guess, called ... pterodactyl. It's really large. The other two were smaller.

D: *All right. Last time you said you saw a type of life that was in the water. Can you see that again?*

F: I'm almost *being* it. Looking out of the water with my eyes. Like stalks. And ... I have a body. ... (Softly) I don't remember it.

D: *You said it had legs, but it didn't have any claws. It lived on the bottom of the water?*

F: Oh, that one, yes. I was looking at a different one. Trying to get my memory clear.

D: *Then there is more than one type there.*

F: Yes. There are fish. And there is this other kind that looks like an underwater spider. It has a body and legs like a spider. It's crawling around. It's about the size of a spider. I don't understand why it's underwater. It doesn't want to come out of the water.

D: *That must be the way it has to live. Then the other one that you were seeing with the eyes on the stalks is a different type of water creature?*

F: It's like a frog, but it has just a little bigger stalks. The eyes bulge out a little bigger, so it can see out of the water. I'm looking out of the water. (Chuckle)

D: *It's a frog-type creature?*

F: The stalks are short, coming down into the head. And eyes on the end of the stalks, but short, coming down into a small body. It has a small mouth on the face of it. And I'm (blowing) pushing out (blowing) gravel. It seems to have a body and mouth and eye stalks.

D: *Does it have legs or arms?*

F: I feel like I can propel my body by moving it through the water. And I just kind of wiggle through the water.

D: *Does it have skin like a frog?*

F: The skin is more like a fish skin. More tough, or sharp, I guess. It's not as soft as a frog.

D: *That's very interesting. Well, you can come out of the water now, back onto the land. Do you see any types of animal life?*

F: Ummm, he's small. A type of ... it almost looks like a monkey, but it's almost like a rat. It's confusing.

D: *Do you mean it's as small as a rat, but it looks like a monkey?*

F: Yes. I don't know what they're called. They might have them somewhere else. I guess a rat, marsupial something. It looks kind of like a possum. It's not a monkey because I saw that tail. It's kind of furry. And it can sit up on its haunches, and scratch itself like a monkey. It's more like a possum. I see it running on the ground, four legs.

D: *Does it have a face like a possum or a rat, with the pointed nose?*

F: It's kind of rounded. It's almost like a monkey's face, but a little bit longer. The chin's long. The face is kind of pointed out like a monkey's but it's long and tapering down like a possum's face. But a small, not a long snout, short, like a baby possum's face. I've never seen anything like that.

D: *What color is it?*

F: Nice brown fur. Soft.

D: *Well, now that you have finished the other job you had to do, do you have an assignment in the world as it looks now, with these animals and these plants?*

F: No.

D: *You're just drifting around and observing?*

F: Yes. I feel more dense now.

D: *Why, because you've been there so long or what?*

F: I feel weighted down, yes.

D: *Was that the only job you had to do while you were there, helping to clean the air?*

F: Yes, before, it was. I don't have a job now. Air isn't the same as it is now. It's still different. There's more odor in it. More ... I guess, sooty. It smells funny.

D: *Does the smell remind you of anything that you are familiar with?*

F: I guess it would be rotten eggs or that sort of smell, sulfur. I've never smelled it. I've smelled dirty industrial air. That's what it reminds me of.

D: *But it must be purified enough to sustain life.*

F: The creatures are breathing.

D: *Before the Earth was very hot, you said, and nothing could live there.*

F: Yes. I was warm.

D: *And there is life there now. So it is purified to that extent anyway. Okay. I want you to look around and see if you can see any other forms of life.* (I was thinking about dinosaurs.)

F: (Pause) Ants.

D: *Insects?*

F: Insects. I mean, ants. (Chuckle) They're ants to me. Black ants.

D: *Are they very large?*

F: No. Similar size as now.

D: *Are you able to drift around this world and see different things?*

F: I almost feel like I have a body. It's like the body I have ... somewhere else. Here, I don't think I'm physical. I think I am lighter than physical. I can jump up in the air real high and come back down. I can fly in this body. It's not a physical body. The animals can't see me.

D: *But you're denser than you were before when you were helping clean the atmosphere.*

F: Yes.

D: *Well, if you can fly, can you fly around the world and see if it's all the same as this place?*

F: Yes. I'm flying in the air. Now I'm down. This area's more rocky, more mountains. I see a lot of wind blowing in this area. There's a lot of dust. I'm going to go some place else.

D: *There's no sign of life there?*

F: No. I'm flying next to the medium sized birds. They seem to be friendly. It's almost like I'm hitching a ride on the back of one. (Grinning) It's a neat experience. I'm holding on to its neck.

D: *They can't see you though, can they?*

F: No. They can't feel me either.

D: *Do these birds have teeth?*

F: No. A bill, a long bill. It's almost like a flamingo bill. Long.

D: *I know what you mean. Well, what do you see from up there?*

F: A lot of water. Not too much land. Enough land, but more like islands. Like a sea full of islands. Big islands. More water now than land.

The Earth had definitely changed since his first assignment. At that time it was mostly molten liquid. Now it had more water in proportion to land. The little creatures that produced water had done their job well.

D: *Can you see any land that looks different?*

F: No.

D: *Then you can come back down to where you were, if you want to. I was just curious if the whole world was the same.*
F: I'm standing on the water.
D: *Oh? Are you near the shore where you started out?*
F: No. I'm ... now I'm back. I just went "zip" back. (Grinned)
D: (Laugh) *Okay. Then do you think the land is either like it is there with the small trees, or rocky like the other part where there was the wind?*
F: My guide's here too talking and helping me understand and translate. He says it's a tropical island type. I guess it's more tropical.
D: *Than the other part you saw with the rocks and the wind.*
F: That was a really desolate area, almost a moonscape-type. It just didn't feel good. Like bad vibrations.
D: *Maybe life hasn't reached that part yet.*
F: I didn't see anything alive there.
D: *But you said the air is still different, and it's very warm.*
F: Yes. It's a ... hundred degrees. It's hot. I just know from somewhere else it would be warm. To me it would be warm when somewhere else.
D: *Well, did you stay there on this planet as it was evolving?*
F: I am back out in space. Ah, it feels so good. I'm flying very fast now.
D: *Where are you going?*
F: I'm going into a bright light. It has circles around it.
D: *Have you been told to do this?*
F: Hmmm, no. It's fun. I like the freedom to fly here. I feel it relaxes me. There's no care here.
D: *Do you think you were released now, that you can go where you want?*
F: I do come back later. This light is more like my home. Like a place to be quiet. By myself. There are others here, but I mean, to be with my own kind. Energies. Not people.
D: *Is that where you go between assignments?*
F: I feel very at home here. It's not like a place. It's like an energy field. It's like golden light, and you go inside it to take refuge. It's like a ball that you go inside, but there's a

tunnel of light entrance to it. Like a vortex. Like another plane inside of the encroaching physical plane. You go into this tunnel and then there's this haven type place. It feels good to be here.

This description sounded very familiar to me, and is described in my book *Between Death and Life*. It has been described in various ways by everyone I have taken through the death experience. In the inbetween lives state, or spirit state, or so-called "dead" state, there are many places where the soul can go. Often they return to what is familiar. This can be a comfortable home comparable to the life they have just left, or it can be the schools or great halls of learning. Other times they may go to the "resting place." This is a place where they can shut out everything and just sleep for a while. This is a place where there is nothing, and is indeed described as a refuge. They can stay there for any length of time before they must return to the wheel of karma, and the lessons of whatever existence they find themselves in. This sounded like the place Fred was describing as his refuge between assignments. It is described by many as "going home." They always feel safe and welcomed there.

D: *Then you know the other energies there. You feel comfortable with them.*

F: Yes. I'm just recuperating for the minute. Now I feel I'm going to another place. I'm back out in space.

D: *Did someone tell you what you had to do?*

F: Yes. It was like I couldn't stay in the recuperating place for very long. It was almost like a finger pointing. Someone with inner knowledge telling me to go back out. I couldn't stay there very long or I'd ... I wasn't supposed to be there very long.

D: *Like a temporary stop over.*

F: Yeah, or refueling.

D: *Or resting place.*

F: Resting place. It was very much like laying in a bed there, but the bed being all the way around you.

D: *But you've been told you have to go somewhere else now?*

F: Yes. I am going to a group of three stars. I'm in space. There are no stars around me, except I seem to be in the middle of these three stars. There are two grouped together and one to the side. I've been there ... not yet, but in the future I remember some place of going here before. But I am in the past to this future event.

D: *Yes, I can understand.*

F: (Grinning) I can't.

D: *That's all right. Don't worry about it.*

F: I'm in this star system. I'm down on the world. This is where I was to go. There's something about getting the assignment for Earth. I've looked at this star pattern before when I was in a dream state. And it was the Sirius star system. But I'm on a blue, no, green sky planet. And there are rounded buildings. They look like bubbles, but oblong like ovals, and on a stem. People can fly here. They don't have to stay on the ground.

D: *Is this one of the planets around the two stars or ....*

F: I see two stars and one over ... here. There are three stars. Two together parallel, two dots on a line. And then one over here.

D: *It's like this planet has three suns? Would that be a way of saying it?*

F: This planet has two suns, but the third star is considered part of the group. (He chuckled) I don't know.

D: *What are those buildings made out of? Do you have any idea?*

F: Looks like what I'd call "plastic". A hard porcelain-like material, like my teeth. It's almost like you could saw it. It'd be like resin, like a plastic.

D: *Then you can't see through it.*

F: No, it's white, but it's hard, malleable. I mean, it could be sawed. It could be heated and changed in shape.

D: *You said there are people there that can fly? What do these creatures look like?*

F: They look like me. (He laughed)

D: (Laugh) *What do* you *look like? Let's put it that way.*

F: I look ... kind of like a body, a round ball. But then I have a gaseous outer covering. Like a body with an outer gas. I've never seen this visualization before. I mean, I *am* it. I'm looking at them. They're kind of roundish, almost like a nut, and then they have this outer form. This is our true form.

D: *Then they more or less float?*

F: We can navigate around, fly around. Not float. It's purposeful flight.

D: *Well, do you consume anything?*

F: (Thoughtful pause.) No. I take whatever I need from universal energy. These are not my words. Universal energy. It's like somebody is talking through me.

D: *That's all right. But I was curious. If you saw buildings, I thought there might be physical people.*

F: No. I see three buildings. There are no doorways. There are windows. You float through this open window, and this is how you get inside. There's no furniture. There are work stations, in order to work with a machine. But there are no hands to work with the machine. You *think* into it, and the machine responds. But the machine was not created with hands.

D: *How was it created then?*

F: I was thinking while I was saying that, it was created through the force of thought. Through mentally creating. I see a thought and then it is manifest in a form, like I was manifest in this form. And then there is a machine there.

D: *What does the machine do?*

F: This one is for computing ... it controls ... a console. It does something ... some kind of experimental thing. It's controlling ... something.

D: *In the atmosphere or in the environment or what?*

F: It's an experiment to control ... something like temperatures. I see waves fluctuating inside, like a oscilloscope. It's controlling these waves, which have something to do with the building itself. It's almost like ... not maintaining the structure, but the structure is sensitive. It's part of the machine. It's almost like going inside the building and being controlled ... like going inside of a tank and controlling the movement of the tank from inside.

D: *That does sound complicated. But if you could manifest these things with your mind with thought, why would you* need *machines.*

F: Words just came through from someone else. They were in preparation for the future of having more complex forms. These are someone else's words.

Fred said later it was as though someone was standing next to him, and was there to give him the answers to anything I did not understand. Perhaps the guide he spoke of earlier.

F: They are preparation for the future of beings having more complex forms. So we are experimenting for the future.

D: *I'm trying to understand. That's why I'm asking so many questions.*

F: That's why we repeated it. (Grinned)

D: (Laugh) *It does sound complex. Then you mean these creatures themselves do not need shelter, or do not need any substances.*

F: No, we do not need more ... (Chuckle) sorry I'm talking this way. This is more the way I would talk there. It's not my words. It's almost like translating.

D: *That's okay. I'm following it. I can understand it. You said they don't really need these buildings then.*

F: No, the outside aura, this film around us absorbs from the atmosphere, from universal light. And then transmutes it to sustain this shell form. This form is oblong. It's not a peanut, but it's almost the shape of a peanut. It has kind of sharp edges, but it's big and puffy in the middle, like a pillow. This is what I and the other persons look like. I was looking at the other people through a *sense*, not as a eye, an eyeball. I was looking at them through feeling what I am and knowing what they are.

D: *And they don't need any food or shelter.*

F: No, we don't.

D: *I was wondering why they had these buildings and the machines, if apparently you can manifest what you want with your mind, by creating with thought. You could just create, you wouldn't have to have a machine to do it. Let me see if I have it correct. You think it's because in the future there will be bodies?*

F: Yes, in the future there will be different bodies, but maybe not for these people. This is coming from someone else. I'm kind of hearing words.

D: *That's all right. Just repeat what they're saying. Then these machines are experimental for these future people?*

F: For people from another place. They're experimenting *here* for people on Earth or some other planet, that will have ... I guess what you would call a "human" body. But their experiment is also to do with the place I'm at. These waves are something to sustain the temperature of the place that I'm at. They're also doing experiments for the future. This building is like a radio tower, to shoot out or monitor universal waves and transmute them into something like temperature and what would be called ... almost like wind. But it's a very stable, peaceful place, so there's no *wind* atmosphere, I guess you would call it.

D: *Then this place has to have its temperature maintained, in order to live there?*

F: No. For maintaining an artificial good temperature. It would be as if I was living in a hot place, and we were cooling it down. Or living in a cool place and we were heating it up, to maintain an *ideal* temperature. It controls the atmosphere of the place where I'm at. That part of the building has something to do with the planet I'm on also. The other experimental things that are being done here are to access how well people will live in a human form. Somehow they're testing a casement of how well the soul will live in a body. There is a test to make sure that the body is stable enough to maintain -- these are not my words -- to maintain this human soul. It's like *building* a body. Not testing anything, we're putting it together.

D: *I think I'm beginning to understand. I hope I am. Then you think this is like a laboratory-type place, where they would be experimenting ....*

F: This building, yes.

D: *Where they would be experimenting with cells or things like that to ....?*

F: It would be more like a future ... like if we were building a robot, as an analogy. We'd have to start with the wiring inside, and then go to the outside. And make the *brain* compatible to the structure. So what we're doing in this experiment is to make sure the soul is compatible with the outside physical organism. To *mate* them, to make sure they are compatible together. That the soul can make the outside form function correctly.

D: (I still did not understand.) *That's why it has to have a certain atmosphere with certain temperatures.*

F: This is part of our experimental things that we're doing inside the building. The building itself is maintained for *us*. We are maintaining the atmosphere, so it will be an ideal temperature for us to live on this planet. It's just like you have a heater in this building, but also in this building you do experiments. So the heater is providing our temperature, and we're doing future experiments on man.

D: *Do they have any human bodies there that they are using, or is it just theoretical?*

F: It's like a *thought*. I see a group of us -- yes, I guess I mean *us*. Because I'm hearing it from someone else, he is the "us". And a group of us, we are *seeing* thoughts, and we're thinking thoughts of a soul. And then we see how to form the structure around the soul. So that, for instance, the fingers will be wired into inner knowledge of it. I don't see personalities as such, yet. It's like a mental construct. And they're thinking these things into what will eventually become a physical organism. But it's like running a program to the computer to stimulate a mating of these units.

D: *Is it like trying to figure out what type of body, or what shape, or how it functions?*

F: Yes. Running a complete program.

D: *Just like building a body from different building blocks to see how it would work.*

F: Yes. It's coming through a lot better now that I'm more away from any interference of this mind.

D: *It would be as though they were experimenting to see what type of body would function the best in the atmosphere it's supposed to be in.*

F: Yes. There are different bodies. We're not just working on humans. We're working on animals, birds, but organic flesh ones. Not vegetables.

D: *But these are not solid.*

F: Not yet.

D: *In other words, they're just mind constructs.*

F: Right now they are. In the future they will be physical forms, if the creative part of the universe wants to project them into matter.

D: *Are you some of the ones that are going to make the decisions on what type of bodies will be put on different planets?*

F: It's like our duty to do the dirty work. (Chuckle) The ground work. The preliminary experimentation. To run the laborious programs, I guess somebody would say. Then it's given up to a panel, so to speak. And then it is *chosen* what forms will be used and where. We do not have anything to do with that part. We are just generating the mechanics of how to put it together. We're building in our lab, this mental lab.

D: *Because certain types wouldn't function in different atmospheres, or they wouldn't be appropriate.*

F: Right. And that is our work assignment, to do these things.

D: *Then these bodies aren't going to be developed full form and placed down on these planets. Do you know anything about what happens after it leaves you, and others begin to ... construct the body?*

F: (Pause) It will be the process of growth, like evolution. I see one form changing to another. A small form growing, and then becoming bigger and more layered, and getting heavier. And then finally having solid form.

D: *I was wondering if they were going to start it out from cell types and let it evolve, or if it would be fully formed.*

F: I see it as a natural form from the planet involved. Somehow there is a starting animal. This starting animal is somehow manifested. I'm trying to look into the future from where I am here. The animal is manifested into a form. And then starts to grow like, I guess, you would in your baby process. And grow up into a human form through different stages of development.

D: *Can you see some of the forms that this machine is designing? You said you could make one appear and then disappear and make another one if it wasn't right.*

F: It's almost like a group effort to think into this, so it wouldn't be just me making it. It would be all of us.

He is either describing a collective mind or individual minds working in tandem. One mind would not be powerful enough to accomplish the task. Rather like the way some groups of aliens operate their spacecraft by combined thought power.

D: *It takes several minds to make this machine operate? Then more or less what you are doing there is working out a blueprint?*

F: Yes. We are putting things together. Taking things apart. Putting this together, putting that together. There was different types almost. Like more arms, more fingers, less arms, less fingers. I see as if we're wiring ... something. We're wiring the soul, so that when the soul commands a certain thing to do something, it will move. Soul -- I guess I could mean "brain" -- eventually. But I'm saying "inner force". You know, like *we* have a soul inside our bodies.

D: *Then it's something more or less electrical that will instruct the different parts to operate.*

F: Yes. I see it similar to how you would program different pathways on a integrated chip.

D: *It sounds very complicated.*

F: It's really very simple, because we think something and then it appears before us. Think something else and then we erase it. It's a mental construct that I'm working with.

D: *But you do need this machine to help with it.*

F: Yes. It somehow combines our energies to have a group effort.

D: *You said you were looking at the future and how these things would evolve. Can you see anything or anybody who would be directing this evolution type process? Or making sure that it turns into the blueprint you started out with?*

F: There is a panel of judges, very bright beings, that choose. Saying, "Thus say us that this will be there. And thus say us this will be here." They choose, almost like a pointer. And that form appears in a starting process, on the world or moon or wherever. These forms also can be planetary forms, like building a rock.

D: *You mean like the elements themselves? It doesn't have to be human then, or organic.*

F: No. Everything is formed this way in the beginning stages.

D: *When these things were put on these planets or wherever, was there anybody that kept an eye on them, or directed their development?*

F: Someone else is kind of speaking, helping me. Yes. I hear the words, "Everyone has his job and his place to do his duty."

D: *Then you had a little part in it. You were one of the people that were directing ....*

F: Legwork, yes.

D: *And developing the blueprints. And then it would be sent to the panel, and they make the decisions. I believe you said, too, that there was a board somewhere that was in charge of making decisions. Well, when you come up with the right plans you think will work, how do they get to the board?*

F: It's almost like I'm being told to do this a certain way, or this other head person is being told. And then we take the appropriate design to the council. Once we're done with it, then we take the finished product to them. There's no review of it.

D: *Did you ever have to take it to the council?*

F: No. *I* didn't. The head person took it. I'm a small person. I'm not very aware. I'm like a worker ant, not a commander. (Chuckle)

D: *But your mind was important for that project, so you were important in that way.*

F: Yes. It's like a radio tube is important to the TV, but not part of the main group that controls.

D: *Yes, but also the radio won't operate without the tube. Everybody has their own little place. I was curious as to where the council was, and what they were like. If someone could tell you the answer to that.*

F: There were three people. I think almost more like angels. It's almost like we were making the people look like these three people. They were more like what I am now. And they're more like, yes, they're like angels.

D: *You mean you were trying to model them after them?*

F: That was the order.

D: *To make the physical appearance be like these main people on the council?*

F: More like the angels. They just happened to be, that's who they were.

D: *I wonder why they wanted them to look like that?*

F: Because they were told by others that is what the plan was. There is an order in the mind of God. And this was interpreted by someone else, then it was given to this planetary group. They farmed out the work order to us. And then we brought back the working model, as if we were the engineers. There were planners and there were engineers, and then we brought the product back to the way it was supposed to function. We built it, more or less.

D: *You were saying that you were able to see these images from the mind with the computer, but you were also able to build the working model to show them?*

F: There is a form that I perceive. It's almost like a clay model made out of energy. Some kind of form, denseness. And we were able to show nerves, for example, and how they would work. The connection between the soul and the energy flows going into the person.

D: *It sounds complicated. But if they wanted changes, would you have to make the changes?*

F: Hmmm. There was no change.

D: *By the time you got it into this form, it was approved?*

F: Just like asking for something perfectly done, you get a ready made thing. You put the money in the machine and you get the Coke. There is no change. (He laughed.)

D: *Yeah, I understand what you mean. I thought maybe if the council didn't approve of it you would have to make some changes.*

F: Right. No, there is no disapproval.

D: *Then you worked it out pretty well.*

F: We just did what we were told. It came out perfectly. And we brought back the finished product. We did not make it there. We made a model of it, but we did not make the final form. It was not our job. We were just working out the possibilities.

D: *Yes, as you said before, the different possible ways, to make sure that the brain or the soul could make the body operate. Then who was in charge of making the finished product? Do you know?*

F: (Pause) I'm looking for it. It seems not to be here. Maybe it's somewhere else. Further in the future.

D: *Then did you see the finished product after it went to the council?*

F: What we made, I saw before it went. Their decisions were not made until later when someone had brought it to that ... place.

D: *What did the form look like when you finished it? Was it like a human form or what?*

F: Yes. I was perceiving what you were going to say way before you said it. I was going to answer before you said it.

D: *It didn't deviate from what we know of as a human form?*

F: Hmmm. I don't see it as such. It's different, it's hairier. It's, I guess, more like a monkey. More hairy, but not a monkey. I see a lot of hair.

D: *So in that way it is different from the model we have nowadays, so to say.*

F: Yes, the beings that we took it to, they were more like us. They were like the body here on the bed. But the one we made is more hairy, and I keep seeing in my mind something like a gorilla. But not an animal. I mean it is an animal in some sense, but not a monkey. It's human, it's got hair on it.

D: *Then the face is not too different?*

F: It's a little bit different.

D: *Very interesting. Now I would like to ask some questions about yourself. If you just developed into the full-blown energy form of this ball or peanut shape, you weren't born or anything then. You just developed this form there on that planet. Is that correct?*

F: I was, I suppose, born as visiting different places gave me more denser form. I have a feeling of energy pulsating in me right now.

D: *But your form, the glowing ball with the gaseous outer layer, is not* born. *It is just* materialized *there?*

F: I was, a long time ago, given *being* as separate from others. That was my first separation from *everything*, into what I guess you would call a *soul.* But then I had to go through gaseous states. (As described earlier.) Now I am in a physical, I suppose, ball with this air around me. Not air, but gas.

D: *Then this is your first* form *of any type*.

F: My first form was on the planet Earth as a denser kind of astral form, but my other ones were more gaseous.

D: *That's what I am trying to figure out. This is your first time as a* solid *form of any type.*

F: Yes.

D: *But that form isn't born or doesn't die on that world that you're on. It just exists until it's ... I keep thinking of things being born and dying.* (Laugh) *I guess it doesn't work that way.*

F: Seeing that I can move freely, when I go back to Earth, I am able to change this form that I fly through space in. And then I go to whatever is chosen for me when I get to the planet. It's just like going to a new city and getting new clothes. They have a clothing shop and they dress you in the clothes of that type of civilization you will be in. I just went into this ball-like gaseous form, because that is natural to this place.

D: *You need something that is natural to the environment then. Do you enjoy your work with these machines and these experiments?*

F: (Pause) I don't know what you mean.

D: *Do you like what you are doing?*

F: I *do* it. (Chuckle) I don't feel particularly happy, sad. There's no happy or sad. I feel gratefulness that I'm *allowed* to do this. Yes, I feel gratitude to the universal -- whatever drives everything -- that I was given this chance to experience. Helping with the -- I guess you would say -- divine plan.

D: *Then that is an emotion you are feeling. That you're glad you're there.*

F: Yes. But as in, "Whoopee, yes, I love my job," I don't understand. (I laughed.)

D: *Then whenever your job there is finished, you will be sent somewhere else. Is that how it works?*

F: Yes. I don't feel I have too much say-so about anything. I have *will.* I can *not* go someplace. But why would I *not* want to do something that's new and unique that I've never done before? Fun equals challenge. It is challenging to do different things, because you experience those things. It wasn't like that gaseous one where I felt I was trapped into doing a *particular* thing. These are more free floating.

D: *I can see that. Why* wouldn't *you want to go on and try something new?*

F: It's almost as if I earned the privilege of being able to do *things.*

D: *It would be very boring if you just stayed in the same place doing the same thing.*

F: I don't understand.

D: *If you get an opportunity to go on somewhere else, I think it would be challenging. It would be interesting to see what's going to happen at the next place.*

F: Yes, I guess. I don't think about it. I do my job, and then when my assignment time is up, it would be like military rotation. You do your job at a duty station -- I don't know where this is coming from -- but do the job at the station or military base, and then you get a new assignment, and then go off to somewhere else.

D: *Yes, that makes sense. Sometimes it is better to leave it up to somebody else, because they can see the overall picture.*

F: That is somebody else's job to make all these decisions. I don't feel I have the rank to make my decisions.

D: *Well, I really appreciate you telling me all these things. I would like to come again and continue asking questions of this type. Would it be all right if I do so?*

F: If it's all right with them, it's all right with me. (He laughed.) Yes, it's all right with me also. (Laugh) Sorry.

D: *Then they don't care if I come and ask more questions?*

F: (Slowly) They think it would be instructional for you to ask questions of me. -- That seems backwards. I don't understand. (Chuckle) But that's what I heard. They ... somebody may give you more if this continues. It seems, I don't know, destined for you to come a few more times again. Whatever is agreeable to both of you.

D: *There are still more things that I need to find out. I have such a great curiosity. And I do appreciate the information you've been giving me. All right. Then I will return at another time.*

F: Yes, you are welcome to.

The story *did* continue at our next session a week later. I returned Fred to the same scene, and the answers came as though there had been no interruption.

D: *What is your job there after this design or blueprint is finished and sent on to the council?*

F: Hmmm. I don't see myself doing anything. Waiting. I'm back out into space. I'm going to that resting area again.

D: *It seems like that's a way station where you can come back to every time, doesn't it?*

F: Not *every* time, but it feels so good to be refreshed. More of my friends are there than other places. But I am not going to stay here long again.

D: *Do you know what your next assignment will be?*

F: I feel that I'm one of the things that were being made. More animal than I was before.

D: *Would this be your first experience of being in a body, of this type?*

F: Yes, of this type. I was going to say, "No," because I was considered a body when I was a round form.

Could this have been a form of karma? Because he had been involved in the creation of this creature, then he had to *become* that creature?

D: *How does this body feel?*

F: I grunt a lot. I'm sorry.

The apology was directed at me, as though he was apologizing for his animal nature.

F: I feel large. No clothes. I can growl. Not speech. I don't think very well.

D: *What are you supposed to be learning by experiencing that?*

F: (Pause) I feel mobility. Touching things. Hands, feet. I'm carrying grass, eating it. I can move around.

D: *Where are you?*

F: I'm here. On the Earth.

D: *Do you see any other beings that look like you?*

F: Yes. There is a woman-type that is near me, to the right.

D: *Are there many others?*

F: I see, I think, ten. I'm being told there are ten in this group.

D: *Are there any other forms of life around?*

F: I see the trees are a lot bigger now.

D: *Different kinds of leaves or what?*

F: No, they're like the palm trees but bigger. They're bushier. And there are some trees that are more like now. They have leaves. I taste them. They don't taste good.

He frowned and then chuckled nervously, because his actions seemed absurd to his partially active conscious mind.

D: *Do you see any other life forms besides plant life?*

F: Small animals and large animals.

D: *What type of large animals do you see?*

F: I see what I guess would be considered a dinosaur type. I know that I'm afraid of them. I growl at them. (Chuckle) But they growl back. And I run away.

D: *Are they larger than you?*

F: Hmmm, yes. Some of them, but not many. But I don't know how to harm them.

D: *They're all different sizes, you mean?*

F: Medium sized ones, not super large ones.

D: *You said dinosaur type, but give me a description of what they look like.*

F: The one I'm looking at has a thin neck on a large body. I've seen this one before. The thin neck, large body, big feet and long tail. But its skin is really rough. I felt it when it wasn't alive, and it was really rough skin, not smooth. Like elephant skin. It feels more rough at the bottom, like it was dragging through the grass. That was the way the skin got rough, because it was dragging its bottom, its stomach, through the leaves and the bushes. It was more rough on the bottom where it was lying down. But this one was dead so it was cold.

D: *What are you going to do with it?*

F: I don't know. Just look at it. It's too big. I could climb up on it and look down.

D: *Then this was a large one.*

F: It was lying on its side, yes. It was dead.

D: *Do you know if those kind eat meat or plants?*

F: They eat what I eat, plants. I don't eat meat. Hmmm, I think I do eat something that's real small. But it has a lot of fur on it. It's hard to eat. My teeth don't seem to be right. I tear at things and I growl a lot. (He laughed.)

D: (Laugh) *I was thinking if the big animal didn't eat meat, why are you afraid of it?*

F: It is bigger. I'm scared of it. I think sometimes it chases. I know we don't like to go around them. They run after people. They're ... I guess I would say medium size. They're ... something ... elephants? A little bit bigger than an elephant. More above medium.

D: *That gives me an idea then. Do you see any other animals that look about that size, or larger?*

F: I see ... it's hard to get my mind clear from knowing, and some other part wants to interfere.

D: *That's all right. You're doing very well. I just wanted a description of some of the other types of animals.*

F: There is one with a bill on it. It has the tail and the arms, and it walks on two legs. But it has the flat bill. It's smaller than the other animal. I don't remember these names.

D: *Larger than you are?* (Yes) *Does that animal eat meat or plants?*

F: Plants. I can't think of these names.

D: *Don't worry about it. In other words, their size is all that's threatening.*

F: I think if you got in the way of these animals they would hurt you. Step on you, I guess. They could bump into you, lie on you. If you were lying down and they were wanting to lie down, they'd crush you. I feel someone got crushed by one. We found them and they were crushed.

D: *And that's why you're afraid of them. Are there any animals that would be dangerous to you in other ways?*

F: I feel ... a small animal. I guess, a cat? A small animal about the size of a cat. A part of me keeps wanting to throw in, "Oh, yes, I know this." Something like a cat, maybe a bobcat size animal. And I feel it could bite you. There are other water animals, like crocodiles, that are dangerous in the water. You don't go near the water. And there's another water animal that's like the large animal. It could bite you if you were near the water. But usually it doesn't ever come out of the water. It swims around in the water. It has fins and a tail.

D: *You mean there's one similar to the large one with the long neck.*

F: Yes, I've seen pictures, but it's hard to remember. I don't know the name now here.

D: *Then there's one type that lives on the land and one type that lives in the water?*

F: Yes, but the water one has sharp teeth, and fins instead of legs.

D: *Okay. What do you do with your time?*

F: I go around with a group. And in the group we eat. And looking around I hit rocks together. I throw things. I am trying to make something. It looks like ... I guess it would be a stone hatchet. You put the stone in a stick and you tie it together. But it's a very sharp stone hatchet, it's not blunt. And I can chop things with it, or it's used for cutting things.

D: *Why would you have to chop things?*

F: I don't know why. I'm looking ... it's to cut that little animal up, cut the skin off it. We eat it raw. It's to skin something. You have to cut it. We could cut its head off and then eat it raw.

D: *How did you know how to make the hatchet? Did someone show you, or did you just know how to do it?*

F: It's something ... others learned.

D: *Do you know what fire is?*

F: I was going to say I didn't know.

D: *You don't use fire then?*

F: No, not now.

D: *Is the hatchet the only type of tools that you made?*

F: There is a pointed thing that we use. It's like a stone with a point on it. It's like a pick, but it's conical to a point, and you almost use it to ... I was poking something's eye out with it. Digging it out, I guess to eat it.

D: *Are those the only type of tools then?*

F: That's all I see, but they just lay around. People carry them and put them in a place. But there's not anything to carry them with. There's no other tool.

D: *Do you have a shelter of any kind, or do you live out in the open?*

F: Yes, there's a place that we lie down, like a cave. And we put grass on the floor to make it softer. And I think we cut, or use the hatchet to put something over the doorway. I guess it's used to make sticks with. You know, to poke things with. Levers or to pry things with. But to put sticks over the entrance, to keep things out.

D: *Is that where the whole group sleeps?*

F: Yes. I see everyone sleeping around ... almost lying on each other, like hibernating. It's to be warm. Not fire. They lie on each other to be warm.

D: *What is the climate like?*

F: It's pretty warm, but not too warm. There is some cold. It's cold at night. And there's also a cold time of year. But it's not too cold.

D: *Well, did anything eventful ever happen when you were in that existence, or was it just the same thing all the time?*

F: I see some kind of volcano going off. It was a loud noise, an explosion. And everyone was scared. All the people ... or (Sigh) I guess, animals. I don't know what to call myself.

They were all screaming and grunting and scared. And I saw the volcano going off. An explosion. The ground was shaking. I see a lot of smoke. It was across the valley from where we were. But it still was loud, and others were screaming and scared. And I was just the same as them. Like a bunch of screaming monkeys.

D: *That would naturally frighten you.*

F: I smell smoke in the air.

D: *Was that the only eventful thing that was out of the ordinary?*

F: I saw the one person get crushed by that large animal. And die? (He seemed unsure of that word.) That was, I guess, eventful.

D: *Otherwise everything is just the same all the time.*

F: Yes. You go out and eat leaves and grass. Eat the seeding grasses.

D: *Then you don't kill any animals for food?*

F: I think we kill that small fuzzy thing. It's like a tapir, I mean, some kind of sloth. It has a lot of hair, but it has like a little bear's head on it.

D: *Then the other things that you eat, you just find something that has already died, like the large animal?*

F: We don't eat them. I don't see anyone ever eating that. I think we're too afraid of it. Even if it's dead people don't go near it, except to poke it with a stick.

D: *You were talking about skinning something. I thought you meant ....*

F: The small ones.

D: *Then you didn't try to skin the large one or eat it?*

F: No. It was just there. I don't even want to be near it.

D: *So you're not aggressive.*

F: No. I think I didn't live too long in this life. I died.

D: *What happened to you?* (Pause) *It's all right. You can watch it. It won't bother you at all. You can look at it objectively if you want to. You don't have to experience it.*

F: I guess I just left that body in the middle of the night. It's just lying there. It doesn't move any more.

D: *Do you think it just got too old?*

F: No. I see it being sick, or cold. Too cold. And dying of cold.

D: *Then you just left it?*

F: Yes. It's there. It's not moving.

D: *Well, do you think that was just a life about learning to experience sensations with a body?*

F: Some sensations. I feel I learned communication with other persons that were in the body, although I feel my mind was very blocked off. All I knew was to grunt and to yell and scream, and make different kinds of noises, and poke at people. And poke at things. (He laughed) Very animalistic.

D: *Yes. But yet you were able to make tools, so in that way you were not totally animalistic. It was more or less a type of learning experience then. Where did you go after you left that body?*

F: I took on another body similar to that one. And I'm with another group of people, if I can call them that.

D: *Are these people doing the same things?*

F: They live down by the water. I see a forked stick stab a fish, and we're eating fish. Something to do with fishing amongst the shallows.

D: *Do these people look the same, with the hairy bodies?*

F: It looks a little changed now, less hair. I feel there are clothes, or wearing something ... like a skin. The women have skins on the lower part, and not on the top. I have skins around my waist. And I'm wearing something wrapped around my feet. I feel there is more communication going on. Pointing, making signs, knowing what to do, sort of like language. There is more knowing what the other person wants out of you.

D: *Do you use words or sounds of any kind?*

F: You grunt and then you point at something. And you know what to do, or to carry something. Everyone knows his place, so if you want to pick up some water or something, then you can take it over. I think we cook things now. Something to do with ... fire, but I feel we cook the fish instead of eating it raw. But you stab it with this forked prong, not just a single stick.

D: *Then you think they use fire in some way. Do you see any other animal life?*

F: What I'd say is a crocodile. And I think I get killed by one of those. But yes, there are those large animals with the sharp teeth. But they don't come near where we are, because they can't come out into the shallows. And there's a lot of fish that come near the shore.

D: *Are there any other types of animals besides that one?*

F: We're down by the shore. It seems to be a real large shore. It's almost like on the shore of an ocean. There doesn't seem to be any animals that come down to the beach area. A lot of rocks. I am trying to bean one of those alligators with a rock. Throw big rocks on it. Trying to kill it, because we don't want them around. They're a nuisance.

D: *Do the rocks do any good?*

F: If we get up to a high place, and we can throw a big enough rock down on it, it'll kill it. I don't see us eating it. But I do see us trying to get together and communicate. And if we see one come in our area, we're territorial, and we throw rocks down on it. I see a cave near the water. That's where we live, but we don't have sticks in front of it. We don't have what we had before.

D: *What else do you eat besides the fish?*

F: I feel I eat other things. Women bring things. I see something. I guess it's the shape of a pear. It's some kind of green fruit. It's hard. It has almost a wooden taste, and it's like a wooden consistency. It's almost like a nut, but it's (made a face) ugh, it's hard to bite into.

D: *Something that must have come off the trees.*

F: I don't know where they got it. It's their job. They go off and collect these things. And I'm standing there with a fork through a fish.

D: *That's your job then.*

F: Yes, and running away from the alligator. (Chuckle) Or finding them and trying to chase them off, but we can't do it very well. They'd come into camp. They'd come into our area. They'd come in and almost chase us. That's why we had to sometimes leave our camp area and get to the higher place and throw things on them from the top of some rocks.

D: *You said you thought that was how you died in that life, from one of the alligators, crocodiles, or whatever they are?*

F: I feel my leg being bitten ... then the mid part of my body being bitten. And screaming and dying, as it is eating me.

D: *Were you on the shore when it came after you?*

F: I couldn't get away. I'd fallen down. And it grabbed my thigh with its mouth. Then it chomped down on the middle of me.

D: *I didn't think you would have gone into the water.*

F: We don't go into the water. It's kind of a marshy area. It's real shallow for a long distance before the deep water comes. That's why those other animals can't come up. Like a wetlands, half dry and half swamp, and then going out into the deep water.

D: *It's not like an ocean beach then, where there's a definite shore line.*

F: There's a shore, but there are small grasses that grow. It's like a swamp, but you could walk and wade out into the swampy water. It got real deep, as it went into the ... it was like an ocean.

D: *Well, when you left your body after the crocodile got you, where did you go?*

F: I went into that resting area again. It's a challenge to be these other ... animals. But I think I like my other jobs better. I'm getting to where I know that I like one thing better than another.

D: *What type?*

F: I like working with *thought* much better than getting eaten. (Chuckle) Because that was very painful that time to get eaten while I was still half alive.

D: *I imagine it would be. But I imagine it was something you were supposed to learn. Maybe that was why you had to experience it. Do you think so?*

F: I don't know.

D: *It seems that if you had something to say about it, you would tell them you would rather do the things with your mind.*

F: I still see myself experiencing without complaining.

D: *Not really telling them what you want to do. Well, where did you go next?*

F: I'm back in space. Now I'm on a planet where I was before. No, no, near there. The planet I first was assigned to, where I was told to go to Earth first.

D: *Do you mean the one where you were radiating or the one where you were in the dome shaped building?*

F: Where I was getting the assignment to go and change the air. There was a group of people there that I was very familiar with. And then I was assigned to go and moderate and change and transform the air.

D: *That was where some of them were also cooling the Earth down?*

F: Yes. That's where I went. Before I went to Earth to transform the atmosphere I was on this place to get the assignment. And then I went to Earth. But I'm now talking with the people, thinking to them on this place. I'm relating to people, just not going anywhere. I'm there on that ... place.

D: *Are you in a body on that place?*

F: I'm more that airy form that I was. There are other airy people here like myself. It feels so good to be out of a body. It wasn't a very pleasant memory of being eaten.

D: *Do you have a job to do there?*

F: I'm talking, thinking to people. I'm sort of in school. I'm learning things.

D: *What kind of things?*

F: I'm learning about stars. I'm learning, it looks like some kind of formula. Some kind of gas converting to something else. To solid. To rock. I'm learning how things are at different levels.

D: *Is this school a physical place?*

F: No. It's a group of us together in a certain area, but there's a person teaching up front. We're all mingled together. But there's a central point where I am, and a central point where someone else is. There's one person projecting like on a ... blackboard or a screen, "Here's gas. Here's denser matter, denser matter, then rock."

D: *Do you know why you have to learn these things?*

F: He is saying, "This is why. This is how matter is coming into being. From thought to gas to denser matter to rock." This is the why. I must know why things are this way.

D: *This is part of your education?*

F: I guess my general education, because I see people asking questions. Why rocks have to be formed? Why things have to be physical?

D: *What was the answer? That's a good question.*

F: The answer is, "Because that is God's plan, that spirit take the body of form. And that the soul experience form. There must be form." Just like ... God must have a form.

D: *What do you think? Do you think God has a form? What is your interpretation of God at that point?*

F: God's plan that must be experienced in form. There must be a body for God. It's almost like creating a physical form for God which must be in the matter. There must be spirit in the matter. God must be experienced in matter. It must be impregnated in matter. Matter is the same as ether. We are learning that each form, each level is just a denser form of spirit. Matter, I mean, ether, God. But spirit, the life force, must impregnate the rocks. Life force must be in everything. Everything must be alive. God *must* have a body.

D: *Then all of these different forms are expressions of God's body?*

F: What I was being shown with the rock, yes. That God must be even in rocks. Physical hard dense forms. Spirit must be able to live in those forms.

D: *That would go along with people saying, "God is everywhere." Of course, we don't normally think of rocks as being alive.*

F: Life force is in them. Not *alive*, not as my soul. The life force is thinner. It keeps what *I am* alive.

D: *Do you stay at that school very long?*

F: I feel I am there for a while. I learn more things.

D: *Can you share with me some of the things you learned? I know it's complicated and it's hard.*

F: No, it's not hard. I learn the reason I am. To express myself as a form. To be, to know, in a movable being. This is why I am, is to express, to know in a movable being, not as a rock.

D: *Why? Because you can learn more that way?*

F: *Yes!* (Chuckle) That really was a strong answer!

D: *Well, it makes sense. You'd be able to learn more with a body than you could as a rock or a tree or something like that.*

F: I feel very simple sometimes, but very complex. I feel that I am to know simplicity, and also complexity. I must know how to put things together for a greater purpose.

D: *Do you know what that means?*

F: Like I do with my inventions. (In his present life.) I'm always putting things together for a greater purpose. I can combine things very easily to make an object.

D: *All right. Is there anything else that you are being taught that you can share with me? I know it is difficult with the language.*

F: No, it's not difficult. I am taught to love things that are greater than myself. I am a little thing, and I must love the great thing. Like God. I must love God. I must embrace the larger thing than I am. I am a little point, and I must expand myself to embrace *all* of God. I must learn to love more.

D: *Then you will stay there in that school for quite a while learning these things?*

F: I seem to be not in the school, per se. I seem to be in a larger space. Almost like my soul is telling you these things.

D: *Maybe these are things they thought you would need to know before you went on to experience other things.*

F: It seems to be a compilation of what I am learning to do as an entity, as a force, as a being. As what I will do in my larger form. I think I am to grow into a larger form than what I am now, in this life. I am to grow into a larger form. I will kind of look like I am now, but more like an angelic larger form, where I will touch and teach and help and *be* with smaller forms, like I am now.

D: *That sounds right, and it sounds like it would be a good thing to do.*

F: Like a guardian angel.

D: *That would be the ultimate destination then, so to speak.*

F: I think that is my destiny, to do this. I am created to do this.

D: *These are all steps along the way then, apparently.*

I brought Fred forward through time to the present day and oriented him, but I did not awaken him yet. I had some work to do with his subconscious. We still had to find the reasons for his physical problems that had prevented him finishing the college classes. The sessions had been beneficial in showing him the first lifetimes he had lived on Earth, but I knew there was more that would explain events in his present life.

It is always a strange phenomenon to actually contact and speak to a person's subconscious. The pattern is always the same and this is unusual enough. The subconscious speaks about the person in the third person, as though it is separate from the subject and his problems. Quite often it will analyze the situation, supply the answers to the problems, and explain how they can be worked out. Other times its attitude is childish. But it is always wise to listen to what the subconscious suggests, because no therapy can be accomplished without its help. It has complete control over the body that it resides in, and once it agrees to work with the therapist amazing changes can occur in the subject's life that would be impossible through psychoanalysis and therapy alone. I respect and recognize the power that the subconscious has, and I always ask for permission to speak to that part of the mind, and try to work with its suggestions and incorporate them into the therapy. The following is a greatly condensed portion of what occurred, and an example of how the subconscious can supply the pertinent information needed to help the subject. The stories I receive are important to me, but the therapy is vital to the subject, so I cannot stop with just the story if the person needs help.

D: *I would like to speak to Fred's subconscious for a few moments. Would your subconscious have any advice or any kind of a message that it would like for you to know?*

F: To be more determined, to stick with things more. (Emphatic) Don't give up, even in the face of adversity. Don't give up. Be determined. Stick with things more. Especially in what he was doing, who he was dealing with. It's a long term project. Don't, don't be afraid of what is being thrown up temporarily as a front. Tell him to be very determined.

D: *But will the subconscious help Fred with these problems in his life?*

F: Maybe. The subconscious is ... we feel very negative sometimes because ... we're not given enough recognition. He yells at us a lot.

D: (Laugh) *That's why I like to recognize the subconscious and try to work with it, whenever possible. The main thing is to help the person. So I would appreciate it if the subconscious would help in every way it can.*

F: (Childish) I will if he will.

D: *He's going to have to learn to recognize you're there, and that you're there to help him.*

F: Oh, he knows I'm here. But he doesn't ... love me.

D: *Well, we'll have to tell him. That's what you really need is self-love. That's the answer to a lot of problems. We'll tell him about it. And we'll try to get him to work with you.*

F: He knows. You just remind him of those things said here.

D: *Okay. That's why I wanted to get a message. But the main thing is we want him to be healthy and happy, and live a* full *life. And we want your cooperation in any way you can give it.*

F: I will give it now.

D: *That's very important. And help take care of his health, too, because you must have a healthy body to carry out the job that we're sent here for.*

F: Yes. I'm no longer angry.

D: *Oh, I'm glad. I really am.*

F: Because I was furious ... because of .... Let's say, I was able to control the first part of life, and then intellect came in. And it has been trying to stifle me. So I don't give. It's been ... it *was* a war until a few years ago. And then I first became the friend. And now I want it as much as he wants, I guess, enlightenment.

D: *That's very good, because we do want you to be friends. And I'm very happy that you're going to work with him.*

During the next session the following week we were able to track down the most recent cause of his stomach and intestinal problems.

D: *I would like to speak to Fred's subconscious before he awakens.*

F: Yes. I am here.

D: *All right. I would like to ask you why he is experiencing these physical problems. Do you know?*

F: Hate.

D: *Hmmm, that's a strong word.*

F: It's a strong feeling.

D: *What does he hate?*

F: His mother.

D: *Does he know this?*

F: Yes, but he denies the core of it.

D: *Then do you think it would be important for him to acknowledge this feeling? And come to terms with it?*

F: Come to the core of it. The reason for hating her.

D: *Then when he comes face to face with it and tries to understand it, then he ....*

F: He will throw it out of himself. It's something to do with ... I keep coming back to telling him of ... the mother had a phrase, "You make me sick to my stomach." It's something to do also with the mother having a similar problem. Being very empathic. I see a line between her problem in the astral and his problem.

D: *And he's identifying with this.*

F: His stomach and everything is functioning a lot better now that we're saying this.

D: *Oh, I'm really glad, because we want him to be healthy. We want him to fulfill what he is meant to do in this life. And it's much easier when he has a healthy body.*

F: He keeps having dreams of throwing this *up*. Throwing *up* the words. The mother always said, "You make me throw up ... because I do not like you." He wants to throw up the reason, and get rid of it totally.

This is a superb example of how literally the subconscious interprets what is going on in the subject's life. It fits perfectly with the saying that your body believes everything you say. If you desire to be sick, then the subconscious is obligated to fulfill your wish, no matter how nonchalantly that wish was expressed. It is thus very important to listen to what we say in idle conversation, especially about our bodies. The subconscious never sleeps and is always paying attention to our remarks.

D: *Will you help him to understand what's going on?*

F: We have been. We must go and tell the mother not to bother us. We have told him this, but he is still running away from her. We must confront her. He knows that it's coming. He is scared of it.

D: *But once it's over with, then he'll be finished with it, won't he? And his physical problems will ease up.*

F: We see it as not as simple as that. It's a little bit more complicated.

D: *But it's a beginning, isn't it?*

F: Yes. Because when the connection is broken between him and her, when the karma is dissolved, then he will ... the stomach is working a lot better now.

D: *Oh, that's really good, just because he's beginning to realize this.*
F: There is karma between him and her.
D: *Well, once he confronts her and works this out, then he will be free to go on and do what he really wants to do.*
F: The chain will be taken off. We all are trying to help him.

When Fred awakened he said he felt hungry and for the first time in weeks he thought he would be able to eat something and keep it down. It was a beginning, because it showed that the subconscious was going to cooperate in the therapy.

We had about four sessions after this, but we did not explore the early lifetimes again. We discovered in all four of these sessions that he had set up a pattern that kept repeating and had followed him into his present lifetime, because the subconscious has no concept of time. It does not always realize that the person is residing in a different body. In the other lifetimes the deaths had all been traumatic and had centered on the stomach and intestinal area of his body: a sword through the stomach, a fall from a cliff, being run over by a carriage and horses, and a wartime shell blast. Not to mention the crocodile sinking its teeth into his mid-section. It was no wonder that in times of stress this most vulnerable part of his body reacted. His problems in early childhood with his mother, who had never wanted him and refused to show him any love, only multiplied the physical condition with her subconscious insinuations.

Fred left our area a few months after our work was completed. At last contact things were working much better for him, and he was functioning normally in a college in another state. I never found out whether or not he gained the courage to confront his mother, but his subconscious said that would have to be done before he would be completely free.

CHAPTER TEN

A LESSON IN SURVIVAL

This case is an example of how an interesting story can be stumbled upon by accident. It also shows how an amateur can begin an experiment and then not know how to progress with it. The questioning and the technique can make a great difference in how the subconscious reveals information. If the appropriate questions are not asked the information will never be uncovered. This is where questioning becomes an art. It also shows how mistakes can be made by an amateur who is not used to working in regressive hypnosis. I found many errors made that restricted the flow of information, but that was only because the operator had a lack of experience. But on the other hand if they had not inadvertently unlocked the door, then this case would never have been uncovered.

The subject was Jack, a young carpenter in his forties, whom I had known for many years. The operator was also one of my subjects who was interested in these types of experiments. In this case she decided to turn the tables, so to speak, and try the role of hypnotist. She discovered it was not as easy as it looks, or as easy as it seems from the subject's viewpoint. There is a lot more to take into consideration, and she felt the tremendous responsibility before the session was over. I commend her for her honesty in admitting she had stumbled into something she did not know how to handle.

This session was conducted by Peggy in her home with her husband and others present. Peggy was mostly doing it as a parlor-game exercise based on the technique which I had used on her in our work together, and on techniques she had observed others use. She was not prepared for what came out, and thought I should explore it further because it was more in my field of research. She wisely had taped the session or many details would have been lost. However, the recorder was sitting at a distance from the participants and several times the words were difficult to transcribe.

Jack had previously asked to have a session with me but since he lives here in Arkansas and there was no hurry we had not set a date. I was trying to have sessions with people who had more urgent problems, or who were only in the area for a short while. Peggy told me briefly what had occurred during this session. Jack had some memories about what he had said, and thought it might have been influenced by the annual UFO conference held in our area a few weeks previously. He definitely questioned the validity and did not accept it totally. Neither Jack nor I had a chance to listen to this tape before we had our session. It was probably just as well, maybe it was meant that we go into it cold without being influenced by what Peggy had discovered. The first time I heard this tape was while I was transcribing it after my session was held.

Peggy said that she used a long induction, probably a lot longer than necessary. She had Jack swinging on a hammock that was attached to two trees, then had the trees disappear until he was swinging in the clouds, then had the hammock disappear, etc. Then had him come down to earth.

Through much questioning he described himself and the surroundings he found himself in. He saw that he was a totally naked young male standing among yellow flowers looking at a river. He reported, "There is a river forking. A waterfall is standing under the river. It's strange the way it's forking off. It's not forking *into* one, it's forking from one into *two*." He had black hair and a tan body, but he had the feeling he had *never* worn clothes. Evidentially he was in a warm climate.

He had the feeling he was all alone, except for the presence of animals. He had no sense of any family or any memory of anyone like himself. He had no home, but slept wherever he found himself. When he was asked to go somewhere else he saw himself floating on his back in a pool of water. He was enjoying the delightful feeling of the sun on his body.

After several minutes of these type of questions it was obvious that Peggy was becoming frustrated and depleted. This type of questioning is very difficult when there seems to be nothing to relate to. The hypnotist is unsure of which direction to take. Peggy decided to let her husband ask questions while she had time to think. He asked about the types of animals in the area, in a hope of determining the location. Jack described only the fish in the water and big birds in the sky. When asked what he ate he mentioned roots, berries and fish. None of this helped in placing the locale or time period. He had no speech or language, but made noises like the animals.

Peggy then decided to take him to an important event in his life. These can be anything, and are not normally what we in our time period would consider important. If the life is mundane, then the event may be mundane. It is at least important enough to break the monotony of a common, boring lifetime. I am often amused by what the personality considers eventful. In this case Jack saw that he was standing on a cliff watching a large hawk.

"I am trying to become the bird. It's in my mind. -- I am the bird. I see myself sitting on the cliff. I feel the wind. I want to fly."

He obviously transferred his consciousness to the bird so he could have this experience. This apparently was possible because he had not been raised with restrictions that told him it was not possible. He said he had been practicing having telepathic communication with other creatures. It may have been a diversion to relieve him of boredom. He then felt the exhilaration of flying and looking down upon the earth.

"The bird chose me. This hawk looks like any other hawk. Except that I recognize it as separate from any other hawk. I don't know why. But I have seen this hawk before. And it has seen me.

I went to the cliff to call this hawk. And he came. I have done this with fish, and with the wolf."

Peggy's husband asked, "What does it feel like when you're with the fish compared to what it feels like when you're with the hawk? How are their consciousnesses different?"

Jack replied, "I can't say. I go into these animals with *my* consciousness and seek what *I* seek. It's fun to run, and it's fun to fly."

These experiences seemed to be the only excitement in his life, yet he felt the need to be searching for purpose. In this way he was different from the animals, because they took their lives for granted. No matter where Peggy tried to take Jack, as he grew older he never saw another human being. He died as an old man with white hair sitting on a cliff. Thus it was impossible to obtain information about his whereabouts and how he happened to be there. Normally this would be considered a simple life with no purpose, but it took a strange twist.

I am well aware that once the soul leaves the body it is released from the restrictions of that body and its limited knowledge. Once the soul enters the spirit realm it has access to all information. I have explored this realm in great detail in my book *Between Death and Life*. Jack described the death experience the same way I have heard it hundreds of times before. He saw a light and felt drawn toward it. When he was enclosed within it he said he felt grateful and loved.

So Peggy at this point decided to ask the man's spirit why it chose this existence of being the only one of its kind. His answer was a complete surprise to Peggy and everyone in the room. Later it was to also startle Jack when he was conscious and curious about the session. He said, "I was an experiment. A seed." They were further startled when he said he was planted by a spaceship. He said he was not the only seed. There were others, but they were planted in other locations. This would explain why he had no further contact with them after reaching the earth.

Peggy's questions were not specific enough to obtain detailed information. He said he grew up on a large craft where there were many people. "I am an experiment. I was created for observation. I was to survive by instinct." He was observed during his entire life on Earth, but did not have conscious communication with the craft after the earlier years. As he grew he forgot about his beginnings. "The experiment was assuredly a success. I grew into an intelligent being. Few memories of creation. My brothers and I -- there were six experiments -- were similar, but different from the creators. I can now see that all six lived, and all six died. The creators wanted to learn the harmony of man with animal, man with nature. The experiment was a success."

P: *Why couldn't these beings experience this harmony for themselves.*
J: Earth was not conducive for their form. They cannot live here.

Peggy asked many questions that led nowhere. She was trying to determine how he was different from the beings on the craft. He was finally able to explain that he was a clone.

P: *Can you describe this cloning process for us?*
J: From the cell ... one goes through embryo state. And is birthed ... or a plastic (unclear, either: door or orb).

The sound quality of the tape was poor and often words were untranscribable. I have seen Peggy's husband operate his tape recorder and he usually sets it in one place and does not use a hand microphone. At times it was not able to pick up Jack's answers, let alone the others' remarks. They were probably sitting further away. There was also a lot of tape noise.

P: *Are you aware of the emotions present at the time of your birth?*
J: No emotions by me, or the other five. Jubilation by the creators.
P: *Have the creators performed this experiment with other beings on other planets?* (Long pause)

J: I don't know.
P: *Have these creators tried this experiment with other beings on* this *planet?*
J: Yes. Clones of plants and animals.
P: *Where are the creators from?*
J: A spaceship.
P: *Where is this spaceship from?*
J: I don't know.

Peggy then tried to take Jack back to before the craft ever came to Earth. She was trying to find where the aliens came from originally. Jack could not do this because he said he was not there. He was not present until he was birthed. Thus he could not follow the line of questioning back to the source of the spacecraft.

It was obvious from listening to the tape that the group was running out of questions. They had been unable to receive sufficient information to carry the story forward. They were trying to bring the session to a close. Peggy asked him what he would do now.

J: I will be born again.
P: *Do you have a plan for that?*
J: Yes. People.

The group laughed. The answer was obvious. He would return in the next life and be living among people, something he had been denied and sensed that he missed. Of course, he had no way of knowing at that time that the interaction with people often does not ease problems but creates them, and in so doing it creates karma, thus creating a vicious cycle of birth and death. Yet at that point in his development the yearning to be with people was uppermost in his consciousness.

When Jack was awakened he had glimpses of bits and pieces of the session, similar to the way we remember snatches of dreams when we awaken in the morning. When I later talked with Jack I found that he remembered a great deal more than was reported on the tape. This is often the case when the operator does not know the questions to ask. The subject will say they saw so much more than they reported, but they could not talk about it because the proper question was not asked. I have learned this the hard way by conducting hundreds of difficult regressions.

Peggy told me about this session the next week and suggested that it might be something I would be interested in. She said that while she was doing this she realized how difficult it was. She also realized that there was a great deal of responsibility involved when you have someone in trance and regressed to a lifetime. She also felt a great deal of love and protectiveness toward the subject, which is the same feeling that I have. Upon listening to the tape I picked up on several mistakes that she made that inhibited the more complete flow of information. Of course, these were things that Peggy would not be aware of, and only come from long practice. She did very well with a difficult regression with all things considered. At least she was able to tap into something that was more in my field and worthy of investigating.

I set up an appointment with Jack after she told me about this case. We did not have a chance to discuss it in much detail. She gave Jack a copy of the tape, and he was supposed to give it to me, so I would know the background of what they had uncovered before I worked with him. But as it turned out, he was unable to get the tape to me beforehand, and handed it to me when I walked into his house. He had also been unable to find time to listen to it. This was probably for the best because we were able to conduct our session without being influenced by the questions Peggy did or did not ask.

Thus when I arrived for the session, I really had very little information outside of what Peggy had mentioned. So I asked Jack what he could remember of the session. He said the scene on board the spaceship was still very clear, so I thought we could begin there. I asked why he thought it was a spaceship, and he said it was because there didn't seem to be much room on it. What he considered to be the most fascinating aspect of Peggy's regression was his ability to communicate with the animals. He said that was something he had always wanted to do in this life. I asked for a description of the beings on board, and he said he didn't think that question had been asked by Peggy.

J: The beings on the ship were four, four and a half feet high. And they had like pointed ears. And possibly the whole head shape was kind of pointed. I had the sense of pointedness. And they didn't speak. They must have communicated telepathically.
D: *What color was their skin?*
J: It was gray.
D: *And any kind of prominent features or anything that stood out?*
J: Ummm. They had big eyes. And it seems like they didn't have a mouth. I don't remember if they ate.
D: *What about anything in the spaceship that you noticed?*
J: Well, it seems like there were a lot of panels with instruments on them.
D: *In the walls or what?*
J: Yeah, along the sides. Yeah, on the walls. It seemed like it was a circular craft, with a room in the middle and then rooms off the center room. That's where the controls and everything were, in the middle. And then it was like ... I suppose a dormitory set-up on the rest of the ship.
D: *Well, we'll find out. But where were the incubator-type things?*

I now know this was not mentioned on the first tape because Peggy did not ask much about the ship. But Jack told me he saw incubator-type arrangements.

J: It was in a room. Not the main room, in an off room.
D: *And you said you thought you were on that ship for about four years?*
J: Three or four years, yeah.
D: *And you thought you were different than they were?* (Uh-huh) *In what way?*

J: Well, my skin color was different. I had a mouth. And my ears weren't pointed. And I was like the other five. You know, we were all children. There were six of us altogether.

D: *Did you have hair?*

J: Yeah. It seems like all of us had dark hair. And brown skin.

D: *Was there anything else different?*

J: No. I think half of us were male and half of us were female.

D: *Did all six of you look humanoid? Or as Peggy suggested, maybe Neanderthal? I mean, did the features look like people, or was there anything different?*

J: (Thinking) Ummm. I guess I perceived myself to look like a person of today. I had, of course, some hair on my body, but not a lot. Which made me think that I was more human than animal. Of course, I'm not familiar with Neanderthals either, but I think they would have a consciousness.

D: *Yeah, I was thinking that their features were more exaggerated, if you go by the pictures. But those pictures are just reconstructions, too, off the skulls.*

J: And I think maybe in Neanderthals, their communication was mental.

D: *That was what you thought you had, just mental communication. You were able to communicate with the animals.*

J: Yeah, because I didn't have a language. I didn't speak. I made noises.

D: *But you never saw anyone that looked like you after you were on the planet?* (No) *All right. Then we'll ask more questions along those lines and see what we can come up with. I just wanted to get the description of the beings on the tape recorder before we started.*

I began the induction and Jack was soon in deep trance.

D: *Let's return to a scene that you saw before and we can explore it again. It was a scene inside a round building, a round place, where there were panels in the walls and strange-looking containers. You felt it was a place that was familiar to you. I would like to return again to that place and we can explore it in more detail. I will count to three and on the count of three we will be there. 1, 2, 3, we've gone back to that scene that you saw before. Can you look around and tell me what it looks like?*

J: Yes. I'm in the central room. I hear a buzzing.

D: *Where is it coming from?*

J: The floor.

D: *Do you know why it is making a noise?*

J: I sense it's the power of the craft.

D: *Is this a craft?* (Yes) *All right. What does the floor look like?*

J: It's shiny, metallic. The buzzing is coming from the center beneath the floor. There's a slight vibration that can be felt by the feet. The craft is in motion. Its destiny. It's going somewhere.

D: *How can you tell it's in motion?*

J: Because of the feel of the vibration and the humming noise.

D: *Is that the only time the humming noise is present?* (Yes) *All right. Look around and see what else you can see in this room.* (Pause)

J: There are four other beings, different from myself, that seem to be monitoring panels. The panels are flat and consist of two walls. If you were standing next to them you would look down at the panels.

D: *Then they're not flush with the walls?*

J: No. They're on like a dash ... sort of, at a forty-five degree angle. No seats.

D: *What is on the panels?*

J: Lights. Knobs. Buttons. One screen.

D: *Is there anything on the screen?*

J: It seems like a star chart. It's not moving. It's stationary. The screen is not paid a lot of attention to. The other dials which control the ship are more important.

D: *Do you understand any of the functions of the dials and buttons and things?*

J: No. They are in communication with each other, by checking and double-checking systems. It seems *all* do *all* work. One person would examine all of the dials and machinery, and so would the other three. And they would communicate to make sure they all came to the same conclusion.

D: *Is it important that they all agree?*

J: Apparently.

D: *What do these beings look like that are doing this work?*

J: They are gray. Pointy. They have arms and legs. Short necks. It seems like the head fits onto the body, but the neck does have movement though. No hair. Their eyes, I think stand out more because of no hair, rather than their actual size.

D: *Do the eyes have pupils?*

J: The eyes are *all* black.

D: *What about a nose or a mouth?*

J: Yes, a nose. And yes, a mouth. They have a slit. I don't ever hear noises from their mouth.

D: *Do they have ears?*

J: Yes. Their ears are pointy and, it seems like a natural part of the head, not separate. They're not like human ears.

D: *Are they wearing any clothes?* (No) *What do their hands look like?*

J: Webbed. Half way between the fingers.

D: *How many fingers?*

J: Four.

D: *Do they have an opposing thumb?*

J: Yes, five including the thumb. There's no webbing between the finger and thumb.

D: *Can you see their feet?*

J: Yes. They are webbed.

D: *The same way the hands are?*

J: Yes. There's more bone structure.

D: *Do you mean the bones are more prominent?*

J: The top of the foot seems to come up, is raised. You can see the bones easier.

D: *Do they have the same amount of digits on the feet?* (Yes) *What do you look like?*

J: I'm a child.

D: *Are you as tall as they are?*

J: No. I'm smaller.

D: *Do you resemble them in your appearance?*

J: No. I have light brown skin. Tan, tan skin. Hair on my head. No webbing on my hands or feet. And the sex organ.

D: *The creatures don't have a sex organ?* (No) *Then you are not wearing clothes either?* (No) *Is there anyone else that looks like you?*

J: Yes. They're in another room.

D: *All right. These other beings, do they eat? Do they consume anything?* (Pause) *Do you know if they need anything to keep them alive?*

J: (Sigh) I'm not familiar. I am cared *for* by them, as are the others. I'm not familiar with their eating or sleeping habits.

D: *You're not where you could observe this then?* (No) *Well, then how do they care for* you? *Do* you *have to eat?*

J: Yes. We're fed. Mostly liquids.

D: *How are you fed these liquids?*

J: In drinking vessels. Like cups. The liquid is different colors. We have white, orange, green. Different tastes.

D: *What does it taste like? Sweet, bitter, sour?*

J: Bland.

D: *All of the different colors?*

J: Well, the white tastes chalky. The orange is ... tangier. And green food is different again. Hmmm, it has a feeling of being more substantial. Lumpy, maybe.

D: *Are you ever given solid foods, or is it mostly liquids?*

J: Yes, we chew. On plants. It is prepared and given us. It's sweet, and to be chewed on, and the cord or the stringy part is spit out.

D: *They feed you and they care for you. What else do they do for you?*

J: They watch us play. Give us blocks and spheres, these types of toys. And we play.

D: *You mentioned that you sleep. Where would you sleep?*

J: All six sleep in the same room. We have a space that's comfortable. It's a mat on the floor. That's all.

D: *Do you all sleep on the same mat?*

J: No, separate mats.

D: *Have you ever been throughout the entire ship to all the rooms?*

J: Yes. There are several rooms off the central room. These rooms have columns. One column in the middle of the room. And there are ... (Sigh) ten rooms?

D: *Altogether? Not counting the central room?*

J: Ten rooms plus the central room, plus our room.

D: *Then there are ten other rooms besides those two. Can you tell me what is in each one?*

J: In each one there is a column in the center. And the walls angle. The ceiling and floor meet a side wall. The side wall having about two or three feet of wall space. (All this with hand motions.) With the ceiling and floor meeting the wall. The pillar would be about six foot high in the center of the room. That's all.

D: *What is the purpose of the pillar?*

J: It is part of the structural supports.

D: *What are the different rooms used for?* (Long pause)

J: I don't know if they have a use. I just wander in and out of the rooms as I go around the ship. I've never been below.

D: *How are they able to go to that section.*

J: (Long pause as though thinking.) Hmmm. I don't know.

D: *Then you and the others have never been allowed down in the other part?*

J: No. (Abruptly) The humming has stopped. That means the ship has stopped moving.

D: *Are there any windows or anything so you can see outside?*

J: Just the screen.

D: *All right. Earlier you mentioned a strange looking apparatus or incubator that you thought you were born into. I would like to count to three and have you go and look at that again and describe it to me. 1, 2, 3, we have returned to that scene once again. Tell me what you see.*

J: There are six cylinders. I'm the first one. Hmmm, three foot high. Narrower, two foot wide. Inside of each cylinder is a womb ... floating.

D: *Transparent?* (Yes) *What is it floating in?*

J: Clear liquid. Warm.

D: *This fluid that you are floating in, is it a certain color?*

J: It's clear.

D: *What is the transparent womb made out of?*

J: Hmmm. Like a jellyfish. A membrane-type thing.

D: *Are you inside one of the wombs looking out or what?*

J: I am looking at myself in one.

D: *What do you look like at this point?*

J: Hmmm. A fetus.

D: *An embryo type?*

J: Yes. Curled up in a ball.

D: *Are the others all alike?* (Yes) *Can you see anything else around this apparatus type thing in that room?*

J: Yes. There are four caretakers that monitor the tubes.

D: *Do these look like the same type of beings?*

J: They are the same. These beings are all alike.

D: *What do the caretakers do when they're monitoring the tubes?*

J: They adjust dials that control the flow of liquid in the cylinders. And just mainly observe. At new stages of growth adjustments are made in the liquid circulation and temperature.

D: *Are there any other apparatus besides just the tubes, the cylinders?*

J: There is a panel with lights and switches on it.

D: *I'm thinking of wires, I guess, wires and tubes and things like that. Does it have anything like that?*

J: Yes. Tubes connect the cylinders that the fluid is in, and the panel.

D: *Are there any colors in that area?*

J: There are colors on the controls. I see red and green lights.

D: *And these four beings, it's their job to monitor the temperature and the flow of the liquids, and to keep track of the growth.*

J: Yes. I sense they communicate with each other. It must be mentally. I don't hear them making any noise.

D: *As long as you are observing in that manner, I'm going to ask you if you can drift even further back and see where these embryos came from that were placed in these cylinders, in these wombs. I think you will have access to that information and you can see where the whole thing began. I will count to three and we will go to that time and you can tell me what you are observing. 1, 2, 3, we've gone to that time when these embryos began. What are you seeing now?*

J: There is a much larger ship. With *many* more people. Much more activity.

D: *The same type of beings?*

J: Some are the same, some are different. Some are humanoid. Some are ... different ... larger.

D: *Larger than humans?*

J: Yes. I sense these beings are the controllers. They wear white robes. They are tall ... white skinned. *Long* fingers. No hair. Large, round heads. No ears.

D: *You said there were others that looked human?*

J: Yes. They're in a room on tables. They're being monitored, I sense, electronically. There is a screen above each one.

D: *Are they conscious?*

J: They seem to be *un*conscious. Yet functioning. Breathing.

D: *Do they look like humans as we know them?*

J: Yes. There are six.

D: *Who is doing the monitoring?*

J: The shorter gray beings that were on the smaller ship.

D: *Can you tell if these humans on the tables are male or female?*

J: Yes. Three men and three women. These are our genetic parents.

D: *How do you know that?*

J: They are experiments. And their cells are being experimented *with*. The taller controllers seem to be working as laboratory technicians. They work in a separate room in another part of this ship. I see a panel desk with instruments and fire and water and ... disks.

D: *Are the fire and water contained in something?*

J: The fire is coming out of a spigot. And the water flows through tubes.

D: *You said there are disks also?*

J: Disks on the desk. They look clear. Shallow disks.

D: *Can you see what these larger beings are doing?*

J: I notice their fingers ... are active. (He made graceful hand motions.) They take the disk, and put it in this area of the table. And run some dials that seems to contain information about what's in the disk.

D: *Can you see anything in the disk?*

J: (Pause) I see a black dot in this disk.

D: *Is it very large?*

J: No. Pretty small. The size of a pupil.

D: *Can you see what they're doing with the water and the fire?*

J: With the fire they seem to experiment with different types of liquid.

D: *What do you mean?*

J: They hold the container with liquid in over the fire, and pass it back and forth across the fire. And they also record. It must be some type of computer.

D: *It sounds like a laboratory type setting. I am interested in the human type beings that you saw on the table. Do you know if they are kept that way permanently, or are they allowed to return to consciousness?*

J: I sense that they stay unconscious during their stay on this ship.

D: *Then they don't stay on the ship the entire time. Can you see where the human cells are taken from?*

J: Yes. From the eye. It seems that is the area of the head they are taking their samples from. I don't know if it's from the meat part of the eye or the liquid part.

D: *That's what I was wondering, if it was something to do with the eyeball itself, or do you think it is just the fluid?*

J: I don't know. I see they are doing something with a sharp object. And depositing something in these disks. (Graceful hand motions again.) Their fingers are so interesting.

D: *Why?*

J: Because they're so long ... delicate. But they seem to hold an instrument ... oh, several inches long. And I feel they go into the corner of the eye around the tear duct part by the nose. And deposit what they come out with in a clear disk.

D: *But you said the instrument is several inches long?*

J: Yes. Long and pointed.

D: *I'm thinking of a nail or a pin ....*

J: A needle.

D: *That small. Then whatever they take out they deposit in the disk. Then at what stage are these cells put on the smaller ships?*

J: After a comfortable stage of growth in the disk. They are developed first within the disk, until they reach the embryo stage. They are put in these containers after the embryo is maybe one month in growth size.

D: *Then am I correct that the developing embryos are raised on these smaller ships and not the larger ones? (Yes) Is there a reason for that?*

J: Possibly.

D: *I would think that the larger ship would be safer. Just conjecture.*

J: The small ship is safe.

D: *Safer than the larger one?*

J: As safe as.

D: *Do you know why?*

J: There is no threat to the smaller ships, or the larger ships.

D: *Why do they transfer it to a smaller ship?*

J: Observation. I suspect that is their purpose, to observe. Whereas the larger ship probably has other things to do.

D: *That would make sense. All right then. I'm going to ask you to move forward, as the embryos are developing within these tubes and are growing to the size that they would be ready to be born, so to speak. Can you see them at that stage?* (Yes) *Can you tell me how they are born?*

J: Yes. The sac they are carried in breaks, and the child inside is just swimming in this liquid. And at that moment the caretakers lift him out of the tube.

D: *It just happens spontaneously when it becomes large enough?* (Yes) *What do they do with it after they take it out of the tube?*

J: They bathe it, in a liquid other than what is in the tube. And feed it.

D: *These newborn babies, do they make any noise?* (Yes) *Because you said the other beings didn't make any sounds, did they?* (No) *What about the larger beings with the long fingers? Did they make any sounds?*

J: (Pause) No. It seems that their motion (hand motions) was nearly musical. Very fluid motions. And I sensed a type of communication in the *flow* as well as in the telepath.

D: *Yes, from the motions you're making it looks very graceful. Then it seems that these newborn babies are the only ones that are making any audible sounds?*

J: Yes. When they're hungry they cry. When they're playful they squeak.

D: (Laugh) *Like babies as we know them. Then they are cared for by these beings. And you saw yourself as a small child. I'm going to count to three and I want you to move ahead to the time that you leave the craft, and tell me how that is accomplished. 1, 2, 3, the time has arrived for you to leave the craft. What is happening?*

J: There is an opening in the craft, through one of the rooms. Where the side wall has come down into a ramp. I am taken down this ramp by two of the helpers. And they go back on the ship. And the ship leaves.

D: *About how large are you now?*

J: I am a child. Three or four years.

D: *Were you able to see the outside of the craft?* (Yes) *What did it look like?*

J: Shiny. Metallic. Much like the floor.

D: *What was the shape?*

J: A circle.

D: *Like a sphere?*

J: It was wider than high.

D: *Where did they leave you?*

J: They left me by a river.

D: *How do you feel about that?*

J: Lonesome.

D: *Do you understand what happened?*

J: No. There was a sense of companionship with the other five. That is not there. I feel sad.

D: *Do you feel frightened, or does it bother you that they left you?*

J: Oh ... I feel sad. I don't think frightened. It seems that I know what to do. I don't know if it is because of preprogramming or instinct. But the water is good. They put me by the water. I drank some, and it was good. And the plant life ... if it's good I eat it, and if it's not I don't.

D: *You instinctively know the right type to eat?*

J: Yes. Some of it leaves a terrible taste, so I do not eat that.

D: *But you're not worried about what's going to happen to you?* (No) *Only the sad feeling of them going away and leaving you. Is that what you mean?* (Yes) *All right then. I want you to move ahead till later in that life, when you have grown and you are an adult of some age. And I want you to look at your life that you lived there. Did you ever see any other beings such as yourself?* (No) *What type of creatures did you see?*

J: I have animal friends I communicate with. A bird. A wolf. A cat. A fish. And a snake.

D: *These are like your companions?* (Yes) *And you can understand each other?* (Yes) *Did you have a certain place where you lived?*

J: Yes. I've lived in a bluff shelter. And also under the stars.

D: *Well, you weren't too lonely then if you had your animal friends?*

J: No. I never considered myself lonely. I seem to always wonder why there were no others like myself.

D: *Did you ever try to find any others like yourself?*

J: Oh, I looked around. I had no recollection of the ship when I was on the earth.

D: *You forgot about it?*

J: Yes. I didn't know where I came from. It seems my consciousness .... Maybe that's when they put me on the earth, when my consciousness started developing. I don't know.

D: *Maybe that was why it was done so young. So you wouldn't be as apt to remember?* (Yes) *You had hair on your head. As an adult is there hair on other parts of your body?*

J: Yes. There is hair on my arms and legs.

D: *Is it thick hair or thin hair or what?*

J: Hmmm. It's thin hair.

D: *Do you have facial hair?* (Yes) *The climate there where you are living, is it warm or cold or what?*

J: Warm. All the time.

D: *Did you ever see any large animals besides your friends?*

J: (Emphatically) Yes!

D: *Can you tell me what kind?* (I was thinking about dinosaurs or extinct animals.)

J: Elephants. Large elephants. There was moose. That was a large animal. And ... oh, there were large water animals. There was hippopotamus. And ....

He seemed to have difficulty finding the names of all of these animals. He hesitated each time.

D: *Did you ever feel any danger from these animals you lived among?* (No) *So living there was just really uneventful, wasn't it?*

J: Ummm. Uneventful. Ummm.

D: *I mean pretty much the same every day?*

J: It was pretty fun.

D: *Oh, you liked it?*

J: It was pretty fun, yeah. It was fun learning about other animals and finding out how they lived.

D: *So it wasn't all lonely then. You did have friends and it was interesting.*

J: Yes, it was fun. I was able to share consciousness with animals. I had friends, friendly animals that I did this with. I didn't do it with all.

D: *Well, that's very good. Thank you for telling me all these different things. I would like you now to leave that scene, and drift away from these things you have been watching.*

I then brought Jack forward to full consciousness, after conditioning him with a keyword to facilitate induction next time. I also gave the suggestion that he would remember some of the details about the ship and be able to reproduce them. When he awakened he drew the star chart that he saw on a screen onboard the craft.

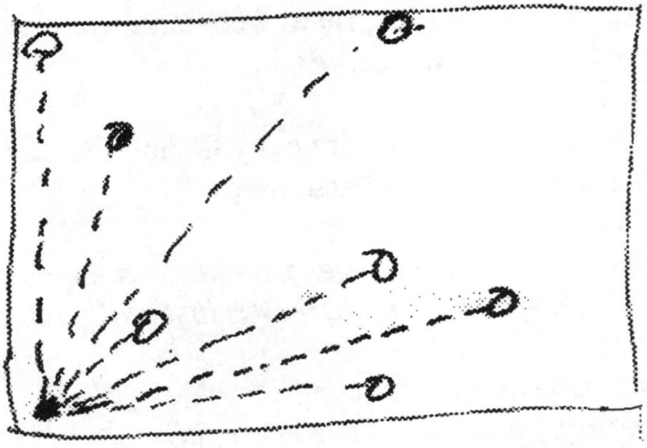

He said the star chart is not exact. There was a central point in the left hand corner which was either the ship or the home planet. There were seven circles and dotted lines going out from the central point. The placement of the seven circles is not exact.

The shape of the exterior of the ship, with ramp coming out of right side.

At first I thought that such an experiment would have been a failure since he did not breed to start the propagation of the race. But maybe that wasn't the purpose. Maybe it was just an early experiment to see if a being of this type would be able to survive in this Earth environment, and how he would adapt. As Jack said, the experiment was a success.

CHAPTER ELEVEN

EVOLUTION IS HELPED ALONG

Tom was a successful freelance magazine writer in his forties. He wanted to try regression to find answers to the confusion that seemed to fill his life. I agreed to work with him even though I suspected his problems were not caused by past lives, but were brought about by present influences. He had recently gone through a divorce, and was having trouble with his teenage son as a result. He had a charming personality, and was considered quite the ladies' man. Several of my friends found him attractive. This could have been one of the causes of his marriage problems, but if the subject does not bring up personal matters, I don't pry. These things are only discussed if they are related to therapy.

We had about five sessions altogether in 1990 before he moved out of the area. The first one was mundane, as the pattern usually is in the first session. He wanted to continue to have a few more sessions, even though I did not think we would discover anything important. I did not think he was capable of deep trance. He was too analytical and had too much conscious mind interference. This session surprised me.

I used my cloud method, and asked him to go to a life that had importance and relevance to this present lifetime.

Tom began to describe a scene. He was standing on a cliff looking down at a stream. As he watched the water flowing away from him, he was aware that he was waiting for someone to come.

He suspected it was a woman, probably a lover. He saw that he was a dark-skinned man with black hair, dressed only in a loin-cloth made out of very soft leather. He said, "I feel very free. I have a young slender body. I guess I must be in my twenties, or early thirties. It's a good body." While he was waiting he decided to go down and wet himself in the stream.

T: I know I'm lying here on the bed in my room, but I can feel the cold water on me. It feels great.

D: *Is it a hot day?*

T: Yes, yes, it is. It's not extremely hot. It's a warm day. And I just piddle around there in the water. The coolness of it feels good all over.

D: *Well, move ahead until something happens.*

T: I can't tell if the woman is there or not. But it's obvious that I'm supposed to meet her there ... to make love. We've done it there. We meet there from time to time. She lives with some people not far away. Not really a village. Just some people that live there.

D: *Do you live in the same place she does?*

T: I stay with her sometimes. Not too much. I travel.

D: *Why do you travel?*

T: (Long pause. Puzzled) I'm a traveler. I'm not carrying anything. I can travel around however I want to, and I seem to be able to get by. I know a lot of people.

D: *You mean you don't have to stay in one place?*

T: No. I move alone. Different groups of people.

D: *Do you have a family?*

T: I have other women like this one. I have children with them, but I don't stay anywhere.

D: *What about a mother or father? That type of a family?*

T: They're gone.

D: *So there is nothing to tie you to a village?*

T: No, nothing except ... they like for me to come around, because there's something I know, something I can say or do for them. It's just strictly intellectual. I tell them things, figure things out for them. Make it easy for them.

D: *See yourself doing whatever that is that you do for these people.*

T: I teach them how to make things. Whatever they need to make. I can do it.

D: *What type of things?*

T: The kinds of things they need to just get by. Tools, weapons, building, whatever. Just help them ... I show them how to do things.

D: *Where did you learn how to do these things?* (Long pause) *What are you seeing?*

T: (Puzzled, trying to understand.) Maybe I came here from a long way off.

D: *What do you mean?*

T: I can't tell where I came from. It's just that I don't know. And I don't know where I learned these things. A lot of it is that I know how to figure things out. And my role is just to go around and show people how to do things. And they're glad to see me come.

D: *But no one in their tribe or in their village knew how to do these things? Is that what you mean?*

T: Not like I can show them. They do things the old ways. I show them how to do things a better way.

D: *That's very helpful for them.*

T: It's a comfortable life.

D: *See yourself doing one of these things, as an example. Of how you showed someone how to do something better.*

T: I can see myself showing some people how to latch some long poles together. They're making the corner of some kind of structure. I don't know what it's for. I'm showing them how to latch them together with some strips of bark, and how to tie the right kind of knots. Simple stuff really.

D: *How did they do it before?*

T: Just half-assed. These people didn't really know how to make anything. Their things were sloppy, and didn't work very well. And I'm showing them how to get things in order. How to control the materials about them. And just make things work for them.

D: *I've always thought that knowledge was handed down in tribes, from one to the other.*

T: No. They'll hand this down for a while, and it'll get askew. And somebody else'll have to show them again.

D: *Is that the way it works?*

T: Yeah. They can't adapt very well.

D: *They can't figure it out?*

T: Not very well.

D: *All right. I want you to see yourself when* you *were being taught these things. Where did you learn them? And you have the answers. You can see where the knowledge comes from.*

T: I got my knowledge in a bright sunny place a long way off. And I don't know how I got from there to where I am.

D: *All right. Tell me about the place where you got the knowledge. What does it look like?*

T: (Surprised) I'll be damned. It's yellow. It's yellow and sandy. I think there's an ocean nearby. It's very flat. And I think I'm probably talking about some aliens. I'm not sure. I don't think I'm one of them, but I'm not sure about that either. And I can't tell you what they look like. They have big black shiny eyes. They don't look like insects, but they .... (confused) I don't know what they look like.

D: *Can you see their faces, or just the eyes?*

T: The eyes are the only thing I can really focus on right now. These big eyes, black eyes, dark. I don't see any pupils in their eyes. They just seem to be great big dark eyes. (Chuckle) They kind of look like sunglasses.

That statement was more important than I realized at the time. I was to encounter the same description when I met the being from the future (Chapter 12).

D: *And you said you don't look like them?*

T: No, no, no. These are probably aliens. I look like a human. I might be ... mixed lineage. I don't know. I know that the children I father are probably going to have a lot easier time than the other ones.

D: *How do you feel about talking with these beings?*

T: I feel as though I'm being manipulated a little bit, but they seem benevolent. I guess it's okay. I'm not really sure why they're doing this.

D: *Can you ask them?*

T: (Pause) I can ask them, but I can't get a straight answer.

D: *What do they say?*

T: A lot of mish-mash about they want to help us, and they like us, and such things as that. And it could be right, but I don't really accept it. But I don't examine it too closely. I think they probably are able to suppress my questions.

D: *But it's not bothering you to talk to them?*

T: No. *They* don't know how to do these things that they're showing me how to do.

D: *They don't?*

T: (Surprised) No. But some way or another they're getting me to figure out how to do the things that need to be done. They don't know what needs to be done, but they can make me able to figure out how to do it. And then after I learn, I go tell all the people.

D: *How are they showing you these things? Are they talking to you or what?*

T: I think they have some kind of telepathy that they use. I can't visualize them talking to me. I can visualize them around watching me do whatever it is they're showing me how to do.

D: *Are you actually doing it, or just seeing it in your mind how to do these things when you're with them.*

T: It could be that I'm just seeing it in my mind, because there's nothing around there. It's just plain yellow. There's nothing there.

D: *Do you feel like you've been there more than this one time?*

T: I don't know. I don't know. I don't even know where it is. It's just some flat yellow place. I feel like there's water nearby.

D: *You said you had a feeling you might be mixed lineage? What did you mean by that?*

T: Yeah. I may be involved in some kind of genetic experiment.

D: *Where is that information coming from?*

T: I have a better mind and a better body than most of the other people. By the time they grow up they're ruined.

D: *From the climate or what?*

T: Just ignorance.

D: *Not knowing how to take care of themselves, you mean?*

T: Yeah. They're not very good in the first place, most of them.

D: *Is that what you meant, that your children will be better?* (Yeah) *All right. I'm going to count to three, and I want you to see how you got to this place where they are teaching you these things. How you arrived there. 1, 2, 3, how did you come to this yellow place?* (Long pause) *What are you seeing?*

T: I can't ... I can't be sure how I got there.

D: *What do you see?*

T: It's in the Mediterranean somewhere. I don't have any way to get there.

D: *What do you mean?*

T: It's in a completely other part of the world. I want to tell you that they're taking me there in some kind of a ship or craft or something, but I can't. I guess I just don't want to answer that question, because I'm afraid I'm making stuff up. I don't know how they got me there.

D: *That's all right. Just trust the answers that come.*

T: Something fast. I feel there are people there that have been in contact with these ... I'm going to say "aliens". I don't know if they're aliens or not. I'm not sure. The whole thing's ridiculous, but it's entertaining, if nothing else.

D: *Something to call them anyway.*

T: I feel it's somewhere around the Mediterranean. And there are people there that have been in contact with these other ... these aliens. And I don't know why they got me involved. But those people are like I am. They have good bodies, they're smart. And when I go out into the jungle, those people are squat and fat and dirty. And not very smart. And I kind of go between the one and the other. (Pleasantly surprised.) And that's the answer that I'm looking for.

D: *What?*

T: I think I'm kind of a link between one group and another group.

D: *Does that make sense to you?*

T: Yeah. Not on any grand scale. I'm not somebody that's a big heavy-duty interpreter for the aliens, or anything like that. I think I've had a role. And it just clicked. This is probably more conscious than unconscious, but it's kind of an epitome that I'm suited for a role of transporting ideas and knowledge from one group to another. I feel like that particular little epitome is going to help me at what I'm doing *here.*

D: *And this is what you think you're best able to do, is be the connection between the two?*

T: Yeah. That's why I'm writing. To transfer ideas.

D: *The main thing is, if it makes sense to you and helps you to understand things.*

T: It hooks together some long-standing fascinations that I've had. That's why I have to suspect whether or not it's an authentic regression into another life. It may be and it may not be. But I think it probably is.

D: *What type of fascinations do you mean?*

T: Thomas has always been fascinated with Phoenicians and Egyptians and Babylonians and South American Indians. And this existence that I'm describing to you, does have a role in all those places and times.

D: *Did you also live in those other times?*

T: I want to say that I did, but I've been fascinated with those times and those places and those peoples, and I've studied about them. So I know enough to say most of the things that I'm saying without having actually been more than just mildly hypnotized. And the alien thing, I probably read enough about them ... that could be a product of reading too.

D: *Yes, but that's the conscious mind trying to analyze.*

T: Why don't you send him out for beer or something.

D: (Chuckle) *That's it. We'll tell the conscious mind to sit over there and talk all it wants, and you're not going to listen to it. But let's go back to that scene, that you said was somewhere in the Mediterranean. And you had the feeling you were moving very fast. Tell me what the surroundings are like when you're moving very fast.*

T: I want to tell you that it's some kind of a flying craft, but I don't entirely trust that.

D: *That's all right. Let your subconscious give you the answers. We will not analyze at this time. We'll do that later. What do you see around you?*

T: Just dark, subdued, kind of gray inside this machine.

D: *Any windows?*

T: In the front, but not back where I am.

D: *Does it have the feeling of being large or small?*

T: Small. Not very big. Kind of a shuttle.

D: *Are you alone, or is there someone with you?*

T: I think there are two aliens operating it. And I can't tell if there are any other humans in it or not. I don't think so. I'm riding in the back. It's some kind of a shuttle craft that they use.

D: *Let's move ahead, and see where the shuttle is taking you. The answers are there. Trust them.*

T: Well, I see it going up to a larger craft. It doesn't come down to the Earth.

D: *How does it enter? Or does it enter?*

T: (Pause) I can't tell.

D: *All right. But do you think that's how you get to the place where the knowledge is given to you?*

T: I don't think they're taking me anyplace else. They're taking me inside this large craft. And maybe that's where it's yellow. I don't know. I don't think so though. I can't tell. I feel like they do something to keep me from being able to tell exactly.

D: *That's all right. You don't want to fight that. Maybe it's for your protection. But you said they give you knowledge, and then you are returned. How are you returned to the place where you have been living?*

T: They fly me back down in the shuttle. And drop me off.

D: *Then you just wander from group to group?*

T: The people in the villages know I'm not like them. They know there are other people like me. They've talked with other people before. They don't know about the aliens.

D: *Is that why they're not afraid of you?*

T: Yeah, they've been helped for a long time.

D: *So they just accept the help?*

T: Yeah. They're good to us when we come around. I don't know any of these other people that do what I do. But I know there are some.

D: *Do the other groups tell you about them?*

T: I'm not sure that they specifically tell me. I don't think they can tell me anything. They don't have languages. They're barely people.

D: *How do they communicate with each other?*

T: They know each other. They live together. They have signs for things. Communicate on an emotional level. They're evolving the means to communicate, but they don't have it yet.

D: *Are they more of an animalistic type of people?*

T: (Long pause) They're not monkeys. They're people. They're just not very well-made.

D: *Do they act animalistic?*

T: No. The animals are clean. These people are not very clean. They're smarter than the animals, but they're weak and dumb. They're evolving.

D: *You said they are not very well-made. What do you mean?*

T: (Long pause) They're not like me. They've got arms and legs and a head, and they don't have any tail. But they're pretty hairy. They don't walk upright all the time. They can, they're just lazy. They're just sorry. It's not their fault.

D: *No, it's not. It sounds like they are a step above the animals.*

T: They're people. They're very early people. Some of them are better than other ones.

D: *This is why your genes will help them? Is that what you mean?* (I thought he might not understand the word "genes".) Your children?

T: I suppose, yes. If they don't kill them off or something.

D: *Is that a possibility?*

T: They'll be different. They'll look more like me.

D: *That's why you're having several children?*

T: No, I'm having several children because it's fun.

D: *That makes sense, too.* (Chuckle) *It sounds like it's also a job.*

T: That's what I do.

D: *These other people that you said were in the Mediterranean, that you saw that were like yourself.* (Yes) *Are they doing the same thing, or do you know?*

T: They're organized. They're not more highly evolved than I am, but they've been doing it longer than I have. Maybe for generations. They're not any smarter. They've just been doing it longer.

D: *They've been doing it in different areas of the world, or what?*

T: It's my perception that these aliens have come and deliberately helped them, and caused these people to evolve.

D: *Do you mean, you think they have helped them to evolve to the state they are?*

T: Yeah, yeah.

D: *And that this is another step?*

T: Yeah. I think probably they're still around.

D: *Still around?*

T: I'm not one of them, I don't think. I don't know. Naw. I think we're getting over into a theory that Thomas carries around with him. And there's probably something more productive to look at.

D: *But do you think the people in the other parts of the world, that these other ones like you are helping, are they all at the same stage of development? I guess I want to say "the natives" that they are helping. Are they all at the same stage of development?*

T: I can't tell. I don't know. I doubt it. On a general evolutionary scale they're all about the same stage probably. But if you were going to compare them with one another, of course some of them are ahead, some of them way behind.

D: *Well, the people you are helping, what type of an environment do they live in?*

T: They live in a jungle, but it's not a tropical jungle. It's not really a forest either. It's not an equatorial jungle. It's away from the equator. It's a subtropical jungle. It has ... I can't tell what kind of trees it has. I don't recognize any of the trees. I don't know what they are.

D: *You mean the leaves look different or what?*

T: They're very tall. I don't see that part of them. I don't see any conifers. Maybe some conifers, but not the same kind. I'm just not familiar with these kind of trees. I don't know what they are.

D: *Is there anything there that is familiar to you?*

T: Fish. Grass. Small animals.

D: *What do the small animals look like?*

T: (Long pause) Birds, monkeys.

D: *Do you see any animals you don't recognize?*

T: I recognize all the animals I see, but I don't know ... I can't tell you what they look like. (Laugh)

D: *They're familiar to you, is that what you mean?* (Uh-huh) *You said the trees were strange. None of the animals are strange to you?*

T: They're different. I'm familiar with the trees and the animals. The person from whose perspective I'm looking is familiar with them, and comfortable among them. But they don't translate. *I* don't know what they are.

D: *They don't translate to Thomas.*

T: No, I don't know what they are.

D: *All right. Do they look like anything Thomas has seen?*

T: Vaguely. They're not bizarre. It's as if you took the trees that *I* know, and crossed them and interbred them and made different species. They'd be recognizable as trees, and they'd seem similar to the ones I know, but they wouldn't be the same. They'd be different.

D: *Is it the same thing with the animals?* (Yeah) *Then it is a basic animal, but it's not something you recognize as Thomas.* (Yeah) *All right then. We can shift back to the other mind, the mind of the eyes that you're looking through. I just wanted to see if there was anything there we could recognize and relate to. And these other people, these ones you are trying to instruct. Do they live in shelters?*

T: Most of them are starting to live in shelters. That's one of the things I'm showing them how to do. They've been shown before.

D: *And they didn't remember, or didn't carry it over, you mean?*

T: It just doesn't stick very long.

D: *Where did they normally live, before you taught them how to build shelters?*

T: They just wandered around and lived wherever they could. Maybe they'd stay in a cave for a while, maybe they'd live in a tree for a while. It's pretty much like they're wild. They just do whatever they have to do.

D: *What do they normally eat?*

T: Roots. Just whatever they can find.

D: *Do they eat meat?*

T: Yeah, they eat anything.

D: *Do they cook it, or can you see them doing anything like that?*

T: I try to show them how to do that, but they don't have the patience. Sometimes they do, sometimes they don't. They're not organized enough to do that.

D: *I'm curious about these people. Can you tell if they have any teeth?*

T: (Pause, as though looking) Yeah, they have teeth.

D: *Are they like your teeth?*

T: (Pause) Their canines are longer. Not a whole lot, just a little.

D: *Then they are able to chew food.*

T: Yeah. They're dirty.

D: *Is that mostly because they're so hairy?*

T: No. They're just dirty. Animals clean themselves. Animals take care of themselves. These people don't do that very much. Even their teeth are dirty. They don't live very long.

D: *Why not?*

T: They're dirty. They don't know how to take care of themselves. They're just lazy, and not very smart. They get hurt, they get sick. They're not much good. It's not their fault.

D: *No. They just don't know any difference. It's no one's fault. Well, the people that are like you, do they live longer?*

T: I can live as long as I want to, I think.

D: *You don't have any set limits?*

T: I'm sure there are some. I'm not immortal. I can get hurt. I can get sick. I can die. I can be killed.

D: *But you think you can live as long as you want, if those things don't happen?*

T: Eventually one of them will happen. Somewhere back in my head I've got the idea that the aliens will protect me. And if I get hurt they'll fix me up. But I don't really believe it. Maybe in as much as it serves their purposes.

D: *And you're pretty much on your own otherwise.* (Yeah) *But when you were given the knowledge that you're supposed to pass on to the natives, do you think it was a one time thing? Or do you go back and forth?* (Long pause) *What feels right?*

T: I think they take me in and check on me from time to time. I don't know what they do. But I kind of feel like it's a sustained contact. Monitoring maybe, more than anything else.

D: *That's what it feels like?*

T: Right now it does, yeah.

D: *I'm going to ask you to drift back to a time when you must have been very young. I want you to see the place you were born and where you grew up. When you must have had parents or something, and you were a child. What does that place look like? What impressions do you get?*

T: An island. A small island.

D: *Tell me about it.*

T: A coastal island. I live by the ocean. Gentle people.

D: *Your parents?*

T: I don't know who my parents are. Everybody takes care of me.

D: *What do they look like?*

T: (Long pause) I can't visualize them. Just people. I keep seeing blond people. I don't know if they're my parents though.

D: *Are there several people there?*

T: There isn't any *where* for these several people to be. When you asked me to visualize my parents, I visualized a few countenances. And the first ones were, I think, blond. And I didn't connect them with any particular place.

D: *But these people are different from the other groups you were looking at.*

T: Yeah, these people are ... *people.* Tall, slender, humans. Nice people.

D: *So that means you didn't grow up with the other group. Is that correct?*

T: That's true.

D: *I'm going to ask your subconscious a question. Just allow whatever it says, whatever impressions, to come forth. That life we are looking at, that entity, was he conceived in the normal way that we consider conception? I'm asking Thomas' subconscious for the information, because it has all the answers. I'm asking Thomas' subconscious if the entity whose lifetime we are looking at, the one who spread the knowledge with the people, was he conceived in a normal manner?*

T: The group that he lived with was genetically engineered. And among them he was conceived normally. His mother was a dark-skinned woman who didn't understand what was happening to her. His father was a human that the aliens had ... made.

D: *I'm trying to understand. Was the dark-skinned woman a member of that hairy group?*

T: No. No, she was a woman they brought to this island.

D: *And the father was who?*

T: He was a human that the aliens had made. He was genetically engineered.

D: *Was he one of the hairy people?*

T: No, no. He was blond, and tall. And he lived on that island with several dark-skinned women who didn't know each other. They came from different places. But they weren't hairy women.

D: *How do you mean the father was genetically engineered?*

T: The aliens brought him there. They made him. They brought the women there, but they collected them from indigenous people.

D: *Then some of the indigenous people on Earth at that time were hairy, and some were not. Is that correct?*

T: That's true.

D: *But the father was made by the aliens. You said engineered. He was created.*

T: Not created. He was made out of flesh, but they arranged his genes to make him the way he was. He wasn't conceived normally.

D: *Did he come from Earth?*

T: I don't know.

D: *But he was ... I'm wanting to say "manipulated" in a laboratory. Would that be right?*

T: His genes were manipulated before he was born. They used a woman. I don't know how they did it, but it wasn't a normal birth.

D: *What is the purpose of that?*

T: (Pause) There's a word. But I can never use the damn word. It gets away from me. I know it. If you say the word to me, I'll recognize it. It's a word that means "take advantage of", but not exactly.

D: (I was trying to think.) *It's not "manipulate."*

T: It's what the white people did to the Indians.

D: *I think I know what you mean. I can't think of the word either. Well, maybe it will come to you. But why would they want to manipulate genes, to make the father and then to interbreed. What would be the purpose of all that?*

T: (Long pause) To evolve humans. To evolve civilization.

D: *It sounds like a good motive really.*

T: Naw, not necessarily.

D: *Why not?*

T: They're going to make something out of it. That word. I can't get that word. But that's what they're doing.

D: *But why wouldn't it be a good thing?*

T: It's not necessarily good, it's not necessarily bad. It's just ....

D: *Well, it's a betterment of the species. Would that be right?*

T: When they came here there were human beings. And the human beings were evolving in their own way. And they changed it. At least temporarily. And they brought some good things, but there's something that they're trying to get out of it.

D: *You mean they had other reasons also.*

T: Sure. They had their own reasons. They turn things to their own purposes.

D: *But if the human beings had been left alone, would they have evolved in the same direction as they have now? That's the question.*

T: I don't think so. Not exactly.

D: *Were the humans that were here the hairy type?*

T: No, no. They were humans that were human. Those other people, that are dumb, are the product of the aliens manipulating the animals and the subhuman species, and evolving them into humans. But the humans that were already here evolved on their own.

D: *I see. I thought you meant that the hairy people were the only ones on Earth at that time. The most advanced species. It wasn't like that?*

T: I don't believe so. I believe there were some humans. It's probably all intermixed by now. That might all be for the best.

D: *Why were they doing all this?*

T: It wasn't moving along fast enough to suit them.

D: *In the natural evolution?*

T: Yeah. They wanted to help it out a little bit.

D: *Do you know if someone told them to do this?*

T: I don't have that information.

D: *All right. Let's return to the person that is teaching the others the knowledge. The man with the dark hair and dark skin. I want you to move ahead in his life. And I want you to go to the last day of his life in that lifetime. And see what happened to him. It won't bother you at all to look at it. You can look at it as an observer if you want to. I will count to three, and we'll move ahead to the last day of his life. 1, 2, 3, we've moved ahead to the last day of his life in that life. What do you see? What's happening?*

T: He's standing on the cliff overlooking the stream. And he just left the stream, and he's walking back through the jungle.

D: (Long pause) *What happens?*

T: He just walks into the jungle and disappears.

D: *How do you mean?*

T: He just disappeared.

D: *His body disappeared or what?*

T: He's gone. He just ... disappeared.

D: *Let's ask your subconscious, what happened to the body?*

T: He just didn't want to be that anymore. So he just quit *being.*

D: *Then what happened to the body?*

T: It just disappeared. It's not there. It's gone. Dissolved. Disappeared. It's gone.

D: *Then the spirit just went on?*

T: Not with that identity. That man said, "I don't want to do this anymore." And he quit. That was all of it. And whatever made up his identity had a life to live spiritually, and went back to wherever it came from. And he just didn't exist anymore.

D: *I see. He left that behind then. All right. I think that was something important for you to find out about. I want you to leave that scene now.*

I brought Tom forward in time and oriented him back to the present day. I did not awaken him yet because I still had a few questions to ask him.

D: *I'm going to ask Thomas' subconscious, is there anything he needs to learn from watching that life, that he can use in his present life? There's something he needs to know. I think he got a part of it a while ago.* (Long pause)

T: Well, he's interested in reasons for why his existence is like it is. I think I got some of the reasons. I don't know what I'm supposed to do with them just offhand. I think it's going to help me make this decision that I've got to make.

D: *There's probably much more there than you realize. It's going to take a while to understand it all, and to apply it to your life now.*

T: I think I'll probably have a dream pretty soon that will tell me what I need to do.

D: *Yes, that would be a very good idea. That is often the way the subconscious chooses to relay information, if we can only understand the symbolism.*

T: That existence that I was just looking at .... Maybe I'm going to have some more contact with that ... I don't know. I'm not sure the guy's body really disappeared. It might be that particular facet of his person just left him at that point.

D: *It's interesting to contemplate. The way you were smiling, it doesn't seem like a negative idea if you did have contact again.*

T: Well, if it could leave like that, that means it could come back like that.

D: *Well, we had access to it just now, so it's always there.*

It would seem that a lifetime where Tom's main job was to impregnate as many women as possible, would be an ideal fantasy trip for a man considered to be a ladies' man and who enjoys the company of women. But it doesn't fit that picture, because it would hardly seem a fantasy to romance women that were hairy, dirty, dumb and utterly repulsive to him. Even though he understood the circumstances, and knew that the condition of these early people was no fault of their own. No, this regression sounds more like a true memory than a romantic fantasy.

It added another piece to the puzzle I was putting together about the origin of life on this planet. It showed the continuing influence of aliens in the evolution and development of our species. All of these stories had a common theme and a pattern unknown to the participants, but which was becoming increasingly more revealed to me.

If all these cases were fantasies, why weren't there blatant and obvious contradictions? Why did they follow a predictable bizarre pattern?

CHAPTER TWELVE

A FUTURE BEING TALKS TO NOW

One theory about present-day sightings of UFOs and aliens is that they may not be from other planets or dimensions. They could be our own descendants. Time travelers from our own future. This case explores this possibility when the subject unexpectedly progressed to a future life, rather than regressing to a past life.

*Pro*gression is as possible as *re*gression since there is no such thing as *time* to the subconscious mind. In Volume Two of *Conversations with Nostradamus* John went forward 200 years to see if Nostradamus' prophecies of our world were true. On many occasions I have progressed an entire room full of people into future lives. It is amazing that many report similar circumstances, environments and events during this type of experiment. One common theme that is repeated in many of these future progressions is that something drastic has happened to the surface of our planet.

One woman saw herself working in a space station laboratory that was obiting the Earth. She was part of a scientific team that was growing food by hydroponic methods in the absence of gravity. Another saw herself working in a submerged underwater laboratory doing the same thing, harvesting food from the sea, kelp, seaweed, etc. In both cases they reported that something had happened and the Earth was no longer able to grow sufficient food. Experiments were being done to provide food for the remaining people of Earth. I have had these type of scenarios come forth not only during group progressions in the United States, but also when I conducted them in England and Australia. I can only hope these people are seeing a possible alternate future, and not a future that necessarily *has* to be. The following case could also be a *probable* future.

Pam was a former school teacher that had moved to our area with her husband. We had worked together off and on for several years, and she had proven to be an excellent subject who was open to experimentation. It had been many months since we had a session, while I was busy with other subjects and topics. She decided to begin sessions again, but we were not looking for anything in particular. On this day in the spring of 1988 when I went to their house for the session, we had no idea what direction it would take. Her husband, Richard, was present and operated his own tape recorder.

There are many methods of induction, but Pam preferred the tunnel method. We decided to try this and just see where it took us, rather than looking for anything specific. In this method I had her walk down a long tunnel, using deepening techniques at the same time. She was instructed to keep walking until she could see a light at the end of the tunnel. She would then tell me what she saw as she emerged from the tunnel into the light. She was so accustomed to this technique that I knew she would subconsciously travel somewhere, although I did not know what scene she would come into.

D: *Now you're out of the tunnel. Look around and tell me what you see.*

P: The tunnel is not a mental trick. It actually does exist. And it seems that I am *in* the planet, under the ground. As I walked down the tunnel, I saw a being standing there and I just moved into this being. I was fascinated by the merging that seemed to take place. So as I continued walking down the tunnel I was aware of wearing a silver suit that covered my entire body. It was a surprise because I now feel as though I am in two places at once. I can move and be with this body. I feel it is *me*, but I'm also observing from a distance.

D: *Maybe that's better. You can be objective that way.*

P: Well, I feel like the reporter. I am fascinated with the tunnel. It is cool, and the walls are totally smooth and seamless. They are purposely constructed, domed so it's like an arch. There seems to be light, but I don't really know where it's coming from. There are no light bulbs. It just seems like the tunnel is bright. And it seemed that, as I put my hand on the side of the tunnel, I could receive information. So it is like a storage center for *much* information. As you were speaking I came to the end of the tunnel, and I was looking into a room that was filled with computer-type things. It looked like the inside of Star Trek, with computer banks all around. The room was round. And all around, from floor to *very* high -- not all the way to the ceiling, because it couldn't be reached -- but there were many, many technology-looking things and technicians who looked just like me. We all seemed to be dressed the same, except that I didn't see faces. Then I seemed to go back into the tunnel. And I saw a *bright* light at the end of the tunnel. And when I got there, it was *blinding* light. That was all I saw, just white, bright. And it was very familiar, because I know this place. So I said to myself to calm down and look around. And when I did, it seemed there was another round room. In the middle there was this big pyramid-shaped object, but it was made out of mineral. It looked like half of a (hard to transcribe because I didn't know what it was) fluorite duodecahedron (phonetic). (Richard seemed to understand.) But it was huge. I don't want to call it a crystal because it didn't actually look like a crystal that I'm familiar with. But it did look like a fluorite shape that I'm familiar with. And it did seem crystalline or glass-*like*, and to be of immense energy and power. It seemed that my function had something to do with this bright room and this pyramid-shaped power source in the middle.

D: *Was it transparent?*

P: You couldn't see all the way through it *clearly*, but, yes, I would consider it transparent, with a violet color cast.

D: *Then it was not opaque.*

P: Not totally. If there were something on the other side of it, you couldn't actually see all the way through it, so it wasn't transparent like glass. But it wasn't totally opaque either.

D: *And it was shaped like a pyramid?*

P: It had four sides that came down. It was on some kind of flat base. The base that I see now looks pretty much like a light box base that I've seen. I'm talking really big though, bigger than a human being. That's all that was in this room, but it was filled with light. I am wondering now if the light came from this crystal object or somewhere else.

D: *You said it was used for some type of power?*

P: It seems to be *filled* with power and energy. Not necessarily generating, but potential energy.

D: *What do you think this power is used for?*

P: I thought if I put my hands on it I would find out. So ....

D: *Are you allowed to do that?*

P: I seem to be sort of in charge of this room. So it seems I can do what I want to. (She laughed)

D: *I was wondering if it would hurt you in any way.*

P: In response to that question, the answer came that if my intent were not right I would be hurt, yes. But I don't have malice or bad intent, so .... Um, that's interesting how it would be able to ascertain what my intent is. I just answered my question on how it would be able to ascertain my intent. It could know my intent because of my vibrations. We are vibrating every moment, and what we hold in our mind does affect our vibration. It is attuned to vibrations, so that was the answer to my query about how it knows what my intent is.

D: *Then what would happen if you touched it?*

P: I'll give it a try. (Long pause) It seems to contain anything you wish to know.

D: *Like an information bank or something?*

P: It is much like the walls of the tunnel, which seem metallic. This seems to be the entire repository. It seems to be -- this is all too weird -- the repository of *all*, everything that people have thought they "know". A repository of all *thought* that has transpired.

D: *I thought when you said it produced power, maybe it was power that was being used for generating, for instance.*

P: I'm pretty sure that it isn't generating, but that it is potential energy. And I believe that it is held in abeyance until called for. At which time whatever the call is, it can generate what that is. What is so strange about it *is* its multi-purpose. You can be as mundane with this great source of power, or as cosmic as your intent guides you to be. I might even be able to generate electrical power for the entire *planet.*

D: *All you have to do is touch it, and you're able to do these things?*

P: *Because* thought is a specific vibration. I don't know how it's stored in there. But the intent of your thoughts is a vibration that connects you with what you are looking *for*. If my intent were to generate electricity, (Surprise) I could do that.

D: *It comes from your mind originally then.*

P: Yes. I get stuff like .... All thought is vibration, and once it is thought it continues to exist. Thoughts aren't destroyed. Thoughts are energy.

This description of the crystal pyramid sounded very familiar to me. In my book *Jesus and the Essenes* there was a similar device in the library at Qumran, the home of the Essenes on the cliffs overlooking the Dead Sea in Israel. A huge pyramid-shaped crystal sat on a pedestal, and the Master of the Mysteries was the only person who knew how to use the energy that it generated. The students would channel their energy to him, so he could direct it in many different ways. In my book *Keepers of the Garden* there were Energy Directors on other planets whose job was to direct energy to be used by the population. That energy could be used as electicity or took many other forms, depending on what was required. Giant crystals were also used to generate energy in the ancient civilization of Atlantis. But in that case the use of the energy was abused, and this was a contributing factor in Atlantis' destruction.

D: *And you said, you are more or less in charge of this room?*
P: Yes. It's a very stark room. It's dome-shaped. Very big. Round. The only thing in the room, as I look around, seems to be this pyramid. It has four sides, but it comes in also on the four sides a small amount before it rests on the base. It looks so much like a fluorite crystal on a light base. But that is all that seems to be in the room. And there are many of these round rooms. It's similar to a whole *ant-farm* down here underground. The rooms and the tunnels all seem to be lined with metallic substance, and they *all* seem to be *filled* with information.
D: *But you think you are associated with that room?*
P: It's a job, and I like it. I can go anywhere in the tunnel though. I don't feel restricted. I'm walking down one, and at the end of *this* tunnel is a door. It's actually two halves together. They slide up and I can go into this big cavernous room. But right now they're closed and I'm just standing there looking at these huge doors.
D: *Is that a room that you often go into?*
P: It doesn't seem off limits. I think I'll have to ask the doors to open. So I will. Now I'm looking in the room. I'm going in a few steps. It's just a bare round, domed room. It's totally flooded with blue light. I can't see where the light's even coming from. It feels good in there.
D: *What is the purpose of that room?*
P: (Sudden laugh.) Wow! It seems that beings that are *off* the planet can be transported into this room, so they can materialize themselves. This is the incoming chamber. The whole room is filled with the blue light, but there's a column

of more intense light beaming down. A beam. And as I stand and look at the column of light, there's a bunch of glitter now. And I know that something is going to materialize in the column of light. Somebody's coming in.

D: *Is this what it looks like, glitter?*

P: Like whirling glitter. Like molecules reassembling, but they're all made of light, so they sparkle. It seems that this is a very critical time. The time of teletransporation, when the -- I want to say the "essences" -- are made physical. So it's really an intense and important time. It seems that at this time of *physical* manifesting in this room, there are not usually observers, because this is *so* critical. I cannot think of the correct term. The process *is* delicate. And surely we want nothing to happen in *this* phase that would in any way inhibit or change or affect the being or beings who are coming in.

D: *Then normally no one is watching when this happens?*

P: That is correct. That is also why there is no object in this room. No *anything* except this light. In the column in the center of the room I see just swirling and glitter, and I know that this will assemble into a being. I know that I'm trying not to breathe very much, because even the act of breathing could affect this very delicate operation. So I'm trying not to inhibit or injure this delicate procedure in any way. I will step outside and allow the doors to close for a moment.

All during this section about the teleportation room her voice was noticeably quivering as well as her hands and body.

P: I am awed that I saw the glitter. It seems that I must not be privy to *every* big thing that happens under here in this city.

D: *Then it is unusual to see that part?*

P: It feels very unusual, very special.

This sounded very similar to Star Trek, "Beam me up, Scotty." But then I wonder where did Gene Roddenberry get his ideas? Maybe science fiction is really more science fact then we realize. In one of my UFO cases a woman reported a room onboard a craft where her molecules were broken down into what appeared to be whirling glitter, and then reassembled.

D: *Are beings transported this way very often?*

P: This is a room specifically designed for that purpose, although it does not seem to be used very often. It seems that it is an occasion that merits great excitement.

D: *Then you don't have visitors come this way very often, in your life then.*

P: No. Only those who spend most of their time *off* the planet. I just realized that I seem to spend most of my time between the room with the large crystal and this room where the teletransportation takes place. And I realized that one of my functions is to *graciously* receive visitors. I must be some kind of greeter. I didn't know that.

D: *Is there equipment there that you have to operate?*

P: No. The equipment is doors that open and close. That is operated by thought. So I don't actually have mechanical apparatus to manipulate. My function seems to be one of greeting and making guests feel at ease and comfortable. It seems that I have a highly developed sense of empathy with a large range of different beings. This is a quality not shared by *all* beings in the tunnel. So that actually qualifies me for the job of greeter. For empathy is not something you could read in a textbook, or even be taught by another individual. It comes from personal experience. So I must be really *old*, I guess.

D: *These type of feelings are something that the others are not as familiar with?*

P: Hmmm. It just seems that I have *more*. And it seems that I have this job because it most -- I was going to say "perfectly", but I don't like that word. -- It most *best* fits my qualifications. It's very hard to feel empathy for some of the visitors that we receive, when they are so very different from us. And yet I seem to be okay with it. I'm not shocked or judgmental or afraid.

D: *You mean that some of the beings that come through the teleportation room do not have the same physical characteristics?*

P: That's correct.

D: *Can you tell me something about these other beings?*

P: I am familiar with hairy-looking things that definitely don't look like us. More like -- well, this is a strange way to say this, but they are similar to artist's renditions of Bigfoot-type beings. I am also familiar with something that is like a mask.

D: *What do you mean?*

P: Their faces look rubbery, like a mask. *Looks* like masks. Like Star Wars' characters.

D: *Do you think it might not be their real faces?*

P: Well, it's their natural appearance. There are millions of different types of beings that exist. Or more than millions, an infinite number. I've seen some pretty strange ones, so I was just trying to describe *in general.*

D: *What do* you *look like?*

P: (Sigh) I can tell you what we look like from the back.

D: *Do you feel uncomfortable looking at the faces?*

P: The face I see is the face that's on the cover of *Communion*, and .... It doesn't bother me. It's just that I feel too left brain, although twelve years ago I also saw this form while in meditation. It has a larger head than proportionate to the way the human head is to the body. The head is larger, thin neck and thinner arms and legs. Small body, maybe four feet or around there. All covered with the same garment. The face ... I just am more comfortable always looking at the back. I can even look at the back of myself. It's weird.

D: *Can you see your hands?*

P: Yes, the fingers are longer. (She laughed.) Well, that's funny. I should have *more* fingers, there are only four. Actually as I'm looking at it now they look skeleton-like. Very bony and long.

D: *What about your feet?*

P: Covered. I can't see my feet. I can feel I am standing secure. I don't actually observe any difference though.

D: *Okay. Do you eat food?*

P: Well, I don't know, so I'll look around and see.

D: *See what comes to mind. What kind of sustenance would you take?*

P: Well, this is really interesting. (She laughed.) It's some kind of very sweet liquid, like a nectar. It's a liquid diet, it's sweet, and it *smells wonderful*.

From her facial indications it was evident that she could really smell it.

D: *Does it remind you of any particular smell?*

P: Of flowers. I thought immediately that it came from flowers.

D: *How do you take it into your body?*

P: I guess I drink it. My mouth's watering. (She laughed.)

D: *See yourself doing it. How would you take it into your body?*

P: (Confused) Well, I almost felt like I *breathed* it in, in a vapor form. That's why it smelled so good. I inhale the elixir, but I can taste it. We do have mouths, and we do swallow. You can inhale through your mouth as well as through your nose. It's a very *thick* essence. (She seemed confused as to how to convey this.)

D: *It has more substance that just the odor then. Does it have a color?*

P: I would say golden would be a good color name.

D: *Do you have any teeth?*

P: I don't appear to have teeth, no. I don't have the chewing sensation, but I do swallow. A tongue. There is taste. But smell is really predominant.

D: *That's one of the main senses? Would that be a right word?*

P: Well, in the *joy* of eating. (She laughed.) Smelling is almost euphoric. It's a wonderful sensation. The aroma is so perfumed. And we know by inhaling this aroma we are perpetuating that physical form, so it's a joyous and conscious thing. Humans aren't aware that when they eat food they're actually replenishing their *living being*. Most humans don't keep those thoughts in mind when they eat. But we *are* aware.

D: *Are you also sensitive to other smells?*

P: Well, we have highly developed olfactory senses.

D: *Do you vocalize? Do you use words in communication?*

P: Very interesting. We do have absolute thought transference, so it is not necessary at all to speak words. However, it seems that we do have vocal cords, because we make a sound that's melodious. And by making different tones we access different -- umm, the word is "emotion". Hmmm, how interesting. Tones, yes, we make, and we understand when we hear a tone what the person is intending.

D: *Is there anything else that is different about the body and the way it functions?*

P: Well, we don't have your usual elimination system.

D: *None at all?*

P: It's through the skin. In humans also, the skin is part of the elimination apparatus. But with us, through skin and suit. More like evaporation. Not an unpleasant or offensive thing in any way to any one.

D: *Then those organs are nonexistent?*

P: They seem to be more like the appendix, sort of remnants but not functioning.

D: *What about lungs? The respiratory system?*

P: It seems that we breathe, definitely. Let's see, lungs seem to be there, heart. There *are* organs.

D: *Blood? Circulatory system?*

P: Yes, I see blood ... I see a heart and I can see all of that. In fact, it seems very similar to the human body internally, although some of the organs just don't function any more, because there's no reason.

D: *Have they become atrophied?*

P: Yeah, atrophied would be a word. But there is a word beyond atrophied that I can't access right at this moment.

D: *I was thinking if they weren't functioning they eventually would just shut down, and disappear.*

P: As the appendix stills remains in humans through many, many, many years of physical evolution, so too do we maintain organs that we no longer use.

D: *What is your skin like?*

P: *Very* thin. As a matter of fact, it's just about transparent. You can definitely see veins.

D: *What color is the skin?*

P: Almost transparent. But very, very, very, very light. Almost white.

D: *Does it seem like human skin, or is it a different consistency to the touch?*

P: These are interesting questions because skin is not something that we look on very often. As I try to really look at a body, everything, even hands and faces, seem to be covered by a protective film that looks like skin. Even though I have on a suit, under the suit I have a film that *entirely* envelops my body, face and hands. The skin is just too fragile, too porous. It has to be protected. All parts.

D: *You mean the skin can be damaged easily?*

P: Oh, yes. Even by just blowing really hard on it.

D: *Does this* film *look like your skin?*

P: Yes. To anyone who is not one of us, they would assume that it is our skin.

D: *It is covering the head and every part of the body under the suit?*

P: Right. But there are holes for our nose and our mouth and our eyes, so it just looks like skin.

D: *This way it would be rather expressionless, wouldn't it?*

P: Oh, we don't have very much in the way of physical facial expressions, because our thoughts and emotions are immediately known to each other. Unlike humans, who *must* use many, many gestures and facial expressions in order to impart what they are *attempting* to say to another.

D: *Yes, we use body language.*

P: It is not necessary, so it seems the facial muscles have long since atrophied too.

D: *Because I was thinking this* mask, *so to speak, would ....*

P: That's a very good way to think of it. Mask-like. Because most beings ... let me think, (Pause) I can't think of any beings that don't, so I'll say *all* that I'm aware of. All beings who are trying to interact with humans don't use vocal or facial or body language to make their thoughts known. It is *all* through the realm of mental telepathy. So humans misinterpret movements and *stiff* faces, as scary or mean or something. When in fact it's just because humans can't read their minds. Their minds are loving.

Imagine how strange we must look to these aliens with our faces constantly moving, especially our mouths grimacing as well as talking. Then add to that how we use our hands to emphasize points of conversations with gestures. We must look pretty bizarre or even frightening to these gentle creatures who long ago learned to communicate in a more fully honest way, with complete mind-to-mind telepathy where no mistakes can be made in interpretation. The first requirement of mental communication is complete honesty, because it would be useless to use trickery when your every thought is known. It also explains why a face with no expression appears frightening to us or makes us feel uneasy. Without body language we have nothing to relate to.

Maybe we will relearn the telepathic form of communication in the future. I say *re*learn it, because in my work with hypnosis and exploring the past I have discovered that the people of Atlantis were extremely adept at using the powers of the mind. These abilities were taken away (and justly so) so they could not be further abused. We are on our way to regaining them. Let us hope that this time we will use them in the proper ways.

I continued with my questioning about the physical makeup of this underground future dweller.

D: *Is this elixir the only thing that you see yourself taking into your body?*

P: Light is the other thing that is essential for continuance in this particular form.

D: *Can you explain what you mean?*

P: We must have light baths pretty regularly.

D: *What is that?*

P: While we're in *inner* space (beneath the surface) we go to a round room in which we lie on tables. Also very stark, like concrete picnic tables. And we're bathed in light. We actually sleep in a light bath also, a different color. It's an indigo when we are sleeping. But when we are taking our fuel bath, it's much brighter. I see it varying in color, depending on the specific need of the individual.

D: *Did you say "fuel" bath?*

P: Fuel, yes. Because like the elixir -- that is what I want to call the food -- the light is fuel.

D: *And the different colors are different types of energies that you would need or what?*

P: It depends on how long we've been away from the light bath. It's almost like recharging a battery. It is just as constant as food and water for humans. Light and elixir are absolutely essential continuing things to keep the body going. If the time period, for some reason, has been an extended one ... and by extended, it seems that I only mean "hours", not days.

D: *You couldn't go too long without it then.*

P: No, and if a *long* period had ensued, more than whatever the prescribed time is, then the intensity would be increased. I see that low ebb requires a sharper red-orange-yellow. Very, very intense. If you went at the prescribed time you would be bathed in a relatively golden glow. That's very beautiful at the end of the bath, because it transmutes into a very soft pink. It's very uplifting and mellow, and you're ready to go back about your business. But while you're receiving the yellow-gold, the regular intensity, if you "light" on schedule -- instead of "eat" on schedule. (Smiling about her pun.) While you're receiving that, it's not quite as mellow. It's just a feeling of rejuvenation.

D: *Then it's more intense if you've gone longer without it.*

P: Absolutely.

D: *What would happen if you didn't get it at the required time?*

P: I think the physical being ceases to function.

D: *They get weaker and weaker?*

P: Let me see. (Pause) Well, there would be no reason that you couldn't get to the light. The variable would be, if for some reason your job kept you from getting there at the necessary time. But it seems that no matter what, if you could not, if you had not the strength to get to the room, that somebody would carry you to the room.

D: *Then there would be no reason you couldn't get to it.*

P: Right. If you couldn't get there on your own, you would be taken care of. I also know that we can go to the surface. At which time we are constantly bathed in a light that is very, very rejuvenating. Very intense. And we can operate for a period of time, but there reaches a point of saturation. At which time we go back to the less intensity of our underground world. It seems that on this planet my society, that I'm viewing now, lives most of the time inside. This could be Earth. I don't have names or anything going through my head as I ask myself.

D: *What is the source of that light on the surface?*

P: Ummm. It's an external orb. Probably another planet reflecting light, or a star or a sun. Looks like *our* sun to me as I look at it.

D: *What about the terrain on the surface? Does it look like Earth or is it different?*

P: I unfortunately see no vegetation.

D: *Do your eyes seem to function?*

P: Yes, they function quite well, although they must be protected. They are covered with a solid black shield of some sort. It reminds me of sunglasses. The eyes are very delicate and sensitive, just like the rest of the body. I don't see the body being able to survive without these protective devices. I have something like a helmet on while I'm on the surface. I have a pack on my back with tubes connected to the helmet. And just my same silver suit. I think it should be noted that we receive light *through* this suit. I don't see us *ever* taking off the suit.

D: *Maybe you use it to process the light in some way.*

P: I don't know. The only thing that's different is this pack and the helmet.

D: *Do you have ears?*

P: (Pause) I can hear. Frankly, looking from the back, I don't see any.

D: *Any kind of opening or anything.*

P: Well, yes, there is like an opening. If you were to cut your external ear off, you'd still have an opening. Yes, that's what it is, because I just turned to the side. It's not as big a hole as a human ear opening, even without the auricle. But I'm totally capable of hearing, really well, actually.

D: *I was curious as to why you had to live underground. Do you have any reason that comes to mind?*

P: Only the gas.

D: *The gas?*

P: One of the reasons we wear a helmet on the surface is because of the odor. Of course, the gases themselves are rather poisonous, so we wouldn't want to breathe them anyway. A small "hit" of the gas without the helmet wouldn't automatically make the physical form collapse and die. It would be some exposure. It's not *that* potent. But the smell is *very* strong and unpleasant.

D: *I was thinking you might be more sensitive than humans would be.*

P: To smells, yes.

D: *Could you think what that gas smells like? Was there a predominant smell in it?*

P: My very first response to that was "rotten eggs".

D: *Sulfur.*

P: A rotten smell. It's thick, too.

D: *The air is thick, you mean, or the smell?*

P: It's a predominant haze, so the gas seems thick. The atmosphere seems so full of this.

I returned to asking questions about the being's physical composition.

D: *Are you any sex? Male or female?*
P: I'm not a sex, but I seem to be a class.
D: *What do you mean?*
P: We don't differentiate by sex. And that made me think of reproduction, and I can't answer that yet. I want to answer your question about class. It seems that it is a privilege to be able to go to the surface at this point in our history. Not *all* of us are allowed to the surface. So instead of *sexual* differentiation there is some kind of "pecking order", I guess.
D: *Like some type of a caste order, you mean?*
P: No, because I feel that it's a very loving, open, equalitarian society. And yet I feel there are privileges extended to *some*, and I'm in that privileged class.
D: *That's what you mean by "class". But there's no sex, per se. Are you androgynous?*
P: Androgynous, to my way of thinking, means possessing both male and female characteristics. I'm looking for physical attributes, because I am only thinking about Earth reproduction. But, in fact, we have cloning down pat. No, there is not sexual reproduction.
D: *Can you explain what you mean? How the procreation process would be done?*
P: (Sadly) Unfortunately I see no new entities. I only see cloning. Because we are sexual creatures we tend to think that every other species throughout the cosmos must be the same. But I am getting the information that androgyny is the *norm* throughout the universe. I do not perceive any male, female per se. There are different personalities who could be *considered* feminine or masculine. Sexuality is unique to humans. It is very unusual to reproduce by using two separate sexes. This is why extraterrestrials are so fascinated with our methods of reproduction.
D: *Then we are the unusual ones, with our two separate sexes.*

P: That we have taken it to this degree, yes. You might even consider it two separate species. (I found that remark intriguing.) Reproducing the species is something necessary to any life form. *Sexual* reproduction, however, does seem to be of, although a *fun* form, a lower vibration. There are times of absolute transcendence that take place during the act of love. During the act of *sex* however, this rarely occurs. So it is not what happens every time there is sexual reproduction. The moments of transcendence that are experienced by Earth beings are also experienced by those who do not have human form. But they don't necessarily come from the same reasons, from a physical union. When the intelligent being reaches the point of total awareness of the cosmic flow, of being one with All That Is, just having that spark of remembrance occur is quite euphoric and sensual. However, I do not see extraterrestrial beings in the act of *mating*. I do see in my mind a pregnant androgynous being, so there apparently is actual physical reproduction. And so I am asking, "Does that mean that there *are* male and female?" And the answer came that, "No, there are parent beings." That is a little unclear, so I am asking, "Can anybody be a parent being?" And the response is something to the effect, "If that is your desire when you have realized that you are capable of any*thing*." That if you wish to have live birth, then that seems to be possible. This is a very difficult area to explain, because different dimensional entities do not perpetuate themselves in the same way that fourth dimensional beings do. This is very difficult ground, because when you have the capability of dematerializing and rematerializing, you don't have an actual need for creating new beings. This, of course, is a generalization. But I might say that although we (here in our underground city) are androgynous, we can manifest -- let me not use that word, because that gives an incorrect picture. We can *act* the way we feel most comfortable *acting*. And some of us "act" ways that can be Earth-labeled "masculine", and Earth ways that can be labeled "feminine".

D: *Then you mean at times you do have this feeling of being more masculine. You more or less play a part, masculine or feminine?*

P: No. Those are terms that we have to use because we are talking *Earth* terms. I just mean that *all* of us are not carbon copies of each other. Some of us enjoy the more physical strength roles, which could be *termed* masculine. *We* don't call them that. This is just a method or manner of approach. A way of being.

D: *It's more of a personality type thing? I imagine you have personalities.*

P: Of course, personality does exist in other beings, not just those from the Earth plane. This concept is very difficult to explain. Because you, the questioner, come from a planet of two sexes, that are actually very different, in order to try to understand masculine and feminine attributes, you would tend to think in Earth terms. It is by using Earth terms that the confusion sets in. So I'll just change it. I will change masculine to lion, and I will change feminine to swan. So some of us are comfortable in dealing with things in a lion-like manner. Others are more comfortable to deal with things in a softer swan-like manner. It does not mean we are lions and swans. It only means that is our basic way of approaching work or life. I personally feel more comfortable with the attributes of the lion. I do identify more strongly with those characteristics.

D: *I can understand that. You seemed to be feeling sadness because there were no children there. Was this feeling or emotion coming from the being or was it coming from you?*

P: It seems that these beings definitely have emotions. Emotion is almost the precipitate of thought. Emotion is a catalyst for movement. Emotion is a very valuable, viable force. And these beings most assuredly possess emotion. Although my human labeling of the emotion may be different than is actually felt, emotion is felt, definitely. I think I could have superimposed the label of sadness. However, emotions definitely exist.

D: *Then this being is capable of feeling ... anger?*

P: Hmmm. Because we work in human terms, yes, I guess you would have to call these feelings "anger, joy, sadness".

D: *Love?*

P: Love. I don't know. Let me see if they would be labeled such by the beings. Well, the response was, "This is just a matter of semantics." So I shouldn't be so picky. (She laughed.) Yes, sadness, yes, you can term it that.

D: *And they can feel love?*

P: Absolutely.

D: *All right. I guess I was trying to distinguish whether or not they are more robot-like.*

P: Doesn't seem to be a bit robot-like.

D: *And we have already established that you are apparently different in your internal makeup. Then the procreation is done by cloning.*

P: Yes, and procreation unfortunately is not an appropriate term, because there are no *new* ... (She had difficulty finding the word.)

D: *Specimens? Or what?*

P: Yes. There are no *babies.*

D: *Then you would all be as carbon copies of each other.*

P: Well, of the *original* ones of us who arrived. It is like unlimited life.

D: *If you're an exact clone there would be no evolutionary process in the disappearance of the unessential organs.*

P: No, it was not evolutionary. The organs atrophied from non-use.

D: *Is this cloning done in a certain type of setting, or have you ever seen where it's done?*

P: Let me think. That is an interesting question. I know this is done if something happens to an original inhabitant. I say the word "original" meaning "original from craft", not indigenous to this planet. Let me think. If an accident were to occur and the life force were to leave, then that "person" would be cloned. But that person's "knowingness" transfers so immediately into the clone, that the clone is the alive person then. So it is like continuous life. There is no break in thought, memory, or awareness. So you asked, have I observed this? I have. (Surprised) I have!

D: *I'm trying to get these terms straight. To me, cloning would start with a cell and have to grow and develop ....*

P: (Interrupted) No! It does not have to grow. That I see. You have two containers similar to a sarcophagus, but the top of the sarcophagus is transparent so you can see in. The only example I've seen is of somebody who was crushed. Their physical form could not continue.

D: *It was by accident?*

P: Yes. So they took the body and put it in sarcophagus No. 1. Sarcophagus No. 2 was totally empty. The *essence* of the crushed body wasn't crushed, only the physical *form* was crushed. Through mechanical means as well as thought transference the same body materialized in the empty sarcophagus No. 2, though not crushed and broken. The "essence" that was in fact making this transfer transferred into the new undamaged body, thereby leaving a crumpled up shell. It's like the same person is now in the second sarcophagus. It's almost like a moth crawling out of a chrysalis. There was no growing. This was very quick.

D: *Then through this process the exact body was recreated cell by cell, particle by particle.*

P: Memory by memory. The *entire* thing.

D: *The cell memory was able to reproduce itself by this machine?*

P: Well, I said through technical as well as thought transference, because the essence *willed* this to happen.

D: *The person whose body was crushed?*

P: Yes. See, the essence wasn't crushed, and cannot be.

D: *It wanted to continue, so it reproduced -- with the help of this machine and the technology -- an exact* copy *of itself and entered into it.*

P: Yes.

D: *Okay. Because I thought that the soul, so to speak, wouldn't remain with the body, and it couldn't be reproduced.*

P: I perhaps used the wrong term when I said "cloned", because this process is a ....

D: (Interrupted) *It's a duplication process.*

P: A duplication. Thank you.

D: *Because I was thinking of our terms of cloning. We take a cell and let it develop and grow, and it takes a long time. And then it might turn into another duplicate.*

P: That's Earth. (She laughed.)

D: *Yes, that's Earth. That's the only thing we have to go on.* (Laugh) *Well, then if the essence didn't want to continue, the new body would just be, what, an empty shell?*

P: It wouldn't work. The ultimate generating source is the *intent* of the essence.

D: *Then without that it wouldn't function or anything.*

P: It wouldn't work. It just wouldn't happen.

D: *You mean, if someone put the body in the sarcophagus and turned the machine on, and the essence didn't want to reenter ....*

P: Then it wouldn't occur.

D: *Then that is the only way you would* die, *is if the essence didn't want to continue?*

P: Death doesn't seem to happen. You see, death would only occur to this species if a planetary catastrophe occurred, in which no one could pick up a body and put it into the sarcophagus. The intent would remain. The essences would not die, but they could not have physical form any longer, if there wasn't *one* left to start this process.

D: *But I thought the essence might decide they wanted to go and do something else.*

P: That's right, then nothing would happen in sarcophagus No. 2, because the *intent* is what propels all energy into matter.

D: *It is interesting that it is* individual *intent. The intent of the others involved is not as important as the individual intent, if I've got it right.*

P: I think you have it absolutely right.

D: *Then they don't procreate* .... (Uncertain how to ask it.)

P: Wait. I'm asking these questions, too. My question is, "How does this society exist if they don't have offspring of some type?" The answer is: We came to *this* planet, but for some reason procreation was not possible here. So all that has happened -- and this is very sad -- has been the cloning of those who originally arrived. I feel sadness, because I think we did live on the surface at one time. It is not possible to live there for any length of time anymore.

D: *When you come out of the tunnel onto the surface, do you come out right on the ground?*

P: Yes, the physical Earth itself. There is like an elevator to an airlock. We don't want the gases that are enveloping the surface to go inside the earth. So there is a ... it's like an airlock. Actually in the distance I can see buildings and spires, and what would look like life on the surface. I guess I could go and see. (Pause) Well, no inhabitants are there. This was either already there when we got here or abandoned. I don't know. I don't have a memory of contact with indigenous beings of the planet that we're now living in. And it seems that the response was that, this society ... ummm, (Surprised) is not indigenous to this planet either.

D: *You said you could see a city of some sort.*

P: I do see the city, and so now I'm asking, "Did the population depart before we arrived?" And my answer is, "Yes, *long* before we departed our home planet." And then my next question was, "Why?" And it was because of the change in the atmosphere. I can see an luminous orb giving light to this planet. I cannot look on the Earth sun for any period of time. But I can look on this luminous orb because of the filter of gas that I'm looking through.

D: *You mean it is different than the Earth's sun.*

P: Well, I have seen the Earth sun look like this. On very, very hazy, cloudy days I can look at the disk and see it. And that's what this luminous orb looks like.

D: *You're looking at it through some kind of a haze then.*

P: Yes. And that is the reason the indigenous population is no longer there. The planet could not sustain life, because of the change in the *gaseous* mixture of the atmosphere.

D: *Do you think they left because of that, or were they destroyed? Is there any record of that information?*

P: (Long pause) I don't see bodies or bones or .... And I don't see records telling that we are leaving and this is why. I can go to where I can look on the city, but I don't think I have walked around there, or dug around there.

D: *Are there any other kinds of lifeforms on the surface?*

P: (Long pause) It seems so barren. I'm not aware of any. Although it seems there are lifeforms like viruses, some microscopic living things, but no complex beings.

D: *What about vegetation or trees?*

P: No plants.

D: *Then there is no form of life except that which exists underneath the planet. Your people. Is that correct?*

P: Yes. Although I think we brought plants with us. There are these flowers. I really think that's what the elixir is. It's a nectar of an actual living flower. It looks kind of like that.

D: *It's something that could be grown beneath the surface then.*

P: Yes, but we have our light sources. This is where we live.

D: *Well, it sounds like you wouldn't have much reason to go to the surface then, would you?*

P: Curiosity. (She laughed.)

D: *That's always a trait.* (Laugh) *Well, apparently your people can't live in that atmosphere either.*

P: No, I don't think we can breathe. No, not without equipment; and it seems that after a while not without the light, for some reason ... not for periods of time, anyway.

D: *Did your people know they wouldn't be able to function on the surface when they chose to come to that planet?*

P: (Long pause) I don't think so. Not to the extent that they found when they got here. I truly believe that our people thought they had scouted a planet that could sustain surface life. Probably through seeing the cities. Not realizing.

D: *That would make sense. If they saw the cities they thought there would be life there. Then they had to create this city beneath the Earth?*

P: Yes. We brought everything. We brought our all-information source. I guess I should call it the crystal because that's what I continue to think of it as. We're very industrious beings.

D: *Did you travel very far, or did you just go to another planet in your own solar system?*

P: (Pause) It seems that a *large* amount of time elapsed, because during the trip inventions that we are using were created. These were things that we had no use for on our home planet, but *thought* to make them en route.

D: *They thought they would need them where they were going. Is that right?*

P: The possibility must have existed. I am also aware that we knew there was *not* vegetation on this planet. So there was already a question as to whether we would live on the surface.

D: *That's probably why they brought their own food source with them. Wouldn't they have been able to go somewhere else when they found out the atmosphere was so bad?*

P: That's a very good question. Although it doesn't seem there was a desire. Let me ... I'll just put my hands on the crystal.

D: *And see what you can find out?*

P: Uh-huh. (Sudden laugh.) Oh! This is really confusing. But it seems that this group that I'm talking about and am now familiar with, has been on this planet long enough to have a very definite attachment and emotion involved with this planet. But they came here from a home planet that *completely* blew up, was destroyed and does not exist, except in its little tiny particles and fragments.

D: *Then did your people leave it before it blew up?*

P: Yes! Definitely! In *mass* exodus. The *knowing* that it would happen was planetary, giving us the ability to leave.

D: *What caused the destruction of the other planet?*

P: (Sadly) We tracked the meteor for many, many years. We were aware of being *immediately* in the path for a long time. When it became absolutely obvious that the collision would take place, we had to abandon. This was a totally natural celestial phenomenon. A collision of a meteor not much smaller than the entire size of our planet.

D: *Then it was nothing that the people themselves did.*

P: No. We had forewarning that this, very sad, but natural thing was going to occur. We had no way of changing the trajectory. It was enormous.

D: *How did you leave the planet?*

P: On craft.

D: *Did you know where you were going when you left?*

P: (Pause) I think so, yes, because many craft landed on this planet.

D: *It was, like you said, a mass exodus.*

P: Yes. They didn't *all* come to this planet though. I have the *real* feeling of some going to other planets. I feel we could travel and visit our brothers and sisters, if you wish to call them that. (Surprised) Oh! There was a reason for them to come to this planet. They're here for a purpose.

D: *What?*

P: As if in the *grand* scope of the cosmos it is another relay station of getting data closer to the primitive lifeforms, i.e.: humans. (She laughed.)

D: *Let's see if I can understand what you mean.*

P: I do. There was a need to leave the home planet because it was facing destruction. Then the choice came of *where* to go. I think that our people believed they were going to find a similar sister planet, and set up life very similar to what it had been. However, it seems that there is a master planner. There is more to this than individual will. There was the plan of things, in order to *get* these people -- who were quite content on their home planet, in order to shake them out of their contentedness -- to remove their home. Thereby forcing them to take flight. Otherwise other people would have taken on this job, other entities. Now the purpose was to get *physically* closer in light years in terms of time and distance, because we are talking about Earth now. I can see the whole progression.

D: *You got the information from the crystal. Do you mean this planet you're talking about is Earth?*

P: No. But these are the people who are charged with the commission of giving this new information *to* Earth. I'm sorry that I'm not making myself clear. ... I understand ....

D: *It's always hard. They say the language is inefficient to translate these things. The planet you're on, is it close to Earth?*

P: It's right out there, *but* it's vibrating differently. It is actually in a different dimension, but proximity-wise, not far.

D: *Is it in the same solar system? Of course, with dimensions I know it's hard to explain.*

P: I think for understanding it would be easier to say that it is close.

D: *It is in proximity. It would just be invisible to us, because it's in another dimension.*

P: Correct.

D: *Then are your type of beings capable of going between dimensions?*

P: Well, yes. You see, we have discovered that capability. We operate in that manner. And we wish to share this information with Earth dwellers, *because* they, too, need to have this information. Or they *will perish* with their planet.

D: *Do you mean it is a similar situation?*

P: (Big sigh) I don't know what I mean. (Big laugh.)

D: (Laugh) *I think you're doing very well. Then is your race of beings aware of Earth?*

P: Oh, yes. (Sigh) I had this strange feeling when I walked out on the surface though, that *I* was future and it *was* Earth. So I have a confusion of future-knowing and the dimension where I am. Because I am trying to work with time and distance, and those are heavy Earth-bound terms. I don't know if I'm on a *totally* different planet in another dimension, or the same planet that is so totally different because it is so far in the future.

D: *Then what do you mean? You're trying to help Earth as it is in the* past?

P: Yes. Past being our *now*. You see, not only are we capable of distance travel. There is no time, so time travel is also possible. I am confused, because when I look on the surface and feel this terrible sadness, I don't know if it is because I am looking at the surface of another planet that I went to, or it's Earth of the future, and I'm trying from the future to tell Earth of *now* what could happen.

D: *Okay. But you are living beneath this planet.*

P: I'm on the inside.

D: *So it would have to be a physical planet that would be incapable of supporting life. This is what confuses me.*

P: You see, I have denial going on, because I feel that I am speaking to you from Earth. That I am a being who lives in the Earth now, and I am not a human. I came from somewhere else. And I know that I can change things. Speaking from the future I can talk to the now and explain the concept of dimensions in such a way that if, in fact, the present Earth were engulfed in noxious gases and life as we know it were no longer capable of existing, I could explain to *humans* who have complex thinking, how they can make a dimensional shift. Thereby still having consciousness in their essence and capable of continuing their form in the future. So I am talking from a distance of space and time.

D: *You also said you were in another dimension.*

P: Definitely! I would have to be in order to accomplish this time-space instantaneousness.

D: *This is why it's hard to phrase questions. But is it part of your plan to incarnate on the Earth from that barren planet?*

P: Incarnate? Let me think of a different term. (Pause) Oh! That's it! That's what I am *wanting* to be able to express, first of all, the concept of "eternal life". The *eternal* existence of the essence, with or without physical form. But if we want to have physical form -- and as human beings physical form is an important attribute -- we can. To express to living beings how they can have, and *are,* everlasting energy and life. They can have form as long as they so choose, but they can also have non-form. To express these things, we have to *look* like humans, *talk* like humans, and be able to *say* these concepts in ways that the human brain can understand. And so it seems that "incarnate" isn't the right word. I guess the proper term is really "walk-in". We merge with already existing humans.

D: *That's a different concept.*

P: Than being born, yes.

The concept of walk-in spirits is discussed more fully in my book, *Between Death and Life.*

D: *To incarnate would be inhabiting a human lifeform from the very beginning, from birth. A walk-in would be an exchange of places.*

P: Yes, or a joining *of,* in this instance.

D: *More of a joining than a trading?*

P: Yes. A joining *of* at a very early age.

D: *The idea of walk-ins, of trading places, has always bothered me. That one of them goes off somewhere. This idea makes more sense. It's more of an integration of another part of* you. *An actual* you. *It's an integration, more than a trade-off.*

P: Like future Pam meets present Pam.

D: *Or past Pam or whatever.* (Laugh) *I just had an idea. Do you suppose that when your people left your planet you landed on the Earth as it is in the future? And you decided to "walk-in" in the Earth's past?*

P: (Excitedly) Yes!

D: *To help it at that future.*

P: Yes!

D: *Then this means we are capable of changing our future?*

P: (Excitedly) Yes! (Happily) Yes! That is the message! Yes! We are!

We know through past-life therapy that we can be influenced by our past lives. If the soul is eternal and there is no such thing as time, can we also be influenced by our *future* lives? This case strongly suggested this possibility.

D: *It's hard to understand. I'm trying to do the best I can.*

P: I know, but *you* are absolutely doing wonderfully well with your human brain. You have done remarkably following this. Every moment of life on physical Earth, in our *density*, has the capability of change. Each thought that takes us into the comprehension of dimensions, and the *belief* of foreverness of consciousness and individuality. Every thought that's generated by a human being helps to move the planet in a direction that will make the future I see -- the barren planet future -- not the one that will be the reality. Thought is energy. Energy creates movement. So it's like lights turning on everywhere. Then it's not dark any more. This is so hard to explain.

D: *You're doing very well. Then what is it that you're trying to tell the people?*

P: First, that thought is a force that is eternal. So the absolute necessity is to think on the highest vibratory level possible. The way to enter another dimension is to raise vibration, or to speed up vibration. The human can do that by using thought. If the human is not aware that they can use their mind to think these thoughts, then they won't do that. They continue having their thoughts on the mundane level. Shoes, food and everything else. The absolute essentialness is of changing our thought, or just broadening our thought. Thoughts are really big things. (She laughed.)

D: *I've heard that before.*

P: With what you do with your thoughts, each individual human has a determining effect on the entire planet. So there must be more people who are tuning into, or generating -- I'll say the word "generating" -- thoughts of the capability of life everlasting, in a *conscious* form. Now actually, I have to regress into a tiny little thing about Jesus, because in basic elementary terms, he was *one* of *us*. Jesus tried to show that if you live a life of high vibration, then you are uplifting yourself and the planet. And when you die you don't die. That was the whole message and the whole thing. And two thousand years ago the capability of Earth destruction, or the Earth as I'm seeing from the future perspective, was evident then from this space of "no time".

D: *It would have been too hard for them to understand.*

P: They didn't. It was attempted. They just didn't get it. *Now* people *can* get it, if they can hear it enough. If it can sink into some place that they can grab onto, they can start. And our job, whether we want it or not, is to tell them. Earth is not the only planet with complex life forms. It does seem that Earth is in the most need of hearing this information, but Earth isn't the only focus of All That Is.

D: *Very interesting. All right. You have the crystal there. You may have access also to your other memories. On the planet that you left, the one that was destroyed, were you normally sexually functioning beings on that planet, or were you always androgynous?*

P: (Pause) I was looking for sexual organs. Well ... that's difficult, because I seem to see smaller *copies*. I would immediately say "children", but .... Either I have no long-term memory or .... I don't see sexual reproduction, even there.

D: *Because you said when you first came to* this *planet they began cloning the originals.*

P: Correct. I also am aware that the apparatus that was used for this purpose was developed en route. So there was a knowing of the necessity for this.

D: *But when your race went to that planet it had physical spaceships, physical vehicles. Is that correct?*

P: That is correct.

D: *Are these vehicles still being used?*

P: Well, you must remember when you operate from a different dimension, that what is physical in that dimension is not necessarily visible in other dimensions. It doesn't appear to be physical in other dimensions. Let us say that Earth in this 1988 is in the third dimension, just for labeling purposes, and we are in the fourth dimension. Fourth dimension life is not that different from third dimension life, only much accelerated. The speed is so different as to render it invisible to third dimension people who cannot at this time comprehend fourth dimension. So we can have craft, cities, planets, bodies. These things are very real to us. Now we have been working on the capability, because we are traveling through time and space, to make our fourth dimension craft visible to third dimension by stepping down vibration to a degree almost unbearable to us, but to make it possible for humans to *see* these craft. It is important that humans actually admit that other life exists. This door must be opened and kept open if the physical form wishes to continue in the future.

D: *This is what you meant by the speed? You meant the vibrations of that dimension are faster?*

P: Yes. Light is a very, very high vibration. Very fast. By high, I mean fast.

D: *But to the people in that dimension everything is physical.*

P: If we so choose, yes.

D: *Are you still working on that, or has it been perfected where you could go into our dimension and be visible?*

P: It seems that not all of the inhabitants of this planet are *willing* to withstand stepping down the vibration. You can imagine not wanting to feel like you weigh two thousand pounds. Or that you are walking through heavy, thick glue that sticks to you. Or that you have infinite difficulty breathing, or moving in *any* way. You can see that many would not choose this. It's not pleasant. But those of us who feel we have a duty to impart this knowledge will make this sacrifice. So ... I think we are all capable and we're working on making it more attractive, like a PR campaign. (She laughed.) But not everybody is making the attempt.

D: *Then even the atmosphere inside the space craft would be difficult, because of the stepping down.*

P: In a change of dimensions every aspect is most assuredly affected. You try to keep it as much like home as you can, but ....

D: *Do you think this is occurring now, where they are coming to Earth, to be visible?*

P: Yes.

D: *Could this be some of the ships and the beings that people have reported seeing?*

P: Sure! Absolutely! This hasn't just been happening within our recent time. Since the 1800s there have been reports and prior to that. And the spaceships of Ezekiel, if you're looking from a future perspective back at present Earth. Present Earth means Earth as it has existed for the past X-million years, since the last major Earth shift. So these attempts have been ongoing in *Earth* history for a long, long, long, long time. It's been a building of acceptance. A tiny, tiny, tiny, gradual, oh-so-small, small opening of the door, that have allowed *more* of us to be brave enough to make this attempt.

D: *What is the main purpose of the visits, if they've been coming for that long?*

P: Humans have the wonderful capability of denying what they see. So, as time has gone on denial has been less, because more people are being brave enough to say they have seen these things. There's now mass communication that's instant. There are many more people on the face of the Earth than there were before. So there are many, many more sightings, and they're more widely reported. And they're becoming more acceptable. The message is very, very succinct, and very clear. From our perspective, human life -- that means human *form*, human physiology -- ceased to exist. Our message is that it need *not* cease to exist if humans want, in their future, to have human physical form.

They may maintain physical form by learning to increase their vibrations. They may increase their vibrations through their thought. Their thought is the primary force of all life, to begin with. So if they *wish* to think greed thoughts, to be heavy and sad, these are low level vibrations. They are slow and low, and do not withstand a vibrational shift which the planet, through its natural evolution, is nearing. So these humans, if they wish to have human forms in the future, have to learn how to speed them up. And that is our message, because from our perspective they didn't *get* it. There are no human *forms* left. Human life, human life force, human essence always remains, because the other part of our message is: You don't die. You don't die, but you can lose your human form.

D: *In other words, in the future you are observing that the human species slowly became extinct?*

P: They *quickly* became extinct. It seems that it was *very* quickly. It was not like, in our particular instance, there was a warning of a giant meteor that had been plotted for years and years. This seemed very quick. You see, I don't wish to have this be the future. It seems that I, the being to whom you wish to speak -- and unfortunately the reporter is doing all the talking. (She laughed.)

D: *That's fine. As long as you're giving me the being's words.*

P: The being has a whole life, a whole scenario, a whole system of operation that seems to have been going on for some period of time. And this being is a future aspect of the person lying here on the bed. That does not mean that is the *only* future aspect of that person. And this being wishes to say that in this string, or line, human life ceased to exist. By dwelling on *that* as the future, *that* happened. It helps to concretize -- if that is a word -- a probability. This is so very difficult for the human mind to comprehend. Not only does this person have *a* future self, this person has *many* future selves, who have had other scenarios played out. It is almost in desperation that this being feels we can get this message about the necessity of raising vibrations to humankind now, because of the *very* possible dimensional shift that will *very* likely occur. If we can get that message through, then that future existence *will not* continue to function. There will be a *new* future existence that this person will be more focused and attuned to.

D: *I am trying to understand what happened.*

P: (Pause as though watching.) I see a change in gravity. I see the planet which normally rotates on an axis, and revolves around the sun. I see this planet ... I want to say "wobbling". What always was a perpetual motion ... changed. This caused planetary climate change instantly, but it seems that something affected the gravity. Almost like it became *so* dense it was pulling down the gases, the elements, toward the surface. Almost like a raining down on the surface of things in space that have been there all along. They have perhaps been in the atmosphere but certainly not pulled to the surface. The gravity seems so dense, so heavy.

D: *Would this be enough to have destroyed all the people?*

P: Oh, yes. I see no one able to breathe.

D: *You saw also that there was no living plant life or anything left.*

P: From my perspective, the shift occurred long before. So by the being's time, of course, there was no vegetation nor any remains of animal life or human life.

D: *Just the remains of their cities. But you claim that even if this event, the shift of the Earth, happens, if human beings can raise their vibrations they would be able to physically survive?*

P: It seems that by raising their vibrations they become open to receiving information that will, yes, enable them to somehow survive. By raising your vibrations you are opening yourself to the inflow of energies that are intelligent and loving, as well as much speeded up. The thoughts of the human can be directed toward, if you please, God. The life force of the universe. The All That Is. Light could be considered synonymous with God. If you can consciously be aware and awake, and also put your thoughts in the realm of everlasting love and light, you *are* raising your vibrations. Light, I continue to think on light.

D: *Light is very important to your race.*

P: Well, it seems to be very important, period. It seems that the human being capable of maintaining physical form in the future will have the awareness of *how* to do this, because of the openness that has occurred due to always pushing their thoughts higher, faster, opener, more cosmic. So my thought keeps coming that they will have forewarning so they can escape.

D: *I thought maybe they were going to invent something that they could use to survive.*

P: Well, they must at this point invent craft, or some way of speeding their vibration so as to not be affected *by* the density of the gravitational pull.

D: *Then you mean they must find a way of escaping. I thought maybe they would invent some way they could survive on the surface.*

P: The question is always maintenance of the *physical* form in the future. Not necessarily physical form of the entire planet. We're speaking of *human* physical form.

D: *And that is important. They don't want the physical human form to become extinct.*

P: It seems that at this point in time humans are very attached to their physicalness. (She laughed.) And I always want to say, *nothing, nothing* is locked in concrete. We *all* affect the future with each passing moment of time that we've made up. It seems that for the continuance of the physical *body*, the human must be aware of how to either reassemble the human body in another dimension, or travel to another dimension.

D: *Does it have to be another dimension, or can it be within this dimension?*

P: This dimension, as we know it, will cease to exist.

D: *The* entire *dimension! I thought maybe it was just our world that was going to ....*

P: Well, I should say for human beings. There will always be a third dimension.

D: *I thought maybe they could travel to another planet in our galaxy, and it would be within this dimension.*

P: Oh, no. That would be nice. But that's not the picture that I see. I see a complete solar system change, if you will. And when we think in terms of a solar system, we believe that's a big picture, but that's a very small picture actually.

D: *Now we're getting into stuff that is complicated. Some of my questions may be naive, but I'm trying to understand it the best I can.*

P: The reporter is having difficulty, too. (She laughed.) I'll tell you the picture that I saw when you said that. This is so funny, this is like a movie.

D: *That's okay. It's coming from somewhere, so let's report it.*

P: I saw something like a giant ... let's call it a "mother" craft. When human form leaves the surface of this planet, it will be because they *know* that the time *has* to be now to leave. They are now in a smaller craft and they are leaving. They all know a dimensional shift is occurring. They know they are undergoing a change that they can't possibly comprehend, until it is in effect ... effected. They are flying out because they know they can't remain on the physical planet. The picture I get is that these craft *see* this huge mother ship. They dock into the mother ship. I cannot possibly explain *how*. They just look like they *fly* into it, to me. Many craft just fly into a big craft. This is like a womb, or a place of incubation. A place where they are taught, perhaps, or helped through this incredibly different change. So there seems to be *help* out there, for those of us who can't possibly comprehend what a change in dimension *really* is. There seems to be a *physical* craft manned -- I might say *personed* -- by very brave individuals.

D: *Where did this mother ship come from?*

P: It seems as if people like this little guy, the future *me*, have constructed it.

D: *Did they also create these smaller craft?*

P: The smaller craft, that we use to leave from Earth seem to have been developed on this planet. With, however, help from "friends".

D: *The mother ship is definitely from another place.*

P: Another dimension. Correct. This seems so fantastic to look upon. The mother craft seems like a giant hospital-school. A place *filled* with this enormous emotion of *great* love. It seems like the merging of human form with the life that exist within this craft. It's this *joyous* occasion of union that is *so* profound and *so* wonderful and so *sought* after by so *many* different consciousnesses. And the pervading thought of the interior of this place of *so* much love is this giant *light*, this *living* light.

D: *So they will stay within this large ship for a certain period of time?*

P: Yes. There will be, of course, a few humans, or hopefully many, who will have mastered the dimensional shift without this help. But basically, the majority did well just to get in the craft and take off.

D: *This whole scenario that you're seeing, is that going to happen within our lifetimes? I hate to pin you down to a time, but ....*

P: Let me say it like this, our lifetimes are forever. This may not take place in the lifetime of our *physical* body.

D: *It wouldn't occur during the time our physical bodies are existing? Okay. That gives us a little better scenario. We don't have to think it's going to happen next* year.

P: Well, I have to tell you that I have an internal feeling of *enormous* urgency. I realize by saying that *perhaps* it will not happen during the life of our physical forms, that takes a slight edge off the urgency of this message. And this message is: we must raise our vibration. And we can do it consciously. It's an absolute essential, imperative thing. So to say that it won't happen in *your* lifetime, or yours or yours or yours. Then everybody breathes a sigh of relief, and says, "Well, then I don't have to do that." But the fact is it is very urgent. It doesn't mean it *won't* happen in this lifetime of our physical form. It just doesn't appear to me to do so at this time.

D: *Yes, that does take the edge off it. -- But now all the little craft get into the mother ship. Then what's going to happen to them? They cannot come back to this planet?*

P: No.

D: *Where are they going to go?*

P: The incredible expansiveness of a fourth dimension makes anything possible. It seems the word "intent" continues to come forth as a response to your question. So, if their intent were to populate a globe and have, say, a global government of love and peace and cooperation, then that could be accomplished. It is the intent of the *individuals*, because each one of course has free will. So if their intent is to remain in the invisible realm, and to travel and observe, to learn, to visit, that, too, is possible. It seems that once they've become aware that they can or cannot have a physical body, then they have free choice to determine.

D: *Because you were talking about the urgency of the* physical *human being continuing. I thought it would have to go somewhere.*

P: They have choice.

Our time was running out and I said I was going to have to end the session for the day.

P: I'm so disappointed.

D: *Why are you disappointed?*

P: Because I just want to stay. I have this feeling of being *so happy* to be *able* to talk.

D: *Well, we know now we can come back. We contacted you, we can come back again.*

P: Yes, come back again! (Emotionally) Thank you. I really thank you.

Pam was really reluctant to leave that scene, but I explained to her that we could come back any time we wanted to.

The story in this chapter did not come forth in one session. It is the result of editing and combining the information from four sessions where the story was continued and moved forward. In each session Pam always seemed to be upset about leaving the tunnel room. She enjoyed the feeling of being there. It always took a firm persuasion to get her to move back up to consciousness. I always promised her we could come back.

A similar future scenario was mentioned in Volume III of my trilogy *Conversations With Nostradamus.* The subject was being shown the Earth after a terrible disaster had struck the Earth and caused mass destruction across the surface of our entire planet. The following is paraphrased from that book:

Subject: Many, many people died. Also many animals and many big trees perished, but not all life.

D: *Then what did humans do?*

S: They started over.

D: *Were they able to?*

S: Yes. There are, right now as we speak, many places that are already built underground. We will go back into the Earth for a period of time, and live under the surface. I say that as a fact. Maybe I should not have said it that way. If the worse-case scenario takes place this is what comes to pass. A scenario of that extent only takes place if humans haven't got their act together to take care of the planet. If that comes to pass it is far in our personal future, but not as far in the future of the Earth.

D: *What do you see at that time?*

S: Just stillness and much darkness. I see an established society *under* the surface. It's been there so long it seems as if that's the natural place to live.

D: *What do those people look like?*

S: They resemble skinnier, spindlier humans with bigger heads and flatter noses. They have smaller mouths with bony plates rather than teeth, and big, big eyes. This is because the darkness factor is greater even though it is illuminated under the surface. When they go out, it's so bright they need to wear black lenses that cover the eyes. They don't have the same muscles either because there's not much physical activity.

D: *Why did they evolve to that state?*

S: I think it was caused by living under the ground for a thousand years. Whatever medium you live in for a thousand years becomes the place you adapt to. If you lived in an aquatic environment over a thousand years, the webbing between your fingers and toes would return. You simply adapt to the environment in which you live.

D: *But in a thousand years wouldn't Earth have straightened out to where they could return to the surface?*

S: This is very interesting speculation. But once a status quo is reached, this is the way it is and this is the way we live. It's not so unusual to think that they would continue this life. It's the same with surface dwellers, we're not in any rush to live underground.

D: *Then what Nostradamus was reporting to us was the absolute worse that can happen. There are many alternatives of lesser degrees in between?*

S: Yes, and even in the absolute worse there is not a total destruction of human life.

D: *So even though they change, humans will survive. It all sounds very strange. But we have to know the worse before we can concentrate on the best.*

It must be remembered that the future is not a time-line that is set in concrete. It consists of many, many time-lines that represent all the probabilities and possibilities. The future for us could be influenced by many little, almost insignificant, twists and turns along the way. Therefore the future path that we walk depends upon what we are programming at the present time.

CHAPTER THIRTEEN

CONCLUSION

Just as in the days of the Inquisition when the Church taught that the Earth was the center of the universe, we, in our narrow thinking, have assumed that *we* are the center and the planets and galaxies revolve around us. It is difficult for us to admit that there are civilizations and cultures that have been around long before our small world was thought into existence. In my book, *Keepers of the Garden,* we were told the story of our creation by our brothers from the stars. When the Earth developed to the point that life could exist here, it was given its life charter. From that point on the creatures that would live here were designed, pruned and cultivated until they had developed into the species we see around us. We have never been alone, our creators have been watching, observing and caring for us since the beginning of life on Earth. They have cheered us on in our advances and victories, and moaned and despaired at our backsliding and mistakes. Why shouldn't they have observed so closely? We are them and they are us. They have wanted desperately for their experiment to succeed, because their blood and their genes are a vital part of us. We were supposed to be the perfect world with the perfect people. It was intended that we would never know disease and never die. Earth was supposed to be the literal Garden of Eden where mankind would live in a virtual paradise. But something went wrong along the way, and the

"Watchers" have been hoping we would be able to repair the damage in some way. It was decided to give this beautiful planet a creature with free will. Give it free will and see what he does with it. Non-interference is the prime directive, just as they say on Star Trek. They cannot interfere on the experiment. Give the creature free will and see where it takes him, and what he will do with it. This could be viewed as a blessing or a curse. I often wonder what they think of us now, whether or not we have lived up to their expectations.

In my work I have found that Earth is unique in many ways from the other civilizations. We live in a world of limitations. We will never realize our full potential while existing in the human body, but that is one of the challenges, and one of the lessons to be learned. Our world is one of the few in our universe that still experiences war and violence. This is one of the reasons the extraterrestrials have not made open contact. We are being quarantined and isolated here in our small corner of the galaxy. They are afraid our childish behavior will contaminate the other worlds. I have been told that we will never truly travel in space, and be allowed to enter the confederation of the other worlds, until we decide to grow up and leave violence and hate behind us. There is no place for such behavior in the councils of planets and solar systems. The time is coming when it will be possible, when they will travel and communicate freely with us. How soon it happens is totally up to us. At that time they will welcome their brothers and sisters home. For we have been on a long journey, and it is time for reuniting with the family.

Not only does their blood and genes flow through our physical bodies, but we have now seen through the cases in this book that our spirits or souls also share the same bodies. We are them and they are us in every respect. We are children of the Stars. This is our legacy and our heritage. We are all aliens and have lived on many other worlds and in many other dimensions, some of which are beyond our comprehension. We are constantly growing and eternally learning. We are like sponges, always absorbing and gaining knowledge and information through our many adventures through life. We make mistakes and hopefully learn from them, and go on to the next lesson in the next classroom, wherever that may be. When we have completed the grades on this planet Earth, where will our new place of education be? There are as many adventures lying before us as we have already traveled through. Our path is like a giant circle with no beginning and no end, always continuing before us and fading into the distance behind us. The only place that is constant is the moment we are living now.

We have learned many things about the aliens in these hypnotic sessions, and also many things about ourselves. They seem to have many features in common that we cannot identify with. They are not sexual creatures. Androgynous beings seem to be the norm, while we are the exception. They have long ago given up verbal communication and have evolved to total telepathy. They are not born and do not die, as we understand those terms. Once they are created they can live as long as they wish, and only cease to exist when they desire to. The majority have no eating habits as we know them. They take their sustenance through light or cosmic energy. Some live communally and seem to have group mind. In these cases they either do not have emotions, or have no understanding of ours. They feel and experience things in a different way. None of these things make them *better* than us or *worse* than us. It only means they are *different* from us. When these things are understood and accepted then the cycle will be completed, and we will be allowed to return to where it all began. We can leave this stopping-off place, Earth, and return to our true home in the stars. This is their legacy to us, and our legacy to ourselves. The fact that we are eternal, our spirits can never die or be destroyed; we are fellow travelers in the game of life, and our destinies are intertwined. This makes us all brothers and sisters in the grand plan of creation. We are them and they are us, and we are all one in the eyes of God. One people. One galactic family. My work with hypnosis has taken me far, yet still I look for more answers to the mysteries of life and death. The search continues.

Dolores Cannon was born in 1931 in St.Louis, Missouri. She was educated and lived in Missouri until her marriage in 1951 to a career Navy man. She spent the next 20 years traveling all over the world as a typical Navy wife and raised her family.

photo by Richard Quick

In 1968 she had her first exposure to reincarnation via regressive hypnosis when her husband, an amateur hypnotist, stumbled across the past life of a woman he was working with who had a weight problem. At that time the "past life" subject was unorthodox and very few people were experimenting in the field. It sparked her interest, but had to be put aside as the demands of family life took precedence.

In 1970 her husband was discharged as a disabled veteran, and they retired to the hills of Arkansas. She then started her writing career and began selling her articles to various magazines and newspapers. When her children began lives of their own, her interest in regressive hypnosis and reincarnation was reawakened. She studied the various hypnosis methods and thus developed her own unique technique which enabled her to gain the most efficient release of information from her subjects. Since 1979 she has regressed and cataloged information gained from hundreds of volunteers. She calls herself a regressionist and a psychic researcher who records "lost" knowledge. She has also worked on UFO cases since 1987.

Her published books include: *Conversations with Nostradamus(3 volumes), Jesus and the Essenes, They Walked with Jesus, Between Death and Life, A Soul Remembers Hiroshima, Keepers of the Garden, The Legend of Starcrash and Legacy from the Stars.*

Jesus and the Essenes & They Walked with Jesus have been published by Gateway Books in England. Several of her books are now available in different languages.

Dolores Cannon has four children and fourteen grandchildren who demand that she be solidly balanced between the "real" world of her family and the "unseen" world of her work. If you wish to correspond with Dolores about her work, you may write to her at the following address.(Please enclose a self-addressed stamped envelope for her reply.)

Dolores Cannon
p.o. Box 754
Huntsville, AR 72740-0754